The state to come . . .

will go the same way with all
the previous ones.

Hold on old mole.

¡Vinceremos!

to CAPPE (esp. Mark, Nicola, Bob)

— CB.

Biosecurity, Economic Collapse, the State to Come

What kind of state emerges from the pandemic? The pandemic caused two crises, in biosecurity and in the economy. The state was forced to tackle both; but subduing one inevitably exacerbated the other. Emerging from the impossible task of handling two conflicting crises is a new form of state, *the state to come.*

To outline the emerging state, this book offers an in-depth critical account of the state's responses to the biosecurity and the economic crises. It is thus the first study to address *both* crises ensuing from the pandemic, *and* to synthesise the responses to them in a comprehensive account of political power. Addressing biosecurity, the book deciphers its key modalities, epistemic premises, its law, the threat it aims to oppose and the ways in which it relates to public health and society — especially its extraordinary power to suspend society. Addressing the economic crisis, the book deciphers the actuality and prospects of both the economy and the state's economic policy. It claims that economic policy is now dual: it adopts countercyclical measures to serve and entrench a neoliberal economy. The responses to the twin crises inform the outline of the emerging state: its structure, logic and legality; its power and its relation to society. This is a state of extraordinary power; but its only purpose is to preserve the social order intact. It is a despotic state: powerful, and set to impose social stasis.

This work offers ground-breaking analysis based on our pandemic experience. It is indispensable for critical scholars and students in Politics, Security Studies, Sociology, Law, Political Economy and Public Health.

Christos Boukalas is a senior lecturer at Northumbria Law School. He develops a political theory of law, based on legal and state theory. His research focuses on the advent of a new form of law and state in the course of the 21st century. He has widely published critical accounts on British and American security law and policy, including the monograph *Homeland Security, its Law and its State*.

Directions and Developments in Criminal Justice and Law

The ways in which crime is constructed in society is of time-honoured interest to criminologists across the globe. The ever-changing landscape of what is criminal and what is not affects scholars and policymakers in their approach to the body of law defining prohibited conduct, how that law evolves, and the modes by which it is administered. Rule of law cannot exist without a transparent legal system, strong enforcement structures and an independent judiciary to protect against the arbitrary use of power. Critical consideration of the mechanisms through which societies attempt to make the rule of law a reality is essential to understanding and developing effectual criminal justice systems. The *Directions and Developments in Criminal Justice and Law* series offers the best research on criminal justice and law around the world, offering original insights on a broadly defined range of socio-legal topics in law, criminal procedure, courts, justice, legislation and jurisprudence. With an eye towards using innovative and advanced methodologies, series monographs offer solid social science scholarship illuminating issues and trends in law, crime and justice. Books in this series will appeal to criminologists, sociologists and other social scientists, as well as policymakers, legal researchers and practitioners.

6. **The Social and Legal Regulation of Domestic Violence in The Kesarwani Community**
   Kolkata, India and Beyond
   Amrita Mukhopadhyay

7. **Biosecurity, Economic Collapse, the State to Come**
   Political Power in the Pandemic and Beyond
   Christos Boukalas

8. **Black Iconography and Colonial (re)production at the ICC**
   (IN)DEPENDENCE CHA CHA CHA?
   Mwangi Wanjiru

9. **Criminal Justice Responses to Domestic Abuse in Northern Ireland**
   Ronagh J.A. McQuigg

For more information about this series, please visit: https://www.routledge.com/Directions-and-Developments-in-Criminal-Justice-and-Law/book-series/DDCJL

Biosecurity, Economic Collapse, the State to Come

Political Power in the Pandemic and Beyond

Christos Boukalas

Routledge
Taylor & Francis Group
LONDON AND NEW YORK

First published 2023
by Routledge
4 Park Square, Milton Park, Abingdon, Oxon OX14 4RN

and by Routledge
605 Third Avenue, New York, NY 10158

Routledge is an imprint of the Taylor & Francis Group, an informa business

British Library Cataloguing-in-Publication Data
A catalogue record for this book is available from the British Library

ISBN: 978-1-032-29999-0 (hbk)
ISBN: 978-1-032-30002-3 (pbk)
ISBN: 978-1-003-30298-8 (ebk)

DOI: 10.4324/9781003302988

Typeset in Times New Roman
by KnowledgeWorks Global Ltd.

To Foteini and her long walk; Salomi and endless patience.

Contents

Acknowledgement

My profound thanks are due to two groups of people: my colleagues in Northumbria for engineering ways to facilitate my writing—especially James Gray, Adam Jackson and Michael Stockdale; and to the Athens Circle—especially Stefi Christidou, Telemachos Doufexis-Antonopoulos, Alexandros Georgiou, Dimitris Koukourakis and Eva Theodoridou—for contributing advice and critique.

Abbreviations

COBRA	Cabinet Office Briefing Room A
CVA	Coronavirus Act 2020
ECB	European Central Bank
EU	European Union
FWNA	Friedmanian, Workfare, National Apparatus
GDP	Gross Domestic Product
HSA	Health Security Agency
JBC	Joint Biosecurity Centre
IT	Information Technology
KWNS	Keynesian, Welfare, National State
MEP	Member of European Parliament
MEAG	Moral and Ethical Advisory Group
NHS	National Health Service
PPE	Personal protective equipment
SAGE	Scientific Advisory Group for Emergencies
SWPR	Schumpeterian Workfare Post-national Regime
TINA	There is no alternative
UK	United Kingdom
US	United States
VIP	Very important person
WEF	World Economic Forum
WIT	Whatever it takes
WTO	World Trade Organisation

Preamble

Here...the greatest calm prevails — a peace of lassitude, a somnolent, yawning peace, where all is still as on a winter's night when all is snow around. All that we hear are small mysterious sounds like water-drops. These are the Rentes, for ever dripping into the iron chests of Capital, which grows and grows and grows — one really seems to hear the growing of the wealth of wealthy men. Yet in it ever and anon there come low sobs of poverty, and yet again there's something like the sharpening of a knife.

Heinrich Heine
(1842: 347)

1 Introduction: The twin crises and the capitalist state

Since the start of the century, the state is doing little else that combating crises — crises that erupt in its two core areas of responsibility: the economy and security. Starting on 11 September 2001, European and North American states have been facing recurring security crises. Between 2007 and 2014, they had to respond to an acute financial crisis and its metastases.

The coronavirus pandemic poses a double challenge for this crisis-fighting veteran. First, the magnitude of the crisis it brings forth is greater than anything western states have faced since World War II. Crudely put, within a couple of years, the death toll of the pandemic is orders of magnitude higher than that caused by jihadis during two decades; and its impact on the economy is more severe than the 2008 financial crisis — which was the biggest economic crisis in a century. Second, the crisis ensuing from the pandemic is dual: it is a security and an economic crisis *at once*. While the state has responded to both security and economic crises, it has faced each type successively and *separately*, employing different sets of policies. Now, both types of crisis hit simultaneously. Worse, they are deeply intertwined: each crisis is pregnant with the other. Anything the state does to ameliorate the security crisis inescapably triggers or exacerbates the economic crisis; and any attempt to ameliorate the latter, reignites the former.

The heart of the problem is that the operational logics of the economy and security contradict each other. They demand contrasting treatment by the state, and so do their crises. Security is founded on fear and constructed around the perception of a threat; it aims to prevent and minimise the threat's growth; it is risk-avert and precautious in its calculi; and it is operationally oriented towards the eradication of threatening agents, phenomena and conditions by isolating and extracting them from the social environment. By contrast, the operation of the economy is premised on optimism — that investment and work will pay off, making the investor rich and the worker better off. It is conductive to calculated risk taking — and even wild, speculative risk. It aims to maximise growth; and it depends on interaction — it therefore seeks not to arrest, isolate and expel, but to enhance interactions to their fruition. In short, the logic of the economy aims to enhance; that of security aims to suppress and extinguish. These

DOI: 10.4324/9781003302988-1

conflicting logics determine the operational framework of the state, and are also its main legitimacy platforms.

In the context of the pandemic, *the state is caught between these two opposing logics and their contradiction is tearing it apart.* This is so because the state is founded on their fault line. The contradiction between economy and security touches on the constitutive tension of the capitalist state as *state* and as *capitalist.* The capitalist state *as state* is primarily concerned with the continuity of the social order it presides upon: the preservation of existing social arrangements, the reproduction of society within their confines, and its own institutional continuity. It is, in one word, concerned with security. There is a "perfect and total" equivalence between the state and security: the state is the guarantor, subject and object of security; and security is the state's primary objective and function. The objective of security operations is the protection of the population living under the aegis of the state (Gros 2019: 73, 146–148). The capitalist state *as capitalist* is primarily concerned with the continuity of capital accumulation: its overall activity aims to provide the social conditions for it. Above all, the state aims to maintain the social relations that underpin capital accumulation: private property, the division of society into capitalists and workers, and the predominance of the former class over the latter (Agnoli 2020; Poulantzas 1973). The twin crises make these two foundational purposes of the capitalist state incompatible with one another. They forcefully pull state policy to opposite directions — and hence state action is confused, hesitant and disoriented.

To complicate matters, while their respective abstract logics are irreconcilable, security and economy depend on one another. The economy cannot function without a secure, pacified social environment; and security cannot operate without support (funding) from the economy. Hence, the state's dilemma is how to *reconcile the contrasting demands of two mutually depended* social practices at the moment when they both face catastrophic crisis. The synthesis — when (and *if*) it is achieved — of their opposing exigencies into a single line of force that allows the state to respond to both crises will be the mould in which the emerging state-form is forged.

Crises are moments of indeterminacy. They disrupt the continuation of social practices along the established ways. By doing so, they can force the re-evaluation and change of social practices, relations, structures and meanings. What direction this change will take or whether it will occur at all, is equally indeterminate. Different designs for post-crisis life are intertwined with contrasting response plans, which are, in turn, defined by different conceptualisations of the crisis as such: its causes, field of impact, effects and its very status as a crisis. The different perceptions of the crisis, the plans for optimal response and the designs for recovery are all promoted by, and express, the interests and strategic calculations of different social forces, and compete for prominence on an uneven terrain that is largely laid, but also destabilised, by the crisis (Jessop 2015). This book is an intervention in this contested field; it addresses the perception of the dual crisis and the response to it. Written as the twin crises are still unfolding, this book unwraps the state responses to each, and their interrelation. On this basis, it tentatively deciphers the state-form that emerges from them. Before this endeavour starts in earnest, it is necessary to clarify its terms of engagement — starting with crisis.

Crisis?

In what sense is the pandemic a *crisis* — rather than an accident, disaster or emergency? In conveying the sense of violent disruption, the four terms bear close resemblance, yet remain distinguishable. Disaster denotes an incident of devastating impact. Emergency refers to a disaster that necessitates drastic decision and action in response — hence it implies the existence of some form of socio-political relations that undertake (or demand) such mobilisation and, possibly, an apparatus to carry it through. Both disaster and emergency remain under the sign of the accident: they refer to occurrences of the "act of god" (or, more fashionably, "black swan") type, i.e. to extraordinary, random events. Like volcanic eruptions or tsunamis, these are instantaneous occurrences. They are also singular, in the sense that, even if repeatable, they are not reproducible. They are not reproducible because they are not the work of society, they are not caused by the society they affect: accidents, disasters and emergencies originate in a non-social beyond. By contrast, crisis is innate. It results from practices, relations and structures that are part of the society — or the specific social (sub)system — that it affects. By this token, crises call into question social relations, practices and structures. Rather than singular, instantaneous occurrences, crises are *processes* with complex causal and temporal determinations. Their causes can be tangled, and their maturation prolonged. While they typically involve an event of "manifestation" akin to disaster, and an acceleration of activity akin to emergency, their initiation is hard to decipher. Their effects can play out over the long haul and are not predetermined. Crises can result to adjustment, recasting or abandonment of specific social practices, relations and institutions, and even of entire social orders; they can also result to no change at all. Even though they can be result-less, causing no change, they are a necessary — but not sufficient — condition for fundamental change to occur: "the eclipse of a way of living and thinking cannot take place without crisis". Radical change is not accomplished by crisis, but it is within the horizon of possibilities that crisis opens (Gramsci 1995: 219–220, 277; also: Aradau and van Munster 2011: 24–25; Jessop 2015: 246–247; Knio and Jessop 2019: 4).

In short, accidents, disasters and emergencies are occurrences stemming from a cause that is external to the social system they disrupt, while crises are systemic processes, caused by (elements of) that very system, which, in turn, they put in question. Because their causes are innate, crises are apocalyptic in the strict sense of the word. They *uncover* the problematic nature of ongoing practices and relations that was hitherto ignored, concealed or tolerated (Knio and Jessop 2019: 8). The crisis is precisely the moment of this apocalypse, the moment when practices and relations cannot continue as usual, for they are revealed to be destructive.

The location (internal or external) of the disruption's origin in relation to society is rarely obvious. Are terrorist attacks, oil spills, worker injuries or fires in high-rise buildings caused by exogenous factors or inherent in social arrangements? The causation of a disruptive occurrence and its classification as crisis cannot be determined *a priory*. It depends on perception, and its perception is the contingent result of contestation. The lines of this contestation are drawn between social forces that aim to change social arrangements and those that desire their preservation. If the disruption is perceived as the outcome of social relations, it could lead to their questioning; if it is perceived as exogenous, existing social arrangements are safe from challenge (Jessop 2019a). The pandemic is subject to such contestation.

At first glance, the pandemic appears to be an act-of-god type occurrence, as exogenous to our social arrangements as a meteorite. The virus is an extra-social being: there is no point in re-examining the prevailing social relations, practices, structures or attitudes, for they are not responsible for the pandemic and the devastation it brings. This perception is promulgated by the state, which framed the pandemic as a natural occurrence and as the invasion of an alien enemy (Primrose, Chang and Loeppky 2020: 20–21). However, this perception is contested.

Jean-Jaques Rousseau was (probably) the first to axiomatically deny that disasters can be caused by extra-social factors, by acts of nature or god. For him, the 1755 Lisbon earthquake — which destroyed most of the city, killed tens of thousands of people and displaced hundreds of thousands — was a human fault. While the earthquake was not caused by human activity, the devastation it caused was. It resulted from the flimsy structures in which the poor were forced to live; the inadequacy of building materials that caused fire to rage though the city; the crammed, narrow alleys that hindered rescue efforts; by the city's proximity to the sea; by the amassing of enormous numbers of people in cities… (Rousseau 1992). In the same wavelength, contemporary treatment of 'natural disasters' highlights the agency (and, indeed, criminality) of the state in bringing them about (Green and Ward 2004: 52–64). In every case, the natural phenomenon, the earthquake, is the trigger, a 'manifestation' event; it manifests the destructive potential of established social relations —and *they* cause the devastation. Strictly speaking, there are no accidents or disasters as such; they are elements of a crisis process.

Through this lens, the epidemic constitutes a phantasmagoria of manifestation. Established social trends are revealed to be generators of, or contributors to, destruction: the operational undermining of health systems; the housing conditions for the poor; the dismal labour conditions in care homes; the systemic inequalities along race, class and gender lines; the chronic operational atrophy of the state; the hand-to-mouth existence of workers; the vandalism of the justice system that would protect elemental rights of workers, renters and welfare recipients; the commercial exploitation of forest land and the mass deforestation that brings wildlife and its viruses in proximity to humans (Justice Alliance 2020; Minakakis 2020: 33–51, Waitzkin 2021). These — and more — are constitutive elements of the crisis. The crisis is only triggered by the virus; its constituent elements are endogenous to our social, economic and political arrangements — and can call them to question.

What crisis?

If the pandemic represents a crisis, the question is what crisis it is. There is a crisis affecting the economy, which, strictly speaking, is not triggered by the pandemic, but by the state's response to it. The crisis that ensues directly from the pandemic is obviously a matter of health. Yet, rather than a public health crisis, I discuss it as a *security* one. This is not an arbitrary choice. The problem with the pandemic is not the illness *per se*, but contagion, its spread through society. Countering contagion calls for managing the proximity among people. Disease control is, more than anything, a matter of policing contact, movement and behaviour; it is an issue of *public order*. Public health is an element of public order; and public order is the overall object of security.

Second, the crisis caused by the pandemic is a security one because *this is how the state treats it* — and this, the state's response, is what this book is concerned with. Since the onset of the pandemic, state leaders in chorus refer to the virus as an "invisible enemy", an enemy against which the nation, and humanity, is "at war". The President of France repeats the term "health war" eight times in his first national address on the issue (Macron 2020). The British Prime Minister relishes on the war-theme, referring to the prospect of a lockdown as "the nuclear option"; to vaccines as "the cavalry"; and declaring hostilities to be "over by Christmas" echoing an equally ill-fated prediction regarding World War I. "In this fight we can be in no doubt that each and every one of us is directly enlisted" and "medical personnel are frontline workers" in a "coronavirus war economy" (Calvert and Arbuthnott 2021: 218–219, 240; HM Government 2020c: 3; Hyde 2020b; Malnick 2020; McQuade and Neocleous 2020: 7). The virus is framed as an enemy, an "unknown and remorseless foe" threatening the nation. Against it, the "overwhelming priority" of the government is "to keep our country safe". To do so, the government must "defeat" the virus. The nation has "made an extraordinary...collective sacrifice" and "should pay tribute to the victims of the virus" (Johnson, 2020b: 3–4). Foe, country, victims, sacrifice: the nation has embarked on a struggle against an existential enemy (Schmitt 1996). This is a pan-social effort: each and all are enlisted. But there is a clear division of labour. The government undertakes the effort in full. It does all the planning, prioritising and acting. Crucially, it is the state that inaugurates the effort and distributes roles therein. Society bears the brand of the "sacrifice" and is responsible for its compliance with whatever the government requests from it: self-isolating, downloading apps, reporting illicit gatherings, getting vaccinated. Both state and society must, in common, "remain alert" (Johnson 2020c: 4). This alertness can mean anything and encompass any conduct. It is a core attitude in which the state inculcates us.

Notably, the invisible enemy, the existential nature of the threat it poses, the combat, the (innocent) victims, the pan-social character of the mobilisation to defeat it, and the respective roles of the state and society therein — all these elements and their articulation are a faithful reproduction of the representation of the terrorist threat, they are lifted from the counterterrorism playbook (Austermühl 2014: 201–219; Boukalas 2014: 46–66, 182–183). Public health policy can smoothly draw its concepts from counterterrorism partly because those were drawn from public health in the first place: the notion of contagion and epidemic spread underpins the state's counter-extremism strategy (Heath-Kelly 2017). In 2003, then Prime Minister Tony Blair diagnosed that a "new and deadly virus has emerged — the virus of terrorism" (McQuade and Neocleous 2020: 7); and the original "invisible enemy" was, according to then President G.W. Bush, the terrorist (Boukalas 2014: 117, 120). Reversely, epidemiologists tend to understand themselves as security agents collecting, analysing and acting on intelligence; they advocate treating pandemics as seriously as military security; and biologists conceptualise some cells as terrorists integrated in the body to prepare a devastating strike (Farrar 2021: 83–84, 213; Samerski 2018: 9).

The state's conceptualisation of the pandemic as a security issue informs its response. The military is mobilised to secure borders (including, in Australia, those of quarantine zones); to repatriate citizens from other countries and to build impromptu hospitals. The police monitors movements and behaviours, advises, cajoles, enforces regulations, ensures quarantines are observed, disperses gatherings. The surveillance mechanism is mobilised to identify, locate and monitor the bearers of the disease and all who contact them. In the UK, the intelligence picture of the pandemic is composed by the Joint Biosecurity Centre. This is modelled on the Joint Terrorism Analysis Centre, is headed (like some of its counterparts in US states) by a senior Counterterrorism official, and communicates threat-levels through a colour-coded system similar to the Homeland Security Advisory system that the US used to visualise the invisible terrorist threat (McQuade and Neocleous 2020: 7). This marriage between epidemiology and intelligence transcends the confines of the coronavirus emergency: the Wellcome Trust, a UK-based international institution concerned with infectious diseases, is led by a former MI5 chief (Farrar 2021: 9–10). The institutional merging of security and public health is complete: since spring 2021, the overall direction of the UK effort is undertaken by the newfound *Health Security Agency*.

These commonalities between counterterrorism and public health point to their common origin in counterinsurgency. The insurgent fighter — terrorist or virus — is seen as circulating imperceptibly among the population. The insurgency, like the epidemic, spreads in and through society — the latter is its conductor, the environment in which it grows. This makes society the par excellence field for intervention for both counterinsurgency and epidemiology (Philippides 2020). Notably, however, while the state relishes combating terrorism, it engages with the threat of the virus reluctantly. The British Prime Minister has foreseen and declared the end of hostilities several times; the then US President exorcised the virus to "just go away" (Pilkington 2020). The capitalist state is *not* eager to exercise coercive powers and impose quarantine. It would prefer to let people continue unobstructed with their proscribed roles in the production and circulation of commodities (Barbaria 2020: 81). This is a fight the state did not pick.

In short, the state response to the epidemic presents strong conceptual, institutional and operational affinities with its response to insurgency and terrorism. These responses are essentially of the same type. They merge to define the response to the pandemic: *biosecurity.*

Crisis of the state

As *crisis*, the pandemic reveals the destructive potential of existing social relations and can put them under scrutiny. This is what governments want to avoid by representing the pandemic as a random, arbitrary event for which no-one and no-thing is responsible. While denying responsibility for the pandemic, governments shoulder the duty to confront it, to protect their citizens. Indeed, denying their duty to protect would undermine the core justification for their existence. When a threat is perceived, the state needs to lead the effort against it.

Because crises are processes that develop over time, they are multifaceted and their locus can shift as they evolve. In our case, the seat of the crisis constantly shifts between biosecurity and the economy — rather, it occupies both seats simultaneously. The opposing exigencies of the twin crises confuse and paralyse the state. As the management, resolution and recovery from the biosecurity crisis exacerbate the economic crisis and vice versa, the two crises combine into an all-encompassing third one, a crisis of crisis management. As the twin crises envelop security and the economy, the two core areas of concern for the capitalist state, the latter is precisely the crisis management mechanism thrown into crisis. This is evident in the institutional inadequacy, the lack of policy cohesion, the strategic indecision and disorientation that the state displays in its response to the twin crises: the state itself is in the throes of crisis; the twin crises combine into a crisis of the state.

As crises open possibilities for re-evaluation, reorientation and alteration of the social relations they involve, the present crisis opens the possibility of an alteration in the form of the state. Whether, and to what extent and direction, such alteration may occur depends on the capacity of different social forces to coalesce around specific demands and projects for social transformation or conservation that include the state. The groundwork for this new state-form is set by a — contingent and, at present, highly uncertain — synthesis of the mode of response to the twin crises, for this would lift the crisis of the state. The new state-form would be one that enables the state to simultaneously handle the twin crises, one that can achieve an apparently impossible synthesis of mutually cancelling modes of crisis management.

The analysis: strategic-relational approach and the neoliberal state

The twin crises and the response to them cause a profound cognitive shock. Few could imagine that the state would mobilise the powers it did in either the economic or the biosecurity field — few even suspected that such powers were at the state's disposal at all. This forces us to re-evaluate our established views on the political and rethink the fundamental categories through which we make sense of our social, political and even personal reality (Tsoukalas 2021: 22).

Confronted with an event of this importance, the intellectual vanguard of the moment addressed it only in order to fit it in their pre-arranged analytical schemata — and thus triumphantly confirm their pre-existing theses. They ignore the specificity, novelty and richness of the pandemic experience — they erase the event (Leoni and Alkamar 2020: 41; Penzin 2020: 11; for relevant efforts by leading political philosophers (including Agamben, Esposito and Latour): Castrillón and Marchevsky 2021). Parallel to these, there is a host of contributions that engage with aspects of the event and employ theoretical perspectives to make sense of it. They often are extremely insightful, and have influenced parts of this study. However these studies address *either* the biosecurity crisis *or* the economic one — and ignore the other. This prevents them from assessing the intertwining of the twin crises, their mutual causation, and the opposite directions in which they pull the state. This duality of the crisis is *precisely* what makes the event of the pandemic historically unique and marks our contemporary reality. By ignoring either security policy or economic policy, these valuable accounts are not only partial (every account is), but one-eyed. They fail to note that state power is simultaneously moving to the opposite direction from that they describe, and is therefore uncertain, unstable and in urgent need of cohesion. For this, they run the danger of providing an inadequate and even misleading understanding of contemporary political reality and dynamics. Even if read in combination, they convey the notion of two separate social realities that run parallel to each other and are governed by two different states.

The distinction, and key contribution, of this book is the synthesis it provides. It addresses the interwoven crises, and the state's response, in both registers; and integrates the resulting analysis into a first comprehensive account of political power during the pandemic and beyond.

This account is made possible by the analytical framework employed in this study. It is provided by the *strategic-relational approach* to the state, and centres on the *state-form*. I briefly explain these terms: outlining them will help the reader to better grasp the overall scope of this study, appreciate its cohesion and judge its success.

The object of this study is *the state*; this term certainly needs explaining. Unlike most political theory, which sees the state either as a subject —a "sovereign" — with its own will, interests and power; or as an instrument, a mechanism that serves whomever grasps and puts it to use, the strategic-relational approach sees the state as a social relation. The state is created by social dynamics: it is instituted to mediate social antagonisms and synthesise conflicting interests (Bratsis 2007: 27–50). The state is born out of social antagonism, and is determined by it. The state is shaped by social struggles, constitutes a terrain in which they are played out, and is a key agency therein. Its institutional framework is the contingent outcome of social struggle. Its structure and logic correspond to, and tend to reproduce, the dominance of some social forces over others. The state does not "possess" its own power; state power is an expression of social dynamics mediated by state institutions. To influence state power, social forces seek to capture, reshape, create or abolish state institutions. Thus, the state is an (uneven) terrain of social antagonism. It is also inexorably involved in it. It selects and combines the strategies of some forces into state power, and helps to organise some forces and their strategies, disorganise others, and even construe some forces as such. Its agency is geared not towards promoting "its own" interests, but towards advancing the interests of the social forces that have privileged access and influence in its institutions (Boukalas 2014: 11–26; Boukalas 2017b; Jessop 1990; Jessop 2016; Poulantzas 1978). The state is, in short, *the official résumé of society* (Marx 1936: 156). Thus, in discussing "the state", studies informed by the strategic-relational approach — including this one — are in fact discussing the social dynamics mediated by the state: affecting and affected by its structure, power and institutions.

Statehood constitutes a radical division of political labour, as the state monopolises decision-making pertaining to the institution, organisation, direction and administration of communal life (Castoriadis 1983). Other than that, discussing the state "in general" becomes problematic: it would mean that Inca kingdoms and contemporary Egypt are addressed in the same framework, as they both are states. To overcome analytical absurdity, the strategic-relational approach develops a typology of states and (thus far) concentrates its focus on those of the capitalist type. These states are premised on a structural separation between politics and the economy, and are overall concerned with promoting and securing the conditions for continuing capital accumulation and the social relations that underpin it, i.e. the rule of the capitalist class over a divided and unequal society (Agnoli 2020; Jessop 2002: 187–152; Poulantzas 1973).

While providing a decisive classification of different states, the *type of state* is still too broad a framework: Sweden under the Palme government and Chile under the Pinochet junta are states of the same, capitalist, type.

Thus, strategic-relational studies are geared towards analyses of the *state-form*, i.e. the *socio-historically specific articulation* between state structure, institutionality, strategy and power, as well as the relations between state and society (Boukalas 2014: 15–26; Jessop 2008; Poulantzas 1978).

The classification of states in types and forms is crucial for this study. First, the notion of the capitalist state is decisive in setting its background: no other type of state — empire, theocracy, the feudal state, oriental despotism, absolute monarchy — would have addressed the twin crises in the way we have experienced. Indeed, *no other type of state would have registered the duality of the crisis*; this could only occur to a state predominately concerned with both security *and* capital accumulation.

Second, classification implies that this is not a study of the state in general, but addresses a specific state-form, namely the neoliberal state in its north-Atlantic configuration. By neoliberal state, I refer to the capitalist state that incorporates (is moulded by and promotes) a neoliberal strategy. The latter is a class strategy aiming at maximising wealth concentration and profitability. It treats labour as a cost of production which it aims to minimise, and seeks to recast all social relations and structures in the image of the market. Accordingly, the neoliberal state is defined by its policies' bias against labour: suppression of wages, withdrawal of public and welfare services, undermining of workers unions and legal protections, and fashioning of state institutions after the "free market" disregarding "dogmatic" legal and democratic principles (for different aspects of the neoliberal state: Brown 2015; Cutler 2003; Davies 2017; Gallas 2017; Handler 2004; Jessop 2018). In short, the overall function of the neoliberal state is to shape society as the optimum terrain for capital's benefit (Demirović 2012). Being an open offensive against popular classes, the neoliberal strategy was first promoted by military juntas: in Chile, Argentina and Brazil. In North America and Western Europe, the adoption of neoliberalism did not involve a radical constitutional break. Thus, the North-Atlantic form of the neoliberal state addressed in this study maintains the liberal-democratic institutional shape, involving representative government, separation of powers, civil liberties — but also, in the course of the 21st century, heightened security sensitivities.

The identification of a North-Atlantic neoliberal form of state is critical for the scope of the analysis developed here. While it draws from developments across Europe and North America, it only examines in depth the response to the twin crises of a singular state: the UK. Certainly, there is considerable variation among these states' handling of the crises — stemming from their differing health care, policing and administrative capacities; and their particular economic composition and political culture. But more remarkable is the *similarity* of their crisis-combating measures, in both the biosecurity and the economic field: most differences are ones of intensity, volume and timing rather than kind. For they are all capitalist states caught in the same existential dilemma posed by the twin crises; and being of the same kind, they react in a similar manner. Thus, the classificatory work informing this study helps it to identify its specific object; and also makes it a point of reference for future comparative studies between states of the same form or across forms (and even types) of state.

Finally, the concept of the state-form provides the heuristic of this book. Throughout the book, the analysis is geared towards outlining the structure and logic of the state, its institutional outlook, the modalities of its power, and its strategic perspectives — in their articulation and in their inscription to the broader field in which they pertain: the relations between state and society.

In short, the strategic-relational approach allows this study to achieve two things. First, as it guides the questioning without offering pre-ordained answers, it allows for theory to move in tandem with the event, with reality, without being paralysed by its novelty, magnitude and complexity and without swallowing it up into prefabricated schemata. Second, by discussing the state as a social relation, the strategic-relational approach guides the analysis towards a rich and multilayered account of the state, as it encompasses not only an institutional ensemble but also the society that shapes it and is shaped by it.

Outline

This is a study in three parts. The first two analyse the state response to the twin crises, the third outlines the emerging state-form. Each part comprises six or seven brief chapters, each making a specific contribution to the broader thematic. Combined, they comprise the only, thus far, study that addresses the responses to *both* crises and synthesises them to into a comprehensive (if tentative) account of the emerging state and its relation to society.

The first part — *Biosecurity* — outlines the response to the biosecurity crisis. Its first chapter (Chapter 2) distils the "pure" form of medical and epidemiological power, thus, offering a first approximation of biosecurity as a modality of power. As biosecurity is a security endeavour, Chapter 3 deciphers the threat biosecurity identifies and opposes. Chapter 4 examines biosecurity law; it thus outlines the institutional blueprint of biosecurity powers and notes their implications for liberal legality. Chapter 5 focuses on public health, the policy at the epicentre of the crisis and Chapter 6 examines how biosecurity meets the broader society, focusing especially on the prerogative to suspend society. Finally, having outlined biosecurity operations and their social, juridical and political meaning, Chapter 7 deciphers the epistemic modalities of biosecurity: the "knowledge" informing its power.

The second part — *Economic Collapse* — outlines the magnitude of the economic crisis that ensues from biosecurity and the contours of the state response. It addresses the question of whether state policy aims to preserve economic trends and relations or alter them — and how. Chapter 8 notes how the state attempts to reconcile the exigencies of the economic crisis with those of biosecurity, and deciphers which crisis the state prioritises. Then, the state's actual response is addressed. Fiscal policy is considered at a programmatic global level in Chapter 9, and as applied policy in Chapter 10. The next three chapters address the class aspects of state policy: the treatment of labour by biosecurity (Chapter 11); the prospects that economic policy opens for labour beyond the pandemic (Chapter 12) and the class differential of distribution policy during the pandemic and beyond (Chapter 13). Chapter 14 combines the insights of earlier chapters to conclude that economic policy has acquired a dual character regarding its temporality and its class orientation; it also notes the emergence of structural shifts in accumulation, which make economic policy unstable.

The third part — *The State to Come* — combines the insights gained from the analysis of the response to the twin crises, to outline the emerging state-form. Chapter 15 deciphers the logic that informs government: it notes the biopolitical character of biosecurity, including its treatment of the body; highlights the capitalist character of biopolitics; and suggests that the latter is replaced by a novel state logic: threat governmentality. Chapter 16 addresses the modality of state power, noting a shift from the "there is no alternative" dogma to a "whatever it takes" mode. Chapter 17 addresses the institutionality of the state. It describes a shift in the juridical paradigm towards a permanent state of pseudo-necessity that reconfigures the liberal juridical constellation. State institutionality, logic and power pertain to the relation between the state and society; the latter is addressed directly in Chapter 18, which discusses this relation in terms of power and responsibility. Chapter 19 completes the account of the emerging state-form. It draws from all proceeding analysis to decipher the strategy and outline the structure of the state to come — and their limitations. It is followed, in Chapter 20, by an assessment of the perils that social resistance represents for the emerging state. The postscript (Chapter 21) juxtaposes the political handling of a major epidemic in ancient Athens to that in our contemporary state, offering an insight on the distance between these two types of democratic polity.

Part I
BIOSECURITY

> Outside: the coffin. Inside: the television, an open window on a closed world!
> Raoul Vaneigem (2020: 2)

First under examination comes the biosecurity crisis. It triggered everything else: the economic crisis and the emergent transformation of the state. The state's response to it is examined in the following six chapters. Collectively, they outline biosecurity as a particular kind of state power. Biosecurity power, the reader hardly needs reminding, is truly extraordinary. Most denizens of Western countries did not imagine, or suspect, that their state could do such things. Its employment constituted a cognitive and affective shock. For many, it was a violent disruption of meaning that forced us to radically reconsider our understanding and relation to our world.

In biosecurity, the state mobilises an astounding array of powers in order to combat an existential threat. These powers are exercised upon society, in order to secure it from a lethal danger, a danger that resides within society. These powers are oriented towards the prospect of universal quarantine. This is their final horizon; they rarely reach it, but are defined by it. Quarantine signifies the suspension of society; through it the state suspends what it exercises power upon. The power to quarantine is the ultimate asymptote of state power: a power so absolute that it eliminates its referent object and fills the social universe only with itself — and thus negates itself. Such power makes no sense, not even in its own terms. It is therefore exercised frugally: the object of power, society, is suspended only momentarily and only inasmuch as it is necessary to secure it from physical extinction. The prospect of this absolute, self-consuming power is inherent in all biosecurity interventions and, hence, even the mildest of them are met with a degree of discomfort; they are justified only by their necessity.

This awesome biosecurity power reveals a state that is (juridically) omnipotent, but, equally, (operationally and strategically) weak. The *neoliberal* state has chronically starved social services to the point that they cannot fulfil their basic functions, let alone respond to the exigencies of the pandemic. This weakness informs the entire biosecurity effort, which

DOI: 10.4324/9781003302988-2

is focused on preventing the collapse of the public health system — on protecting, in other words, from exposure the state's incapacity to provide this basic social good.

Further, the state mobilises extraordinary biosecurity power, but it is unclear *what for*. The purpose of the biosecurity effort is undefined. It is neither to eradicate the virus nor to let it run through society unhindered. It is to control the progress of the virus — and this can mean virtually anything. There is notable equivocation towards biosecurity interventions: typically the state embarks on them later than the epidemiological situation demands, and lifts them earlier than it allows. This strategic indecision is because the state is not managing only the biosecurity crisis but also its twin: the economic crisis, triggered by biosecurity, which for the capitalist state is equally urgent and existential, and pulls its powers to the opposite direction. In short, each of the two crises is contained in, and informs, the state's response to the other. They are interwoven.

Still, as they erupt in different fields of state activity and demand opposing responses, they are analytically distinct. Part II will discuss the economic crisis; this Part is dedicated to biosecurity. Chapter 2 distils medical and epidemiological power in their "pure" form. Such pure form is never met in reality, but its underlying logic is shared with biosecurity and can offer a first, abstract approximation of its power. As we are dealing with a security crisis and effort, Chapter 3 identifies the threat biosecurity sets out to counter: the threat of the epidemic is in contagion; and contagion is in society. The next three chapters discuss the state response to the crisis. Chapter 4 observes the abstract summoning of biosecurity powers in legislation — and their effects on the liberal juridical constellation. Chapter 5 focuses on public health policy during the pandemic; and Chapter 6 offers a broader discussion of biosecurity and society, concentrating especially on the power of the state to suspend society. Finally, having outlined biosecurity operations and their socio-political meaning, Chapter 7 deciphers the epistemology of biosecurity: its epistemic modalities, and its relation to science and intelligence.

2 Medical power

Biosecurity, as experienced during the pandemic, outlines a novel configuration of power. It combines the repressive and exclusionary modality of security with the paternalist, caring power associated with medicine.

The doctor dictator

Medical power is the most authoritarian form of power. Throughout modern history, dictators sought to justify their usurpation of power on its basis. At the dawn of modernity, in Renaissance Italy, Rinaldo degli Albizzi attempted a coup on Florence in order to cure the city from its illness (Machiavelli 2021: V, 8). In the 19th century, Juan Donoso Cortés, the great reactionary philosopher whose thought has marked conservative and counter-revolutionary politics, conceptualised society as a quasi-human body that can be offended by illness — and cured by dictatorship (Cortés 2000). Indeed, the conceptualisation of the polity as a quasi-biological structure, as "body politic", already contains the preoccupation with its health, illness and doctoring. This preoccupation — and the biologisation of politics — reached its paroxystic apogee in Nazism. Nazism outlined a medical-biological programme that saw Jews, communists, homosexuals, gypsies, delinquents and "degenerates" as offences to the health of the German race: as viruses, bacteria, parasites, bacilli, cancer and syphilis as well as rats and lice. It embarked on a "social disinfection", which offered Nazi doctors total power over life and death; and hailed Hitler as "the great German doctor" (Esposito 2008: 112–117; Sontag 1978). Since then, it is a staple of fascist and/or dictatorial political discourse and programme of government, as seen in the proclamations of juntas to stop the spread of the "Marxist disease" in their respective countries. In liberal states, the invocation of medical/biological terms used to alarm even moderately conservative thinkers. The diagnosis of a "sick society" is direct invitation to a dictatorial "law and order" hardening of the state. It is a most dangerous development, for "[t]he sicker the patient is supposed to be, the more likely that the surgeon will have the last word" (Arendt 1970: 75).

DOI: 10.4324/9781003302988-3

It is worth noting that this tendency to assume the role of shaman that would heal the nation from deadly illness pertains to dictators, not to despots. Dictatorship constitutes a violent rupture in a political arrangement that involves the people as an active element. Therefore, dictators need to justify their usurpation. This does not apply to despots, whose ascendancy is in continuity with the existing political form; and, even in the case of dynastic disruption, they do not need to justify their authority to society, but only to cliques of nobility. In other words, the medical metaphor in politics is a legitimacy platform; and the need for legitimacy implies a politically involved people. This legitimacy is typically articulated on the basis of a lethal threat to the "body politic". The dictator then exercises medical power to erase the disease from the suffering body. The dictator's power is therefore rooted in, and motivated by, care. It is also dictated by necessity, its exercise is a question of life and death. This makes it limitless: it can employ all means available; it must, and will, *do whatever it takes.* The disease, and the body politic, are, of course, metaphors. During the coronavirus pandemic, they became literal; so did the state's exercise of medical power.

The pastor doctor

Medical power is based on expertise. It can be legitimately exercised only by qualified scientists, acknowledged as such by their peers. The knowledge on which it is based is secluded from the non-experts (Foucault 1996: 115). Indeed, medical power is constituted as such by depriving the people from the knowledge and ability to care for and treat themselves (Illitch 1982: 12). This expertise-based power makes illness a matter of technical understanding and treatment, dissociating it from its social causes, like pollution, stress, working conditions, poverty. Medical power turns health from a social issue to a technical-clinical problem. In doing so, it exonerates the social order, deflects its questioning and shields it from change (Illitch 1982: 71, 96–98, 121).

Medical power strives to counteract the disease, which it understands as a natural occurrence governed by its own laws and regularities (Foucault 1996: 7–9). Its method involves identification (of symptoms), classification (of diseases' types and symptoms pertinent to each), and distribution (attachment of symptoms to diseases, and of diseases to bodies). Notably, medical power tends to decipher the necessity of its intervention: doctors are reluctant to diagnose the absence of illness; they assume that, unless proven healthy, the person before them is ill (Illitch 1982: 55–56, 70). Medical power is self-confirmatory.

Medical knowledge continuously moves form abstract to specific: to identify the disease, it subtracts the individual from its specificity, turning it into a mere vessel of the disease; to treat it, it needs to know the individual in all his specifying detail: his means, environment, habits, desires, relations, attitudes. It is therefore concerned with both the abstract, universal and objective knowledge of the disease; *and* with the specific, particular and subjective knowledge of each individual that bears it (Foucault 1996: 7–9, 15).

To attain this knowledge that spans abstract universality and minute specificity, medical power is surveillant: it constantly extracts, assesses and revises information. It is based on perpetual, expansive, detailed and open-ended surveillance of both the patient and the disease within her (Foucault 1996: 29, 60). Medical power is, indeed, based on observation: it monitors, watches and develops technologies of super-vision that penetrate the skin and the opacity it introduces. Thus, medical power renders its objects, the patients, fully transparent. More than (supra-)empirical, it is analytical and combinatory. Medical power deciphers reality by articulating disperse elements acquired through observation, which in isolation may have no meaning, into a meaningful, conclusive whole (Foucault 1996: 114–120). On this basis, its interventions are based on calculations of probabilities for optimum outcomes and set to produce decisive effects in specific conjunctures in the development of the disease (Foucault 1996: 88–89). Medical power is acutely tactical.

Morally, medical power is profane: it defies and resists limitations posed by sacredness or by a popular sense of decency (Foucault 1996: 124–125; Linebaugh 2011). It develops its own morality, one defined by care. It is kind, gentle and considerate to the patient. It is prudent and attentive to the patient's needs and limitations. It is concerned with what we need to do and with what we are actually doing (Foucault 1996: 60, 121; Mol 2008). It is persistent but patient, calm and forgiving. It does not force the patient to conform with abstract principles, but only with specific actions that would bear optimum results for her specific case (Mol 2008: 5, 23). And, it does not demand obedience (Mol 2008: 25); it is not a coercive power. Coercion does not emanate from the doctor but from the illness; and both the patient and the doctor face it together. For the former, this is a necessity; for the latter, an ethos. Thus, the exercise of medical power is a collaborative venture, where the doctor seeks the deepest, and deeply sympathetic, understanding of the patient, her circumstances, attitudes, capabilities and limitations. On this basis, the doctor adjusts the treatment to the patient and nudges her to adopt it — and this involves guiding her to alter her attitudes, overcome her limitations, expand her capabilities (Mol 2008). In this common effort the responsibility for a successful outcome lies not so much on the quality of the doctor's proscriptions, but on their accommodation by the patient. Due to its empathetic and collaborative nature, medical power is irresistible — resisting a course of action co-defined by one's participation is absurd, especially when such action is necessary. Coercion is external to this relation: the patient can ignore the doctor's advice; the consequences will not be brought by the doctor, but by the illness. The nature of these consequences makes medical power not only irresistible, but undeniable: medical power springs from necessity, it is dictated by the illness. For this, it is immanently absolute and decisionist. At the limit case, the doctor can, and will, intuitively determine the life prospects of different patients and decide who is to be treated and who left to die (Illitch 1982: 146).

There is no power without an object. The object of medical power is the patient; and the entire power relation is established on the premise of the patient's vulnerability (Mol 2008: 25). In this relation, the patient is an object of knowledge and intervention. As an object of knowledge the patient is, on the one hand, abstracted. She is merely the container of the disease, and her specific qualities are subtracted and ignored. Yet, on the other hand, she is also the support of the disease and, for contagious diseases, its medium. In her treatment, the patient is both a subject helped to become cured, and a body to be mended — an object of technical dispatch. The extent and manner in which she participates in her treatment are determined by the doctor. Whether more or less passive or "activated", the patient remains the last cog in a one-way traffic of instruction. She is also the least reliable cog, the unstable factor in a technical process. Yet, the outcome will largely depend on her, on her compliance with the doctor's instructions (Illitch 1982: 135, 146).

Thus, medical power establishes a relation of dependency. The need for healing and the means thereof, the suffering and the absolution from it, are firmly attached to different parties in this relation. However collaborative the treatment might be, and however much it is defined by the patient's condition, it is determined by the doctor; the patient is the, prone or reluctant, executant of the doctor's orders. There is therefore an asymmetry in the treatment relation: rule-making is monopolised by one party, while their implementation is left with the other, who also suffers or enjoys the consequences. The doctor sets out rules that the patient does not have, but needs, to follow; the patient needs to comply with rules she cannot co-author. At the extreme case, when the patient does not have her senses, when in a ventilator, for instance, or in induced coma, she is the passive object of treatment. In short, medical power describes a benevolent but also profoundly heteronomous relation (Illitch 1982: 126).

Doctoring the population

The illness caused by coronavirus is not contained or isolated within each individual body it offends. It is contagious, transmitted across bodies through their proximity and contact. This has drastic implications for the character of biosecurity, starting from the type of medical power mobilised against it: epidemiology.

Epidemiology diverts the attentions of medical power from the individual to society, to what it calls "the population". It is not concerned with any specific individual but with their social aggregate, and address the individual only as an atom within the latter. Its primary focus is not to match bodies to illnesses, but to understand transmission and its modalities. It is therefore preoccupied with the contagious properties specific to the disease and, chiefly, with individual's behaviours, flows and contacts. It is, in short, relational.

However, its operational modality is the same with individualised medical power —it is a distinct configuration of medical power, not a different type of power. Epidemiology perpetually extracts information, evaluates it, and intervenes in order to constrain the spread of disease. To do these at the level of the population it is supplemented by a police apparatus (Foucault 1995: 195–228; 1996: 25–26): a mechanism of intelligence and enforcement that extracts knowledge from society, organises it and, on its basis, intervenes to forcefully rearrange society (Neocleous 2000). Indeed, in epidemiology, medical power is exercised through a policing mechanism, it is expressed as policing. This is so because, in its epidemiological iteration, medical power traverses and penetrates social space in its entirety (Foucault 1996: 31). Thus, medical power becomes political *strictu sensu*. Its terrain of application is no longer the individual body, but the collective body of the population.

By transferring its attentions from the individual to the collective organism of the population, epidemiology expands the scope of medical power. The latter now comes to bear not only in the molecular level of the natural properties of a disease; but mainly on the disease-generating conditions. These may include anything: from practices and attitudes concerning health, work, leisure, sex, friendship and family life; to natural and build environment; from dietary habits, physical care and hygiene; to publicly circulating opinions regarding all the above. Epidemiological power is premised on an evolving, meticulous knowledge of humans: as natural *and* as social beings (Foucault 1996: 34–35). As it addresses the population, epidemiology is, more than anything, a practice of surveillance, and it is future-oriented: the population it constantly monitors is healthy. Rather: it is not ill *yet*. Epidemiological knowledge continuously moves from the individual to the aggregate and back, in a seamless surveillance of a totality it considers as potentially ill and contagious (Armstrong 1995; Samerski 2018). In its epidemiological guise, medical power is political and *total*. Its knowledge and intervention can encompass everything, from the relation of individual with her body; to the broadest socio-political arrangements and structures. Epidemiology can envelop the totality of social relations to intervene on specific — actual *and* anticipated — conjunctures and their exigencies. Epidemiology is certainly tactical; it can also be strategic.

Thus, to control the epidemic means to control society. Society is the overall environment within which diseases spread. To control society means to control the contact and proximity of individuals, its purpose, modalities, duration and rhythm. Individualised medical power institutes, and is exercised through, particular spatio-temporal separations and regimentations. Its fortress, the hospital, encapsulates this: as a structure, the hospital is nothing but spatio-temporal regimentation. It is separate from the broader society, and a society within itself, with relations and hierarchies that are specific to it and active (or conceivable) only within it. Its patients are sequestered according to the classification and intensity of their ailment into parallel spatio-temporal worlds. The limit case of this regime of separation and regimentation, the extremity of medical power, is the quarantine: the regimentation pertinent to the hospital comes to apply to the broader society. Epidemiology shifts the parameters of this power. Rather than turning society into a hospital, it breaks the confines of the latter to encompass society where, and as, it is. Accordingly, the epidemiology apparatus and operation is not centralised and regimented, but open-ended and defused. Its target is not only coextensive with society; it is society as such: the totality of interactions between not-yet-ill individuals. If society is the disease-generating environment, its suspension eliminates disease.

To control the epidemic means to control society: For epidemiology, society is not only the generating environment of the disease. It is also the patient. The vulnerable, rudderless entity whose survival depends on the benign expert interventions of medical power is no longer an atomised individual, but society as a complex, singular body. Society is also the misbehaving cog that threatens to sabotage its own rescue by misapplying the prescriptions handed to it. In epidemiology, the doctor's prescriptions may encompass anything, from toilet manners to urban designs; and they are addressed not only to unfolding epidemics but also anticipated ones. In short, epidemiology not only examines and intervenes in society, but actually shapes it, in order to proof it from the possibility of disease. In epidemiology, medical power is no longer an individualised relation between doctor and patient, but a political relation between the state and society.

Medical power

In sum, medical power is a benevolent power. It is premised on the perception of human vulnerability and aims to ameliorate it. It is a caring power, reluctant to coerce. It is a knowledge-based power, constituted upon scientific knowledge of illnesses and cures, which it tends to systematise and seclude into a monopoly of expertise. It also necessitates the minute knowledge of each individual body, the interaction between bodies, and their general social environment. It seeks the fullest possible knowledge of each individual and of their dynamic aggregation into a society. This knowledge concerns the present but also the past — the medical history of patients and their progenitors; the "underlying conditions" each person or group may carry. Even more, it is concerned with the future: dormant dangers, risky behaviours, prospective outcomes of interventions, vulnerabilities of individual bodies and of the population, and prophylactic reshaping of their physicality and behaviour.

Coextensive with its object of knowledge, the scope of its intervention is virtually unlimited. It can encompass anything from medical prescriptions and individual treatments, to food quality standards, irrigation projects, or energy production and waste disposal methods. Across its countless areas of application, its interventions are flexible: not determined by principle, they are practical, case-specific and proceed through trial and error. They are aimed to specific outcomes in specific conjunctures — actual, anticipated, or merely possible.

Medical power is also undeniable. While it does not coerce, it can neither be ignored at a personal or social level. The cost of ignoring its proscriptions is illness and, ultimately, death. On this basis, medical power institutes a relation of dependency. Whether it applies to specific individuals or to the population, it represents an heteronomous condition, where all decisions and rules are produced by one party; while all the dangers are run by another party which is excluded from their production but should, nonetheless, obey them.

This power construes its object as afflicted, lacking, deficient, damaged and needy. The patient — individual or collective — is a pathetic subjectivity. She utterly depends on the doctor. The utmost of her agency is to resist (ignore or misapply) the doctor's decrees and, thus, undermine her recovery and hasten her demise. Responsibility for failure lies not with the doctor who devised the treatment, but with the insubordinate patient. Medical power is, therefore, a responsibilising power; and this is another sense in which it is undeniable: it is always right, even when its undertake fails.

In one word, this is pastoral power. A gentle, benevolent power, reluctant to coerce, and stemming from care for the flock and for each individual member thereof (Foucault 2007). It is a paternalist, heteronomous, power, that is based on dependency and denies the possibility of individual or social autonomy. It is an irresistible power, for its exercised not only on but also through its object. In its context, politics, the question of social organisation, direction and purpose, cannot be raised because it is already settled. Medical power is an undeniable, limitless power that neutralises the political faculty of society in order to save society from itself. This is the power that defines biosecurity and is exercised through it. It is the modality of state power we have come to experience. It is mobilised to save us from a threat.

3 The threat

Security is always constituted in relation to a threat. It identifies the threat that calls it forth, and is largely defined by it — security defines the threat that defines it. Biosecurity is defined by the threat posed by covid-19. Yet, for this to occur, biosecurity defines the threat posed by the virus: the nature of its threat, and its nature *as* a threat. The threat posed by covid-19 — or rather its perception by the fledging state logic and the apparatus that is formed in order to counter it — is that of an intangible, invisible and potentially lethal entity that is easily transmitted from human to human.

Biosecurity then is a regime, organisation and apparatus of security directed to life. It aims to preserve the integrity of a given life form from the danger posed by the intrusion of factors foreign to it — animate and inanimate, organic and inorganic. Notably, for the neoliberal configuration of biosecurity, the threat emanates *only* from *surplus* — when something, like a virus, is superimposed to the life-form, intrudes and penetrates it. The threat never occurs through *deficit*. Neoliberal biosecurity does not contemplate the possibility of threat residing in the life-form's *lacking*: of water, food, medicine, healthcare and shelter.

In the coronavirus pandemic, the threat is posed to the human life-form, by its intrusion from another form, a viral one. This form maintains the basic attributes of life: it is distinguishable and differentiated from its environment, and presents propensities, vulnerabilities, adaptabilities and malleabilities specific to itself. But it lacks the faculties of reflection, planning or forming intension — strictly speaking, the virus lacks the faculty of action. It is passive, predictable and controllable. As the virus is incapable of it, all action is done by humans. The intrusion of the virus-form in the human-form occurs through the proximity and contact between humans. Thus, for biosecurity, in the context of the pandemic, human life is the object of protection, but also the means through which the viral threat circulates and multiplies.

It is its contagious nature, its ability to spread until it potentially envelops all human-forms, that defines the parameters of the threat. The threat resides on its potentiality for expansion. Its spread is can envelop the entire society. The atomic agent of this spread is the individual who, affected by

DOI: 10.4324/9781003302988-4

the virus, becomes its conductor. The threat then resides in inter-individuality. This means that the individual comes to be closely related to the threat; she comes to be defined by her relation to the threat, as its sufferer and as its bearer.

The individual is conceived as the victim of the threat. She is the nodal point at which the entirety of biosecurity efforts converge. Biosecurity is concerned with her rescue, its apparatus and interventions are designed to achieve this. Biosecurity's rescuing endeavour combines two aspects differentiated in terms of operation and temporality: a recovering and a preventive one. The first, recovery, aims to save the individual that has fallen victim of the threat, that has been inflicted by the virus. The second, prevention, aims to prevent the individual from being inflicted by the threat, to reduce or eliminate such possibility. Biosecurity's recovery operation unfolds through medical interventions on the individual, conducted in medical institutions through the personnel, practices and protocols pertinent to them. Its preventive operation is not centred on any specific individual, but on all. It is concerned not with the relation between each individual and the virus, but with the relation between each individual and the others. It is not enclosed in specific institutions, but expands throughout the space that these interactions occupy and in which they occur — the social space. And, it is not carried out by medical personnel, practices and protocols, but by police and intelligence. In short, biosecurity interventions modulate between being strictly medical and "integrally" medical: epidemiological. The former apply primarily to the individual, the latter to society; the former address the threat in its actuality, the latter address the threat as a potentiality.

Crucially, the individual is not only the, actual or potential, victim of the threat. She is also its bearer. The threat exists and acts only through her. It is, hence, the individual herself that threatens others: the victim is the threat — and the victim is subject of concern only inasmuch as she represents a threat. Replicating the modality of counterterrorism, biosecurity conceptualises the citizen as both a potential victim and a suspect (Boukalas 2019). Crucially, she can be both without anyone knowing, not even herself. Both infliction and transmission of the illness can be asymptomatic, and this is a key element in defining the threat. It is estimated that up to half of the transmissions of the disease occurred through people who, at that moment, were displaying no symptoms; and that almost a fifth of inflicted people remained asymptomatic throughout their illness (The Economist 2020e: 66). Thus, the threat can grow, in and through, individuals whose threatened and threatening status is not manifest — and this, more than its infinitesimal size, makes the "enemy" invisible. Even those individuals who were tested negative were healthy only up to the moment of the test. They may have since been infected and can therefore be threatening. Affirming the epistemological dogma of pre-emptive security, when the virus is concerned, "the absence of evidence is not evidence of absence" (Rumsfeld 2002). The asymptomatic modality of the threat introduces an acute condition of suspicion: one cannot trust oneself. She may be unknowingly infected and unwittingly harming others; she may be a threat without knowing it. Thus, being human comes to mean being the potential bearer and spreader of the virus; life becomes coterminous with threat.

The threat of the disease is in its spreading. While the threat is ultimately located in its individual victim and bearer, it is its transmission across them that makes it a threat. And it spreads through proximity: approach, contact, talk and touch. The threat, in short, resides in the very act of society; society is the threat. The threat is coextensive with society, it spreads through and exists in social interaction. The threat resides in and encompasses society as such.

On this basis, suspicion becomes the universal currency. It permeates all social relations, including those between state and society. Suspicion becomes the social meta-relation, that encompasses all others. Its object is everyone, especially those closer to the individual: friends, lovers, colleagues and relatives. In this context, social relations become relations of mutual policing. They are marked by mistrust and fear of the other's proximity, and are expressed in flight from it and in a moralist normativity as individuals catechise and judge each other on their performance of biosecurity protocols. The self cannot be trusted either: as the absence of evidence is not evidence of absence, one maybe a threat to others without knowing it. He must therefore — always — assume that he is threatening and act accordingly. The asymptotic presence of the threat is particularly common in children — who tend to not to suffer from the illness, but can be its bearers and spreaders. Here, the threat effectuates a perversion of morality. The children, the subject culturally enveloped by notions of innocence, becomes the most threatening one. More than that, the threat constitutes a perversion of security. More than the epitome of innocence, children are, due to their fragile nature, the par excellence and universal object of protection — so universal, that we may call it *instinctive*. They are constantly in danger from the catastrophic intrusion of corrupting influences: physical, emotional, intellectual and moral. Now, children become silent marauders: the most stealthily dangerous conduits of the threat. From *the* object of protection, children become the subject of threat. Innocence is danger. Even in the form of a child's face, the other is fore-mostly a potential killer. Thus, the elemental relation of trust that is necessary for society collapses. Long before any quarantine is imposed, the possibility of society as a set of actions and relations is cancelled at a conceptual and affective level. Premised on universalised fear and suspicion, this cancelling of society underwrites all measures for physical distancing and quarantine, and runs deeper than them. They are its official expression and organisation. Isolation, the suspension of contact, is but the logical outcome of the collapse of trust needed for society.

In conceptualising society as a threat, biosecurity effectuates a fundamental reversal of society's meaning. While it is impossible to reduce society to security, the latter is a relation deeply inscribed in the social texture. Human beings are patently ill equipped to survive in a multifariously hostile nature *alone* — either as infants or as fully hatched Robinsons. Our life utterly depends on society: the relations of association, community and mutual aid that comprise it and the various forms of collaboration, knowledge, care and material resourcing they entail (Kropotkin 1902). Thus, while every society is much more than security, while it covers and creates a myriad more needs, security remains a fundamental social relation, purpose and function — a relation that cannot exist without society. Society cannot be reduced to security, but security does not exist without society. Biosecurity effectuates a reversal of this relation. From a necessary condition of life's security and safety, society becomes their negation, a threat to the survival of the individual. In this sense, biosecurity perfects (completes and exacerbates) the fundamental liberal imaginary, which sets the individual and its innate "rights" in juxtaposition, antagonism and mistrust to the others — to society — which is in principle an entity hostile to the independent individual in the centre of the liberal universe (Locke 2016). While liberalism placed an element of danger and suspicion within society, biosecurity turns society as such into danger and suspicion, perfecting its reversal from a place of security into one of threat.

To conclude: Security is premised on fear — there is no (need for) security without threat, and there is no threat without fear. Still, security is not the elimination of fear, but its organisation. Every security endeavour is constituted on promulgating insecurity, on sublimating, reproducing and even instilling fear, and managing it: setting up its parameters, intensity and meanings. This organisation of fear decisively depends on the definition of the threat that security sets out to confront. Biosecurity locates the threat posed by covid-19 in its transmission, in the potential for the virus to spread. This makes every individual an — actual or potential — victim and bearer of the threat, a threatened and, simultaneously, threatening subject. While the virus is always located in, and transmitted across, individuals, the threat resides in their interaction. It resides, in other words, in the acts that constitute society, and the space and time that these describe. The threat, therefore is not merely *in* society, in the space and time of interaction; it *is* society, it is the interaction. Transmuted at the social level, the dual conceptualisation of the individual as a patient and a spreader, becomes a conceptualisation of the citizen as both victim and suspect. In turn, each individual is suspected by, and suspects, everyone else: society as such is suspect. Suspicion then becomes a universal attitude and the overarching social relation; and this has a deleterious effect on the relations of trust that are necessary for society. The conceptualisation of the citizen as a suspect, a potential bearer of threat; and the generalisation of relations of mutual suspicion among individuals, were tropes of the counterterrorism endeavour (Boukalas 2019; 2020; Guittet and Brion 2017). Indeed, more than the undermining of rights and the rule of law, they are the most deeply authoritarian trends of counterterrorism and its most profound legacy. In biosecurity, these trends are reiterated and perfected. For, in counterterrorism, a specific citizen can — regardless of the suspicion with which the state and even her peers confront her — know herself to not be a terrorist, to *not* be a threat. There is a limit to suspicion. In biosecurity, this is no longer possible; suspicion has no limit. The citizen cannot know herself as non-threatening, and cannot act as if such was the case. She must always assume herself a threat, she must always suspect herself. The deleterious effect of security on the trust that underpins and enables social relations, comes now to also encompass the relations that constitute the self. There is no room for no-suspicion, safety is inconceivable. In counterterrorism, this undermining of social trust designates a relation of dependency on the state, as social relations come to be mediated by the logic and the operation of the security apparatus. In biosecurity, this dependency is complete: the citizen cannot know the truth regarding the status, intentions and effects, not only of others, but also of herself. She utterly depends on the state to learn who she is and what she means for others. In biosecurity all truth emanates, exclusively and undeniably, from the state — and the truth is: *you are a threat.*

Biosecurity conceptualises (everyone in) society as the threat; accordingly its operational logic tends towards erasing society. Erasing society is the way for biosecurity to deliver its mission, to defeat the threat. With society cancelled, the only actor in the social field is the state. We turn to see its operation in biosecurity's social void.

4 Biosecurity law

Law is the blueprint in which state powers are outlined and state strategies become decipherable, in abstract. Moreover, the legal blueprint involves in its production key state institutions — at minimum the legislature and the executive — and therefore the law-making process offers indications not only regarding the direction the state is taking but also about the shape of its institutions. Accordingly, our examination of the biosecurity state starts with its law.

The state response to the biosecurity crisis is defined by the spectre of quarantine. It comprises interventions imposing separation, isolation, immobilisation and closure: social distancing, lockdowns, self-isolation, prohibition of gatherings and quarantine proper. These apply to individuals, workplaces, public institutions, localities, regions as well as entire state territories and their citizenry. While these interventions vary in scope, intensity, time and duration, their ultimate horizon, which determines them even when not present, is quarantine: the complete isolation and confinement of every individual in a suspended time.

Biosecurity is a state operation. Its limit concept, quarantine, is also a limit concept of state power — for it suspends society. It is not only an extraordinary measure but also one that liberal states tend to be uncomfortable with. Here, I examine how such a state, the UK, vested itself with such powers: I examine the law of biosecurity. Readers beyond the UK will, probably, find a lot that is similar to the legal architecture of biosecurity in their country; they will also spot a lot of differences — and this can be the first step towards a comparative account. A first such similarity is that, in most countries, biosecurity interventions are conducted through Executive decree. A first difference is that, in most European and North American countries, under either parliamentary or presidential systems, the power of the Executive to issue such decrees is inscribed in their constitution — in the context of constitutionally predicted "exception", "necessity" or other such vehicle. In Britain, this capacity must be codified in legislation issued by Parliament. The key legislation here is the Coronavirus Act 2020.

DOI: 10.4324/9781003302988-5

Coronavirus Act: a state of siege

The purpose of the Coronavirus Act (CVA or the Act), stated in its accompanying Explanatory Notes, is to help the government: (a) increase the available health and social care workforce; (b) ease the burden on front-line staff; (c) contain the virus and slow its spread down; and (d) "support people" (House of Lords 2020: 5). This last objective is formulated in terms so general that it stands out as odd, even in an era where open-endedness and lack of definition has become a hallmark of law making (Boukalas 2017; Scheuerman 2004). It is completely unclear what constitutes "support", under what circumstances it is to be delivered, or to whom. Similarly, it is completely unclear what "people" is: citizens, denizens, individuals, associations, corporations — are these all "people"? Further, there is no outline of the means of support, of limits to it and no consideration of whether supporting some people could harm others. While this is just a statement of intent, its vagueness and open-endedness shows the Act is inclined to allow governmental discretion.

The first two stated purposes (to increase the available health and social care workforce; and to ease the burden on front-line staff) describe an attempt to strengthen the healthcare mechanism. To this end, the Act provides arrangements for the emergency registration of healthcare and social care professionals (sections 2–5 and 6–7; Schedules 1–4 and 5–6). It also provides for the compensation and employment rights of emergency volunteers in these sectors (s.9; House of Lords 2020: 7); and removes obstacles preventing retired National Health Service (NHS) personnel from returning to work (s.45). Further, the Act indemnifies health workers from clinical tort liability for negligence in any NHS "business as usual" activity, including diagnosis, care and treatment, that results to a patient's death (s.11; House of Lords 2020: 34). The Act also removes NHS personnel's duty of care towards its patients, and thus exempts them from criminal liability ensuing from this duty (s.14). It also relieves hospitals from their duty to assess patients' need for continuation of healthcare provision and removes relevant regulatory requirements (s.18). Similarly, the CVA relieves local authorities from their duty to meet citizens' needs for care and support. Finally, the Act suspends the requirement for inquest by jury when covid-19 is a suspected contributor to a death (s.30). Somewhat unexpectedly, it reduces the statutory requirement for doctors' opinions necessary for the detention and treatment of mental health patients, from two to one; and also lifts the limits to their detention, rendering it indefinite (s.10; Sch.8–11; House of Lords 2020: 30–31).

Beyond healthcare, the state is concerned with security and its apparatus. The CVA grants the Secretary of State for Agriculture unlimited powers to request and acquire information on any aspect of the food supply chain from anyone working within relevant industries, in order to identify disruption risks (ss.25–29; Sch.15(7); House of Lords 2020: 13). Further, it allowed the Home Secretary to extend for 6 months the retention of fingerprints and DNA profiles if she considered that the pandemic may have "an adverse effect" in preventing Police chiefs from making such determinations (s.24). These powers were stroke down by the government in March 2021. They were exclusively dictated by counterterrorism exigencies. Its purpose is to identify travellers to Syria; identify terrorism suspects amongst asylum applicants; provide evidence for "potential" terrorism offences; and to match terrorism suspects' data to other countries' relevant databases (House of Lords 2020: 12).

Finally, the Act provides for the emergency hiring of judges to approve surveillance warrants (s. 23). This is done through regulations and statutory instruments issued by the Home Secretary upon request from the Investigatory Powers Commissioner, a senior judge who leads a small cohort of judges whose approval is necessary for the validity of surveillance warrants. The Act also creates a regulation-making power that allows the Secretary to quadruple the time (from 3 to 12 days) for which surveillance operations can continue without judicial approval. These powers anticipate, and aim to ameliorate, a potential disruption to warrant-approval processes by afflicting those responsible for that work. It is, however, worth noting that these powers are not part of the arsenal against the pandemic: the track-and-trace surveillance pertinent to biosecurity uses "relational data", which is freely available to public institutions without judicial involvement. Instead, the judicial approvals, whose smooth production the Act seeks to secure, are only needed in the context of highly intrusive surveillance. These CVA provisions are designed to safeguard the customary operations of the intelligence apparatus from possible disruption.

Thus far, these powers describe a state of siege. In anticipation of a devastating blow to the continuity of its operations, the state strengthens its capacity to dispatch its most basic functions uninterrupted. It seeks to safeguard the food supply and to guarantee the continuity of its policing operations, especially those undertaken by the intelligence apparatus. Above all, it seeks to bolster the healthcare system, its fortress in the war against the invisible enemy. It rapidly pulls in everyone that can lend a hand in the fight — with the notable exception of private healthcare equipment and personnel. In relieving health workers from legal responsibilities towards their patients, it frees their minds from worrying about the consequences of their acts and omissions. It is remarkable that this strengthening of the healthcare *system* is enabled by a diminishing of healthcare *duties*. This implies a circumscription of citizens' rights, including their right to health. This move will be fleshed out in subsequent Chapters (5 and 17); but is already programmatically present in the abstract blueprint of state power, in legislation. The Act indicates that strengthening the state involves its departure from responsibility towards society; it suggests that the strength of the state resides precisely in its freedom from responsibility.

The law of biosecurity

More than state institutions and functions, the state of siege implicit in the CVA encompasses society and resets the state's relation to it. This resetting is marked by a temporal suspension of civil liberties and the empowerment of the Executive to impose it unilaterally.

Schedule 22 of the CVA grands the Health Secretary authority to declare a threat to public health due to coronavirus. He can do so at any time he "is of the view" that coronavirus constitutes a serious and immanent threat to public health. Upon such realisation he can exercise any powers he finds to be "an effective means" for preventing, protecting against, delaying "or otherwise controlling" the transmission of the disease; or facilitating the deployment of medical or emergency personnel and resources. The declaration of imminent threat initiates a "public health response period" which ends when the Secretary revokes the declaration. During this period, the Secretary can restrict and prohibit any type of public or private events and gatherings; and restrict access and order the closure of any type of premises. Failure to comply is a criminal offence punished by fine, without right to appeal.

This is the legal power from which the British measures emanate, like the obligation for those who present suspect symptoms and for anyone that has been in contact with them to isolate; the closure of all but "essential" businesses; the prohibition of all travel but for "essential purposes"; the obligatory testing of those arriving from abroad; the permission to exit the home only for essential work, food shopping and limited exercise. All it takes to trigger such powers and restrictions is for the Health Secretary to be "of the view" that there is a threat to public health, and that the powers he institutes are "an effective means" to counter it. Through what considerations the Secretary may come to this view is unknown. Similarly unspecified are the consultations and deliberations through which the Secretary determines the effectiveness of the measures he imposes. Notably, there is no requirement that the measures are *proportionate* to the threat; or *necessary* for countering it; or that they are the optimum way for doing so. The Act allows the Secretary to ignore requirements for the necessity of the powers, and to exceed even the elastic limitations posed by proportionality. Indeed, the Act does not require any link between the measures and the threat. It does not define, or even outline, what can be classed as a threat — what type of phenomenon, with how harmful effects and what probabilities of them coming to pass must the Secretary contemplate before he becomes "of the view" that there is a threat; and his measures only need to be however effective he thinks them to be. In short, the Act allows the Secretary to decide whether a threat is present or imminent; and, on this basis, dictate whatever measures he wants, as long as he thinks they are likely to help counter the threat — somewhat and somehow.

Once they had voted for the Act, parliamentarians realised it marginalises them. Despite introducing "some of the most sweeping powers seen in modern times" the CVA was inadequately scrutinised; and its parliamentary review process does not allow parliament to amend or repeal specific provisions, but only to extend or revoke the Act as a whole (Joint Committee on Human Rights 2020: 14, 67). Notably, the actual regulations that most heavily contravene civil liberties are not subject to parliamentary review at all. For they are not issued under the CVA, which is an emergency law with inbuilt review procedures, but under the Public Health Act 1984, a permanent legislation to which review procedures do not apply. On its basis, most of the coronavirus-related statutory instruments that ministers issue were subject to the weakest parliamentary review and typically came to force without parliamentary approval (Joint Committee on Human Rights 2020: 68–69). By early 2021 more than 370 sets of regulations had been issued in this way, prompting high ranking civil servants to note that the unceasing issuing of hastily enacted, unscrutinised, contradictory and vague rules could become a permanent feature of government, undermining the state's ability to govern through law (Jones 2021). The government, in other words, is observing the appearances of exercising power through rule of law processes, while it is in fact ruling by decree. Essentially, the Act grants the Secretary the power to curve a whole in time — a "public health response period" — during which his commands are law. Rather: there is no law in the "response" period; only power. It is impossible for the Secretary to abuse his powers, to overstep their limits — for there are none. In the CVA, parliament has authorised the government to exercise power at its discretion. This power applies to society.

Schedule 21 of the CVA authorises health officials, police constables and migration officers to test individuals for the virus, including through force; and to restrict or cancel individuals' movement, association (meeting specific people and people in general) and activity — activity of any kind, including that necessary for their livelihood. It also authorises public health officers to order the quarantining of an individual. This quarantine may last up to 14 days, but can be extended, for another 14, if the public health officer reasonably suspects that the person will be potentially infectious at the end of the quarantine period, or that the restrictions are still necessary[1]. The "reasonable suspicion" requirement needed to trigger these powers is the lowest possible threshold, it is as close as can be to unconditional licence without being it. Moreover, there are no specified criteria or processes through which this reasonable suspicion is determined. The officer's decision-making process and the decision itself are reviewed by no one. In essence, a singular state employee can issue orders that completely cancel a person's social life on the basis of his suspicion that the person is "potentially infectious". A person is, or can be, potentially infectious if she is *possibly* contaminated with coronavirus or has been in an area abroad infected with coronavirus — in short, anyone, (from) anywhere. The measures must be necessary and proportionate to the interests of the individual, the interests of others, or the maintenance of public health. This requirement allows the affected individual to apply for a review of the orders by a magistrate. But, if the order is not obviously unlawful, irrational or procedurally flawed, the magistrate has no grounds to quash it. Moreover, the peculiar interplay of interests to be protected (of the person subjected to the order, of anyone else, or of the public in general) assure that any order would satisfy its purpose, it would be to someone's interest. Effectively, the law only requires the officer to produce some justification for the issuing of the order — it is as close as possible to full licence without being it. Again, failure to comply is a criminal offence, punished by a fine.

This is the legal arsenal of the state in its fight against the threat. The powers the Act grants the Executive materialise in the Regulations that the Secretary of Health hectically issues, which impose "the most wide-ranging restrictions on individual liberties, affecting the greatest number of people" since the Defence Regulations during WWII. These Regulations reverse the, quintessential of liberal jurisprudence, presumption that people are free to act as they want unless there is explicit prohibition in law. Under the Regulations, people are prohibited from doing anything that is not explicitly allowed by the government (Joint Committee on Human Rights 2020: 16). The CVA authorisations to screen, assess and isolate; to require biological samples, contact details and documents; to restrict travel; and to detain for up to 28 days those who they deem to be potentially infectious, "inevitably engage" Article 5 of the European Convection on Human Rights, as they allow deprivation of liberty on the basis of an amorphous categorisation ("potentially infectious") that is essentially determined by officers' discretion, while failure to comply constitutes an automatic criminal conviction, without trial or appeal (Joint Committee on Human Rights 2020: 45–47).

The relentless issuing of regulations that are not the outcome of deliberation or strategic coordination, but merely a Secretary's reflex response to the weekly trends of the pandemic (and the economy), results to regulatory chaos. The speed and frequency with which national and local lockdown laws change sabotages legal certainty. Neither citizens nor police forces can keep on top of what is legally required or what is reasonably expected of them. Implementation of the regulations is thronged with confusion and misunderstanding. These are exacerbated by the uncertain demarcation of government guidance from legally binding regulations. As a result, *all* people prosecuted under the CVA until, at least, June 2020 were found to have been wrongly charged (Joint Committee on Human Rights 2020: 5–6, 20–24). The disruption of legal certainty results to arbitrariness: parliamentarians find "unacceptable" the fining of thousands of citizens on the basis of regulations that contain unclear and ambiguous language, are not fully understood by the police, and do not include right to appeal (Joint Committee on Human Rights 2020: 25).

Further, biosecurity's reliance on surveillance undermines the right to privacy and, as surveillance is primarily targeting interaction, it implicates association. The track-and-trace system involves mass collection of sensitive personal data regarding someone's health; and maps out people's social, professional and circumstantial contacts, but does not contain any safeguards for privacy or data protection — it is even exempt from the requirements of the General Data Protection Regulation (GDPR). The government has explicitly rejected parliamentarians' recommendations to align its biosecurity surveillance regime with basic protections of privacy. Instead, it shares this data with private companies, and allows them to keep it for seven years and exploit it for their purposes (Joint Committee on Human Rights 2020: 6, 49–52). In short, for reasons of biosecurity, the government jettisons the right to privacy and engages in deliberate, systematic and massive mining of personal and relational data. This data includes citizens' vaccination status. Through various "vaccination passport" schemes citizens are additionally obliged to publicise this sensitive information to a motley array of institutions — from airlines to nightclubs — who are, in turn, obligated to police their clients.

There is no remedy for these violations of basic rights. The closure of courts during lockdown has denied citizens access to justice, and internet-mediated hearings have potentially impacted fairness. Defendants are often denied legal representation in hearings — which are often *in camera* — and do not have confidential lines of communication with their solicitors. At the same time, pre-charge detention is extended, from 182 to 238 days — almost eight months (Joint Committee on Human Rights 2020: 16, 59–61). Citizens cannot seek redress collectively either: protest has not been included as a "reasonable excuse" in any of the regulations that prohibit gatherings. This right is effectively cancelled, and it is unclear if this is a necessary and proportionate intervention with the rights to expression, association and assembly in Articles 10 and 11 of the ECHR (Joint Committee on Human Rights 2020: 16, 25).

Finally, Parliament was alarmed by the number of deaths of health care personnel, care workers, police officers and transport workers due to lack of adequate personal protective equipment (PPE), as well as the deaths in care homes ensuing from early and unsafe release of their residents from hospitals. The government rejected or ignored the calls of parliamentary Committees for inquiries into the reasons for these deaths, as well as the deaths in custody and in care homes, and of deaths due to denial of access to treatment (Joint Committee on Human Rights 2020: 6, 27, 65–66). In its endeavour to protect life, government seems uninterested in the death of certain categories of people; and hostile to the prospect of acknowledging responsibility for them. This responsibility goes beyond mere negligence. The government's directive for blanket implementation of the Do Not Attempt Cardiopulmonary Resuscitation (DNACPR) protocol at care homes was issued without consideration of patients' interests and applies without their consent. It is seen as a violation of the right to life, a violation that systematically discriminates on the basis of age and disability (Joint Committee on Human Rights 2020: 5, 26–31; Tapper 2021). Oddly, in its effort to protect life the state renounces responsibility for doing so.

Indeed, the most extraordinary feature of the Coronavirus Act is that, while it grants the Executive extraordinary powers upon society, it does not impose any obligation on it. The state *can* do all manners of things in order to combat the threat, but it does not *have to* do anything. The law does not require the state to help, support, compensate, or save anyone; to increase healthcare capacity; to keep hospitals open for necessary diagnosis and treatment; or to increase "front line" stuff, raise their salaries, or provide them with the necessary protective equipment. The state can do any of the above and more, but at its discretion. It does not even have to utilise any of the powers the Act grants it. Put schematically, the state *can* do everything but there is nothing it *must* do. Being, at its core, medical power — mobilised to save life — the power of biosecurity pulls all the stops. In conveys only powers, no responsibilities, to the state. Biosecurity power is *limitless* and *irresponsible*. Moreover, while the state response to the pandemic is founded in, and supported by, the CVA, it is not set in law. Essentially, all the Act does is authorise the Executive to respond to the crisis by issuing regulations or other statutory instruments at its discretion, and legalises these instruments in advance. Effectively, the Act is an invitation to government by decree. Given the absence of substantive standards, criteria and limitations, this invitation is open, a carte blanche.

Vaccinating against autonomy

Finally, biosecurity law, in the form of vaccine passports and mandatory vaccination, intervenes at the molecular level of the relation between the citizen and her body. The development of covid-19 vaccines was the *deus ex machina* that would smash the vicious circle of the twin crises. By neutralising the virus, it would resolve the biosecurity crisis, allowing the economy to operate unhindered. The state would thus be able to swiftly let society return to pre-pandemic normality and escape its own crisis without having to reflect, adjust or change. Accordingly, the state's eagerness to promote mass vaccination was matched by its escalating intolerance to those blocking the avenue to normality, those that refuse to get vaccinated. By excluding them from several kinds of employment and social life, the state reduces them to social pariahs, and seems keen to also force them into illegality.

Across Europe, with Britain a relative laggard, vaccination is becoming compulsory. It is being set as a requirement for continuing to enjoy commerce-mediated leisure and social life, from football to opera. For workers in such settings, vaccination has become *de facto* obligatory on penalty of suspension and even dismissal. It has become *de jure* obligatory for those who wish to continue their employment in health and care settings. In the US, a series of Presidential Orders make vaccination obligatory for the vast majority of (public and private sector) workers (White House 2021b; 2021c; 2021d), while almost all private employers demand vaccination certificates of their staff (White House 2021d). Austria has driven this inexorable trend to its conclusion: it is the first country to make vaccination mandatory for all its citizens (Oltermann 2021).

The implications of compulsory vaccination for the juridical framework and culture are multifarious and profound. First, compulsory vaccination runs roughshod over labour law. It allows, even dictates, the abrupt and unilateral re-writing of employment contracts; and allows for a sensitive decision concerning the personal health of the worker to constitute legitimate grounds for her dismissal.

Further, a person who is vaccinated, but refuses to divulge this fact upon request, is subject to all exclusions, from work and social life, as a person who is not vaccinated. Effectively, compulsory vaccination cancels medical confidentiality. The right to privacy is jettisoned as information pertaining to her medical record, i.e. the most sensitive, personal and protected type of information, must be freely disclosed to a random and endless array of parties: from hotel receptionists to cafeteria workers, and from all sorts of employers to vast IT corporations that harvest vaccine certification data submitted online (Big Brother Watch 2021: 22, annex p.15).

Finally, compulsory vaccination is discriminating. It discriminates on the basis of class: those who do not need to work in order to live are free from compulsion. They have a genuine choice whether to get vaccinated or not — even as they force their employees to do so. As for their social life, this mainly moves in secluded, private circles anyway, by choice; and they travel in their own boats and airplanes. The exclusion imposed by vaccine passports does not affect them. Finally, even when issued with fines for rule-breaking, this represent a truly insignificant sum that hardly registers as an inconvenience. For them, biosecurity law contains no punishment.

This discriminatory condition is largely lifted when vaccination ceases to be compulsory *de facto*, and becomes mandated *de jure*. This, however comes at a cost. In mandatory vaccination the state forces all its citizens to execute a medical intervention upon themselves. Vaccination is effectively imposed upon society and every individual as a duty — a duty to fellow citizens, to public health, to the economy. Thus, the person, in her relationship to her body, ceases to be an end in herself and instead becomes a means for the achievement of the aims of public policy. In short, *autonomy*, the cornerstone of liberal judicial civilisation, is undermined (Kant 2017). The corollary of diminished individual autonomy is an omnipotent state. Indeed, it is hard to envision many limits to the power of a state that can force each and all its citizens to subject themselves to a medical act.

Liberal ruins

To highlight the nature of pandemic control as a security endeavour, it is worth noting that the legal architecture of biosecurity replicates that of counterterrorism. Just like epidemic-control orders, the Terrorism Prevention and Investigation Measures (TPIMs), can apply on anyone and are triggered on reasonable suspicion. They can impose all manner of restrictions on liberty, movement, association, employment and more. Both types of orders are issued unilaterally by Executive personnel on the basis of unspecified criteria and determinations; and the power to issue them stems from statutory authorisation. Their review is weak, post-festum and failure to comply constitutes a criminal offence. Importantly, both counterterrorism and biosecurity measures are pre-emptive: they apply on individuals not because they have caused harm; but because they may do. They do not seek to redress harm, but to neutralise its potentiality (Boukalas 2017a; Hunt 2013; Zedner 2007). There are, of course, important differences. Biosecurity measures can apply not just on anyone, but on everyone, simultaneously. Restrictions on specific individuals can, in biosecurity, be imposed by low-level health and police personnel — counterterrorism restrictions (and blanket biosecurity ones) must be authorised by a Secretary of State. Counterterrorism orders must be necessary and proportionate to their purpose; but failure to comply carries a ten-year a maximum sentence — not a fine. Crucially, counterterrorism orders are a permanent addition to the state's legal arsenal; biosecurity ones are meant to be temporary. These differences, important as they are, are differences of degree; the legal structure of the two regimes is virtually identical. Biosecurity law does not innovate: it expands and further deregulates counterterrorism law, on a temporary basis and with drastically reduced intensity. Importantly, it extends the counterterrorism structure, so that a (heavily ameliorated) version of counterterrorism law is now applicable to — and experienced by — everyone.

It is worth appreciating where this universalisation of the hitherto most deregulated regime of legal coercion leaves the legal relation between the state and society. It is worth contemplating the legal landscape biosecurity has arranged. Everyday life is determined in minute detail by laws issued unilaterally by the Executive, often on the basis of considerations and determinations known only to it. They combine into a chaotic compound of ad hoc, short-leaved, haphazard law, that is hard for citizens and law-enforcement authorities to abide with, implement, or even fathom (Cowan 2021). They engage the whole of society across the spectrum of its relations, from the individual's bodily integrity, to its ability to assemble with others — and, hence, society's capacity to exist as such. At the same time, they do not confer to the state any responsibility towards society. Nonetheless, and while the input of the Legislature and the Judiciary in the production and administration of this law is restricted to vanishing point, this does *not* represent an Executive coup: ministers draw their open-ended powers from properly (if hastily) enacted Acts of Parliament that authorise them to act; and Parliament maintains the power to withdraw this authorisation at any time. There is no clash between state branches: each holds its institutional shape and executes its functions in perfect accordance with the constitution. If anything, Parliament's urge to authorise open-ended Executive powers shows that the two branches are operating in synergy. Similarly, there is no jettisoning of the rule of law:

government by decree has come about through rule of law processes. Armed with the legal power to rule by decree, and under the imperative to save life, the government has suspended a host of liberties and rights fundamental to a liberal polity. Liberty, privacy, access to justice and due process, association, assembly, even, paradoxically, the right to life, and autonomy, the cornerstone of liberal law, are all undermined. Rights and liberties are now reduced to exceptions, to be granted to citizens by the state, if, when, and to the extent the latter sees fit. In short, the legal landscape of biosecurity shows nothing but ruins: of liberties, rights, the rule of law, the balance of powers, the capacity of physical self-determination — the ruins of liberal democracy.

Note

1. In practice, the quarantine period is subject to repeated discounts: it started at 14 days, was reduced at 10 and currently stands at 7 with a view to be lowered at 5.

5 Protect the NHS (the spectacle of public health)

The biosecurity effort was communicated to UK citizens through the governmental slogan: "stay home — protect the NHS — save lives". Its simplicity, verbal economy, rhythm and *ad nauseam* repetition over the early phase of the pandemic, tattooed it onto citizens minds. It consists of three instructions expressed with commanding gravitas. The three commandments are not merely added to one another. They are interrelated: each is present in the next as its consequence. The citizen is ordered to "save lives"; to do so he must "protect the NHS"; for this, he needs to "stay home" — essentially this last is all that he really needs to do; the rest will result from it.

For the government, these orders translate into priorities, and they are configured differently. The government cannot "stay at home"; but should keep everyone else in. Its purpose is to "save lives". To achieve this, it must "protect the NHS". Thus, rather than saving lives by any means, the focus of state policy was the protection and strengthening of the NHS (Penzin 2020: 14–17). The prospect of an NHS collapse, a prospect that the experience of Italy showed to be very real, is what "terrified" the British government into action (Johnson in House of Commons Liaison Committee 2020: question 102; also: Farrar 2021: 116–117). The two — to "protect the NHS" and to "save lives" — are intertwined, the former is means to the latter and therefore contains it. But they are analytically distinct, and their distinction reveals political considerations and priorities.

The British government was reluctant to take measures to restrict the spread of the pandemic. While the devastation the latter could cause was already *known* from Italy and Spain, the government refused to close the country's borders and allowed mass gatherings to go on, despite expressions of concern by scientists that echoed across civil society. Government officials, including the Prime Minister, would not observe social distancing and continued to shake hands, including with hospital workers and patients. In a state of fear, civil society — and the markets — started adopting epidemic control measures before they were imposed by the government: universities send their students home, football games were played without spectators, employers ordered workers to work from home, shops shut, parents kept their children off school, the stock exchange crashed (Calvert and

DOI: 10.4324/9781003302988-6

Arbuthnott 2021: 145, 177, 183, 195; Farrar 2021: 139; The Economist 2020i; Tooze 2021: 96). France was similarly tardy in imposing a lockdown — and there too society acted before the state did, and demanded the latter's protective intervention and coercion (Boyer 2021: 62; Leoni and Alkamar 2020: 42–43). Thus, the early reaction of the state was to do as little as possible, to adopt a *laissez faire* approach that would allow the virus to run through the population until it eventually achieved what epidemiologists call "herd immunity". This approach was followed, in different manners and with wildly varying results, by Brazil, Sweden and the US; for Britain too this was the initial strategy; it was not carried through, but neither was it replaced with another (Farrar 2021: 108, 129–130). The trigger for the shift in British policy was a "model", an epidemiological projection. Issued in mid-March 2020, it predicted that, if the virus were allowed to spread unchecked, the NHS would be overwhelmed, leading to half a million deaths (Ferguson, Laydon and Nedjati-Gilani 2020: 6–7). In short, a *laissez faire* approach was abruptly reversed when the magnitude of the threat to the NHS became apparent. Britain imposed a nationwide lockdown on 23 March 2020.

Similarly, the only identifiable purpose of the restrictions imposed in late autumn 2020 was to avoid the NHS being put under "intolerable pressure" as the seasonal winter surge in cardio-respiratory infections would couple with a surge in covid-19 infections (HM Government 2020c: 6; HM Government 2020b: 14–17); and the pressure that the Omicron variant would put on the health system was the only reason for the restrictions imposed in December 2021 upon a largely vaccinated population. Protecting the NHS was an aim already obvious in the abstract terms of biosecurity legislation; it is now shown to be the focal point of biosecurity policy throughout the pandemic.

To protect the NHS, the Department of Health led a frantic effort to procure ventilators. It promised to buy as many as offered, and mobilised a range of private sector entities — from universities to vacuum cleaner manufacturers — in the effort. As with all panic buys, it paid extortionate amounts, and much of its purchase proved useless. Still, it did bolster the system's intensive care capacity. Similarly, the army, in conjuncture with public health authorities, transformed several large conference and concert venues across the country that were abandoned during lockdown, into impromptu hospital wings — and collectively named them after Florence Nightingale. The Nightingale units augmented the capacity of the health system. Yet, they were hardly used. They lay empty, and plans to build more of them were quietly forgotten. The reason was that, first, there was not enough personnel to make them work (Farrar 2021: 143). The state had failed to appreciate that it is easier to build a hospital unit or make a ventilator than to "make" a nurse. And, second, there was no demand. Despite Britain having extremely high infection numbers, hospitalisations did not exceed existing hospital capacity — mainly, as we shall see, because the NHS was defended from patients that needed it (Calvert and Arbuthnott 2021: 227, 246).

Protecting the NHS was the decisive factor for imposing restrictions. Conversely, the NHS capacity to respond to pressures was the key consideration in lifting lockdown measures. Among the five factors that guide such decisions in Britain, three, including the first and the last, are concerned with the NHS capacity to respond (LBC 2020). Indeed, the British Prime Minister appreciates that avoiding an NHS collapse was his major achievement (Johnson in the House of Commons Liaison Committee 2020: q.102).

The concern with healthcare capacity is self-explanatory in an epidemic. Yet, there is an added reason for it: the capacity was not there. The suppression of the social wage and the shrinking of the welfare state are programmatic staples of neoliberal policy (Handler 2004). Ergo, as soon as a neoliberal strategy was adopted (for most European and North American countries during the 1980s or 1990s), the healthcare system came under pressure. Expenditure in health was considered a source of economic inefficiency detrimental to good macroeconomic performance. The overall target of public health policy is the restructuring of institutions to become more cost effective, eclipsing consideration for people and their health problems (Waitzkin 2016: 129). In this context, privatisation of health service provision became the preferred solution. It mainly took the form of public funding for services offered by private, profit-seeking, enterprises — and resulted to both social exclusion from health services and the ratcheting up of their cost. As public health became a commodity, companies would inevitably transport key production sites — including for PPE, medical equipment and medicines — to countries with low labour costs. Similarly, states would suppress health workers' wage to the point that it would actively deter people from engaging with the profession (Boyer 2021: 128–134; Caduff 2020). This chronic situation accelerated and intensified in Britain and southern Europe after the 2008 financial crisis, as their governments severely curtailed public spending. The pre-covid treatment of the NHS consisted of cuts on staff, which drastically worsened retention and work conditions for the remaining workforce and led to the first doctors' strike; drastic decline in hospital beds and intensive care units; and the neutering of the Health Protection Agency. Between 2011 and 2020 the NHS suffered £33 billion of cuts in funding, and since the late 1980s it has lost more than 160,000 beds — whilst the citizenry was both growing and ageing. Thus, the UK came to be amongst the European countries with less hospital beds (2.76) and doctors (2.8) for every thousand people. Its threadbare ("lean and mean") service is governed by just-in-time policies, as, in order to achieve the targets on which their funding depends, hospitals shorten hospitalisation time, and reduce diagnostic tests (Frade 2020: 16; Minakakis 2020: 69; Primrose, Chang and Loeppky 2020). On the eve of the coronavirus pandemic, Operation Cygnus, a nationwide exercise testing the response of the healthcare system to an influenza epidemic, concluded that the NHS was seriously underprepared to cope due to lack of intensive care equipment and PPE. Since, the government decimated PPE and ventilator stocks even further (Calvert and Arbuthnott 2021: 89–80). In short, hospitals are governed as if they were factories, where idle capacity is not tolerated. Its being there in standby in case anyone needs it is seen as as an irrational cost that must be (and was) erased. Public health as well as most public services — from schools to courts — are subjected to the principles that govern supply, while they are in reality institutions dealing with demand.

Further afield, between 2011 and 2018, the EU Commission directed member states 63 times to reduce health expenditure and to proceed to privatisation of health services. This was the Commission's second most persistent request, following that for increasing the pension age (solicited 105 times), and followed by those for wage cuts (50 times) and reduction in unemployment and disability benefits (Martin Schirdewan MEP in Minakakis 2020: 68). As in the UK, the destruction of European public health systems resulted from a combination of funding scarcity and the adoption of supply-side management marked by zero stocks, just-in-time production, and overwhelming consideration with "value for money" (Leoni and Alkamar 2020: 41).

Thus, when the pandemic arrived, British and European governments faced the immediate prospect of having a popular institution collapsing at the moment it was most needed, leading to an escalation of deaths. Crucially, they faced the prospect of taking the blame for this; and the risk of a spontaneous social eruption that would implicate the legitimacy of entrenched policies (Antithesis 2020: 27). Put schematically, the government is concerned with "protecting the NHS" in order to protect "itself" from a questioning of the overall social and economic strategy it has been pursuing for 40 years. In the "chaos" ensuing from an NHS collapse "the whole grip of government might collapse with all sorts of terrible consequences" — this is, reportedly, what his chief adviser told the Prime Minister to shake him off his reluctancy to take restrictive measures (Farrar 2021: 122). A crisis of public health could spiral into a crisis of neoliberalism — protecting the NHS is, ultimately, meant to avert this prospect. The government was not aiming to "save lives" *per se*, but to save the social order that it promotes and over which it presides from potential upset.

Protecting the NHS is strongly related to saving lives but not identical to it. The tentative tension between the two imperatives is worth exploring, as it offers important insights on biosecurity, and thus helps make sense of our adventures in its realm.

In March 2020, when the pandemic hit the UK in earnest, the NHS had half the intensive care capacity of its Italian counterpart. The government was anxious that critical care units should not be visibly overrun as they had been in Italy. The first move in defending the NHS was to empty out its hospitals. Hospital managers were ordered to free up a third of UK hospital capacity. This involved postponing 15,000 scheduled operations and ejecting another 15,000 patients from their beds. As the Coronavirus Act lifted the duty to assess patients' need for continuing health care, NHS managers were absolved from liability (Calvert and Arbuthnott 2021: 202–203).

Another trench of NHS defence were the triaging instructions implemented throughout the first year of the pandemic. Tellingly, the decision that elderly covid patients should be denied life-saving treatment was taken on the day the "protect the NHS" slogan was launched (Calvert and Arbuthnott 2021: 161–162, 213, 224–225). Charged with setting out triaging guidelines was the government's Moral and Ethical Advisory Group (MEAG). It produced a vulnerability scoring system, through which doctors could make quick selections on who would be admitted to intensive care. It essentially instructed that everyone over 75; as well as those over 65 that had an underlying health condition, including diabetes or high blood pressure, would be excluded from intensive care treatment. It is not clear if this is what the MEAG really suggested, for its members find these instructions to range from "extremely crude" to "disgusting" and "nazi-like" (Calvert and Arbuthnott 2021: 227–229, 243).

During the first peak of the pandemic, triaging contributed to a rather strange outcome: nine in ten deaths in hospital occurred outside intensive care units. Critically ill patients were simply being denied access due to their vulnerability profile. They were placed in "death wards" and were effectively left to die. They received no mechanical ventilation, and were offered medicine, food, or water only occasionally (Calvert and Arbuthnott 2021: 242–246, 249–251). Essentially, government policy was to exclude from care those who needed it most — and this allowed the government to claim that intensive care capacity was not breached (Calvert and Arbuthnott 2021: 250, 261). Strictly speaking, this was true. Patient selection, and the expulsion of the most needy, was enforced so rigidly that many intensive care beds remained empty, reserved for those with the "greatest chance of survival" (Calvert and Arbuthnott 2021: 257–259). During the second wave, in autumn 2020, up to 80 percent of patients needing intensive care were denied it. Some patients were not even offered standard, non-invasive ventilation due to lack of personnel capable of using it (Calvert and Arbuthnott 2021: 374, 378). Protecting the NHS entailed the exclusion from critical care of patients who could have survived if they had received it; in entailed a massive cost to life.

The defence of the NHS starts before the patient reaches the hospital. It involves the exclusion of needy patients from hospitalisation *tout court*. While, during the first six months of the pandemic, deaths in hospital increased by less than 8,000 compared to the rolling five-year average; deaths in care homes and private homes increased by more than 50,000 (Calvert and Arbuthnott 2021: 263–264). This was a direct outcome of public health policy. The NHS was transformed to a single-illness service. All treatment for non-covid conditions, including those that would normally be classed as urgent, was suspended — resulting to considerable loss of life and the accumulation of 6 million patients (nine percent of the UK population) awaiting treatment (Quinn, Thomas and McIntyre 2021). Even most covid patients were kept away. First, politicians and scientists were relentlessly admonishing that people should avoid contacting the NHS unless their symptoms were severe. Indeed, the plea to "protect the NHS" led to patients refraining from burdening the health service until it was too late for them to recover (Calvert and Arbuthnott 2021: 273–275). At the same time GPs were requested to persuade their elderly patients to sign "no resuscitation" agreements; and to identify all their patients who are frail or depending on care so that they could be denied hospital admission (Calvert and Arbuthnott 2021: 267–269). These people were denied entry to hospital or access to an ambulance. Ambulance staff were moreover ordered to triage patients' circumstances on the spot, and leave the frail ones were they found them.

Finally, care homes became the advanced detachment of NHS defence. Their residents suffered blanket exclusion form hospital treatment. However ill, or "likely to survive" they were, they were left in situ. The only treatment available to them was palliative. Indeed, the movement of patients between hospitals and care homes was reversed. Elderly patients were hastily ejected from hospitals and returned to care homes, to make room for younger, more robust ones. An estimated 25,000 of them were discharged without previously being tested for the virus, and some were discharged despite having tested positive (Amnesty International 2020). Thus, frail people highly likely to be infected were introduced en mass to the most infection-sensitive of environments. As relevant instructions were a state secret — and did not officially exist — the Prime Minister explained this phenomenon by placing the blame on the doctors that issued the discharge documents (Johnson in House of Commons Liaison Committee 2020: q.43–44). The elderly patients cast out of hospitals were not the only ones spreading the virus in care homes. Their carers, compelled by their meagre income to work across several homes — untested, even when they presented coronavirus symptoms — also became major conduits of disease. As a result, care homes became a site of massacre: in 2020, they suffered 26,000 excess deaths and were the locus of almost half the covid death toll (Amnesty International 2020; Calvert and Arbuthnott 2021: 280–284; Harding 2021: 120–122). Their residents were deprived of their most elemental rights: right to health, to life, to freedom from subjection to inhuman and degrading treatment and, as visits were banned, the right to family life. The suspension of these rights stems from the residents' status as either old or disabled; it entails a suspension of freedom from discrimination (Amnesty International 2020: 45–47; Tarrant and Hayes 2021).

To cope with the collapse of the public health system, the government set out to conceal it. Hospitals were out of limits for visitors; and care homes were completely closed to the outside world: access was forbidden to visitors and doctors, and their inspections abruptly stopped (Amnesty International 2020: 34–36; Tarrant and Hayes 2021). The only witness of the situation in both sites was their staff. They were directed to refrain from undermining morale by exposing the reality in their workplaces, to not mention staff deaths, and to not make calls for PPE donations. They had their social media accounts policed, and faced intimidation and threats of redundancy for no compliance. Hospitals and care homes were under omertà (Calvert and Arbuthnott 2021: 247–248, 261, 397). This vacuum of information was filled by the government. It set up a dedicated propaganda unit, spreading positive news from the pandemic front and intimidating anyone who would indicate that reality was different. Ministers would repeat *ad nauseam* that "world beating" care was available to everyone that needed it; the Secretary of Health declared that his department had placed a protective "ring of steel" around care homes (possibly meaning that there was no way in or out). The prime minister congratulated himself that the UK "had defied all expectations" in not running out of hospital beds and ventilators; and in late December 2020, as the UK was leading the body count in Europe and already in the grip of a third surge, the Home Secretary was boasting that "the government has consistently throughout this year been ahead of the curve in terms of proactive measures with regards to coronavirus" (Calvert and Arbuthnott 2021: 296, 400). The grimmest the reality, the louder the government's triumphalism. The government was resorting to cognitive dissonance, forcing journalists to sum up its communications effort as "gas-lighting" and to resurrect the old slogan: *Do not adjust your mind — there is a fault with reality* (Hyde 2020a). When everything else failed, the government simply changed the way it counted deaths, so that the numbers became, on the stroke of a pen, more palatable (Calvert and Arbuthnott 2021: 280, 286–288). To date, the government resists calls for an inquiry into its workings during the pandemic; and the Prime Minister refuses to meet with bereaved families' representatives (Calvert and Arbuthnott 2021: 402).

Thus, the NHS was protected, at the cost of letting die thousands of people that would have overcome their illness if they had been offered appropriate care (Calvert and Arbuthnott 2021: 276). The NHS *appeared* to cope with the pandemic at the expense of fulfilling its service. Indeed, the key concern of the government throughout the pandemic was optics. The ultimate drive of state policy was the fear of the Italian experience: of endless news coverage of people dying "in hospital corridors or banked up in ambulances" (Calvert and Arbuthnott 2021: 273).

During the biosecurity crisis, the "save lives" and "protect the NHS" imperatives were at cross-purposes. Prioritising the latter caused a monumental loss of life. The NHS coped only by abandoning its purpose; it succeeded by failing. This paradox of coping by no coping is lifted if we consider that the core objective never was to protect the NHS — that would be strange for a state hell-bend on destroying it; but to protect *the image* of the NHS. It was not that the NHS was not overrun, but not overrun *visibly. Biosecurity is the spectacle of public health* (Debord 1994). It is the triumphant image of public health when public health is no more. The Nightingale, the hospital without doctors or patients, is its emblem.

The spectacular nature of biosecurity is evident in its obsession with images at the expanse of animating materiality: labour. Labour constitutes a persistent blind spot in the biosecurity enterprise. The Nightingales are the spectacle of hospital: spatial arrangements of beds without the labour — nurses, doctors, cooks, cleaners — needed to *be* hospitals. Similarly, "protect the NHS" by no means involved protecting its workers. The lack of PPE for healthcare personnel was acute and persisted for almost a year. Having repleted NHS stockpiles as part of the drive to cut expenditure, the government had moved the NHS from a just-in-case model involving warehousing stocks, to a just-in-time one, relying on contracts arranged on demand. Having caused this jeopardy in the course of a decade, the Department of Health was late to even realise the lack of PPE. Health ministers were unaware of the alarming findings of the 2016 Operations Cygnus, which highlighted the inadequacy of PPE stockpiles (Calvert and Arbuthnott 2021: 85–96, 122). The government was forced to action by urgent public calls from medical workers and NHS trusts and the images of nurses and doctors using homemade substitutes, including cooking aprons and bin bags. Its attempt to replenish its stocks and to distribute the equipment were, for months, grossly inadequate, revealing a state without the capacity for basic logistics. By autumn 2020, care home workers still had no access to PPE — prompting Parliament's Public Accounts Committee to describe government treatment of care homes as "reckless" and "appalling" and to accuse them of "throwing care homes to the wolves" (Calvert and Arbuthnott 2021: 333).

The response to the PPE procurement failure bears the government's standards: concealment, repression, deception. Medical staff were ordered to not refer to "political matters" like PPE shortages. Those who did were disciplined by management: accused of insulting their heroic colleagues and undermining morale and public trust, and threatened with redundancy. In an unprecedented scientific breakthrough, PPE was found to be reusable, and medical personnel was requested to use the same mask for several days. Another scientific marvel found coronavirus to not be a High Consequence Infectious disease, hence its treatment did not necessitate high grade protective equipment (Calvert and Arbuthnott 2021: 207–208) — which begs the question of what the whole biosecurity endeavour was about. The Health Secretary blamed the lack of equipment on doctors for "overusing" it (Stewart and Campbell 2020); and boasted that he had provided "billions" of PPE items — which were found to be: inadequate; irrelevant; in transit; and inflated by the inclusion of body bags, bin bags, cleaning materials and the double counting of every pair of gloves, as they comprised a left and a right "item" (BBC 2020; Bloom 2020).

Unsurprisingly, Britain presents the highest mortality rate for medical personnel in Europe. Its "frontline" staff is cannon fodder. The concern with the robustness of the institution does not include the workers that make the institution function. This is paradoxical, illogical even; but it is aligned with the deep premise of neoliberal strategy, which sees the worker as a cost and hence ignores her needs and diminishes her rewards. She is held liable, and sacrificed, for the smooth operation of the system — or the appearance thereof.

Having thus bolstered its defences, and its excuses, the state goes on to address the par excellence terrain of the epidemic: society.

6 Cancel society

Biosecurity measures are anti-social in the true sense of the word: they seek to stop the activities necessary for society and dissolve it into isolated atoms. They culminate in, and are defined by the prospect of, quarantine. Quarantine represents the utmost of state power. Through it, the state does not merely control, manage or even oppress society; it cancels it. It replaces it with atomised units, individuals or households, in isolation from each other. These units are now scattered in the space that was once social. They do not, *strictu sensu*, constitute a society. They communicate only through technological mediations, they avoid approaching each other, and, apart from some activities permitted by the state and aiming to secure their biological existence, they do not act. This radical condition, the suspension of society, is not imposed by the state through awesome violence. It is desired and observed by society itself. In a situation where the threat resides in every other, and in the self, the only certain protection from it is the elimination of contact. As both state and society are captured by the security imperative, the state's demands are society's wishes. The suspension of society is society's act — the last. Thus, biosecurity brings forth a specific reconfiguration and an emphatic affirmation of Margaret Thatcher's view of society. Now, there *really* is no such thing as society, only threatened and threatening individuals and families, living parallel to each other.

Except, this is not exactly so. What replaces society is not Thatcher's individuals and *families*, but individuals and *households*. While many, possibly most, households are defined by a family, this replacement is not innocuous. The family, a unit determined by affective and carnal ties, relations of strong dependency and solidarity, and millennia of moral investment, is replaced by the household, a unit of administrative dispatch. The non-society of biosecurity has shred the last remains of conservative idyl off the neoliberal state, leaving only dry bureaucracy.

Welcome to the household (there is no way out)

The elevation of the household to core social unit — the social *cell* in both senses of the word — poses some serious questions for the liberal way of living and understanding life. The liberal household is, first of all, a "hold":

DOI: 10.4324/9781003302988-7

property owned by individuals; property that moreover, in the surviving pre-capitalist sense of the noun "hold", denotes a defensible position. As a unit, the household is inherently spatial: it is a "house", defined by walls and rooted in place. This spatially fixed property is an enclosure. The household is not only spatially distinct, but secluded from the its outside: from other privately secluded individual house-holds; and from the public, the common, the political. It is the liberal Englishman's castle: the household is a prohibition to external intervention to its interiority. Reversely, occurrences interior to the household are kept therein. They are "private", secluded from "publicity", from external knowledge and interference. The inviolable internality of the household consists of close, often intimate, interpersonal relations. These relations, and the overall functionality of the household, are ones of reproduction. The household is the par excellence reproductive unit, involving work, consumption and leisure aimed at the physical creation and renewal of the productive capacities of its members and at their cognitive, affective, moral and social education. The simple cell of the household is, then, a relation of relations: a complex relation among spatial, property, interpersonal and reproductive relations. Under biosecurity, these relations — and, therefore, the household-relation — change considerably.

Biosecurity has forced the household to become not just the par excellence unit for social reproduction, but the *only* one. With schools, nightclubs, churches, cinemas, gyms, hairdressers and pubs gone, the household has to cope with all reproductive functions by, and within, itself without aid from the outside — for there is no outside to speak of. Further, with the closure of workplaces, and the advent of home-work, the household becomes site of a function that, in capitalist societies, it seldom undertakes and for which it is not designed. It becomes the site of production, of work undertaken on somebody else's terms, designs and purposes, to somebody else's benefit, for which the worker receives compensation. Thus, a foreign set of relations invades the household: work, a relation of exchange marked by compulsion and underpinned by the angst of survival. These are relations that do not belong there; the household was meant to provide refuge and respite from them. Thus, the household becomes the site of virtually *all* social relations — productive and reproductive. It is, subsequently, forced to cope with the different, and largely irreconcilable, functions, purposes, logics, aims and temporalities that these relations involve and the pressures they bear. The task is likely impossible. It moreover introduces a radical shift in the household's spatial constitution.

On the one hand, the assumption of all reproductive and socialising functions signifies that the household is radically secluded from its outside. As its outside has ceased to exist or is too dangerous to exit to, the household cannot access it. On the other hand, the insertion of productive functions signifies that the household remains open to the outside: it assumes the function of the workplace, and inherits the relations and pressures pertinent to the latter. Once they enter the realm of the household, these relations and pressures remain therein — for the household cannot access the outside. The outside enters the household, but the household cannot get out. Its spatial seclusion has become one-way only: it absorbs its outside, but cannot let it out. The liberal castle has been breached and turned into a *trap*: people, relations and tensions enter and cannot escape.

In its ideological investment, the household is routinely represented, and idealised, as the place of peace and enjoyment. It is the shelter from the outside world, from its crime, pollution, violence, noise and toil — from a social world that, in the core of liberal ideology, is hostile to the individual. In biosecurity conditions, this place of safety from external threats doubles up as a place of safety from the threat of the virus that thrives in the public domain. But, biosecurity also sees the household as a threat: once the virus is inserted therein, the household becomes a threat to the public; it must be sealed off and its inhabitants trapped in what now is a zone of danger. Again, things — relations, pressures and threats — enter the household, but cannot leave. In a reversal of liberal ideology, the private is seen as a potential threat to the public.

The shelter has become a trap. As it is shouldered with reproductive and productive functions in full and in isolation, the household has to cope not only with the tensions that reproductive functions entail, but also with the tensions inherent in productive relations *and* those that arise *between* productive and reproductive functions and relations, as well as the tensions between private and public health. Worse, all these tensions cannot escape the household; they must be resolved within and by it. Ill-suited to cope with an entire world of proliferating, inescapable tensions, the household breaks down. From the idyllic haven of liberal ideology, it turns into a site of violence: interpersonal violence its members exercise on one another — typically the men on the women and children — that has multiplied under biosecurity; and intra-personal violence exercised against the self and registered as an explosion of mental health breakdown.

As the private realm of the household becomes the site of tension, danger and violence, shelter and safety are to be sought in the public space. People need recourse to it to escape danger; and the publication of the violence they suffer is a first step to its curtailment. Thus, the liberal relations between public, private, threat and safety are reversed. People need to escape the private trap and gain recourse to the public; they need, first, to create it.

Finally, a word of analytical caution. Strictly speaking, none of this is new. It would be absurd to imply that worries about work only infiltrated the household thanks to biosecurity, or that domestic violence first occurred in March 2020. It would, however — and this is the point — be equally absurd to carry on with liberal "common sense" significations of public and private, danger and security. Once again, the crisis has played a revelatory role: by intensifying what was already there, it uncovers and highlights it. There is also something novel that biosecurity brings: a paradox. By saturating the isolation — the privacy — of the household, biosecurity tends to lift it: it turns the household and what occurs therein into a social phenomenon, into an affair of, and for, the public.

Quarantined politics: space, time, flows and contact

The suspension of society leaves the state as the only active agent, which now occupies the entirety of public space. It thus removes the physical proximity necessary for politics, leaving the state as the only political actor. Under quarantine, politics shrank into the spectacle of a government minister, flanked with scientific advisers, informing and admonishing a nation of atoms and then responding to questions from select journalists. In Britain, even official politics could be cancelled. The Health Secretary is authorised to postpone elections (CVA, ss.59–63); and to assume the capacity of local authorities to meet, discuss and decide — but not the duty to dispatch their regular services to citizens (CVA s.78; House of Lords 2020: 20). Biosecurity involves a monopolisation of politics by and within the state, its perfect concentration at the centre.

While mostly conceived as spatial arrangement, quarantine is, equally, a temporal one. The emptying of space and the suspension of movement it imposes entails a suspension of time: when nothing happens (in space), nothing changes — hence time is suspended. During quarantine, everything is preserved as is, hoping to resume from the point when time and motion stopped. Quarantine aims to stop time; but fails. In suspending movement, the quarantine renders occurrences and events impossible — hence, it freezes time. But, in freezing time, the quarantine shatters regular, quotidian, routine time. Thus, the frozen time it imposes is uneventful, but also *an event in itself.* Because it negates events, the quarantine is, as such, one. Thus, in deep freeze time goes on and can even accelerate. Under the icy crust of quarantine, time, events and politics persist. But in another register, with different forms, directions and rhythms. They move underground and carry on unbeknown.

Crucially, quarantine did not, in practice, suspend movement completely. Even during the strictest lockdown, people could go to the supermarket, walk a dog or ride a bicycle. Movement was restricted, controlled and subdued, but not cancelled. Instead, what was cancelled was *meeting.* There were regulations imposing social distancing, one-way movement for pedestrians, protective screens, as well as the shutdown of all possible meeting places: cafeterias, workplaces, schools, bars, churches, nightclubs. The City of New York recommended that its denizens should restrict themselves to masturbation for the duration of the pandemic (Tooze 2021: 98). In short, flows were *not* suspended, *contact* was. It was the suspension of contact that lead to an atrophy of flows. This observation forces as to reflect on these two and their relation. The quarantine appears to target flows; but seeks to eliminate contact.

At first glance, contagion, the pandemic as such, resides in flows. It spreads through them. To counter it, flows must be disrupted. But, diseases do not spread through abstract, free-flowing flows. They spread through their convergence, punctuation and articulation in points of contact: schools, bars, factories — ultimately, bodies. The threat does not reside in the flow, but in the contact: "It's not how you fall that matters; it's how you land" (Kassovitz 1995). State policy centres not on disrupting flows, but on erasing points of contact: meetings and gatherings at any place, for any reason. Society is not flows, but contacts. It is cancelled not through the elimination of flows, but of contact. Flows as such are insignificant; it is contacts that specify them and render them meaningful — and threatening.

Chaotic biosecurity

Biosecurity policy is overdetermined by the spectre of the twin crises and the dilemma they pose for the capitalist state. Biosecurity is paramount for the capitalist *state*; but it causes a collapse of capital accumulation — it is therefore an anathema for the *capitalist* state. In trying to navigate the Symplegades of the twin crises, the state is disoriented, undecided, reluctant and, ultimately, lost. Piled upon this fundamental indecisiveness is the state's policy-making processes. Drawing authority from carte blanche licence granted in constitutions or legislation, biosecurity policy is designed and imposed by a tiny junta of Ministers and advisers. Its formation does not benefit from processes of consultation, deliberation and codification. Instead, it reacts to the exigencies of the moment and is pulled in different directions by different concerns and interests. It is therefore ad hoc, particularistic and unprincipled; it lacks cohesion and strategic orientation, and consists of knee-jerk reactions to occurrences and pressures as they arise. As with all government by decree, it results to ill thought out, contradictory and haphazard measures (Chapoutot 2021: 94–95, 112–113; Neumann 1995: 118–138; Poulantzas 1978: 218–231, 241–247; Scheuerman 1994: 126–140). Simply put, the state (the Executive) can do what it wants; but cannot decide what that is. The outcome is, necessarily, chaos.

A systematic account of haphazard occurrences would preoccupy both author and reader for a long while. I will simply mention a few examples from the British context chosen (like the measures themselves?) at random. Thus, for instance, the list of businesses providing essential services that could remain open during general lockdown included, along with supermarkets, banks and pharmacies, bicycle shops, dry cleaners and breweries[1]. Later on, as the country was gradually exiting lockdown, cinemas were allowed to open, theatres were not. Britain did not impose a requirement to incoming travellers to self-isolate upon entering the country when contagion within it was low; but (in June 2020) imposed it on arrivals from countries with lower infection rates. That restriction was soon perforated by a long list of countries exempt from the requirement; and soon after some countries were made exempt from the exception. The requirement to wear masks initially applied to banks, but not to "premises offering financial services"; it applied to post offices, but not to libraries or museums. In all cases, it applied to customers but not to workers; their mask-wearing was left to the discretion of the employer[2]. Further, under the tier system introduced in autumn 2020, pubs in "tier 2" locations were ordered to close, unless they served their customers a "substantial meal" to accompany alcohol consumption — resulting to debates on the "substantiality" of a Scottish egg and a slice of pizza (HM Government 2020c: 6; also: Farrar 2021: 186). As no explanation or justification is provided for these discrepancies and contradictions, the overall notion they convey is absurdity. Summing up the degree of confusion, the Prime Minister summarised the "vital messages" of his government as "stay at home if you can; go to work if you must — although this will change, obviously, for some sectors", before giving up and making a plea to individuals' "common sense" (Johnson in Hansard 2020b: c.30; Johnson in House of Commons Liaison Committee 2020: q.24). The restrictions imposed over a "local area" of five million people, were announced by a Health Secretary twitter message late at night.

In short, measures are unfathomable and, therefore, unimplementable (Halliday 2020). In a public address to the nation, the British Prime Minister recited the regulations wrongly, and several of his ministers did the same or, more wisely, declared they were uncertain of the rules (Murphy and Bland 2020; Parveen, Stewart and Halliday 2020). Incomprehension became, in January 2022, the last line of defence of an entrenched prime minister: he claimed that none of his aides explained to him that it was against the rules to throw parties in 10 Downing Street during a time when his government had banned social gatherings (Elgot 2022).

The situation did not improve with time. In July 2021, the government lifted virtually all biosecurity restrictions, but nonetheless instructed citizens to keep implementing some (Davis, Walker and Campbell 2021). At the same time, as a new wave of infections was spreading, millions of citizens that had been in contact with someone infected were placed into quarantine. But when the Chancellor and the Prime Minister were put in this position, they tried to evade isolation and ministers claimed that the isolation of contacts was not a rule, that relevant requests were merely "advisory" and meant to help citizens "make informed decisions" (Ross 2021). Consequently, the government undertook to produce a list of key workers who, if vaccinated, could escape isolation; then it dropped this task, and this resulted to disruptions in food supply (Kollewe 2021b). In short, the partial, patchy, ephemeral and contradictory nature of regulations as well as their sheer volume, result to chaotic uncertainty. The requirement for legal clarity and stability is jettisoned, and this is matched by a collapse of the legislative function: the legislators do not know the rules they make.

As the first wave subsided in summer 2020, European countries all too promptly eased restrictions opened their borders, and allowed economic activity to resume in full. When, as a result, by mid-autumn, a second wave of infections and hospitalisations engulfed them, state response lost all strategic coherence. The tactic of locally targeted measures was abandoned, for the 'local' spread of the epidemic was seen to encompass enormous parts of the population (about 20 million people in the UK), while the mosaic of incomprehensible measures had no effect on the situation. In response, European governments improvised a range of tactics: tier systems (France, Greece, UK); "circuit breakers" and partial lockdowns (Germany, Wales); border closures (*including* between Wales, Scotland and England); universal mask-wearing; and night time curfew (Belgium, Italy, France, Greece, Spain). The latter was not experienced since these countries were under military occupation or dictatorship; it makes no sense as a measure of epidemic control, but highlights epidemiology's affinity with counterinsurgency and the inherently oppressive nature of biosecurity.

These measures were spasmodically adopted, dropped, replaced and intensified by governments in panic before the pandemic's resurgence. The latter, unlike the first wave, was predictable, predicted and, indeed, certain; and states had done nothing to prepare for it — except causing it by opening the economy. They adopted those halfway measures aiming to slow down transmission without having to impose a second lockdown. They invariably failed, and — reluctantly — imposed lockdowns again. Or, rather, they introduced a new form of lockdown during which most work, economic activity and education continued. Ever since, the only thing banned during a lockdown is sociability: gatherings in public and private settings.

During that period, from autumn 2020 to summer 2021, the uncertainty regarding biosecurity measures became systemic. It enveloped the process and criteria by which measures were imposed or lifted. There were no epidemiological thresholds that a locality or a country needed to cross in order to enter a stricter regime of measures; or of the improvement needed for measures to be eased or lifted. Indeed, criteria for locking and unlocking were so broad and undefined that they could justify any decision at any moment (Calvert and Arbuthnott 2021: 316). The only definite criterion was not, *strictu sensu*, epidemiological: it was the immediate prospect of health system collapse (Stewart 2020b). Similarly, different restriction levels did not correspond to differences in state mobilisation. What state mechanisms will be employed, to what extent, for what purpose; or what means of economic support will be available to affected businesses and workers — all these were determined ad hoc, on the basis of unknown standards and criteria; they appear to result from improvisation.

Crucially, there is no sense of purpose or strategic cohesion. It is not clear what the state aims to achieve with this plethora of measures. They are all imposed so that they can be lifted: To quell the spread of the virus, so that they can be removed, which will lead to a resurgence of transmissions to be quelled by the re-imposition of restrictions. In Britain, throughout the course of the pandemic, the scientists advising the government were exacerbated by its lack of strategy against the pandemic and with ministers' fixation with next day's headlines at the expense of long term action (Farrar 2021: 93, 104–105; 108, 125, 184).

Indeed, by autumn 2020 any pretence that biosecurity responses were scientifically guided was cast aside. The Prime Minister admitted that he does not read the scientific advice meant to inform his decision-making, and tended to be unaware of basic data regarding the epidemic situation; and the emergency (COBRA) meetings were not setting out action plans, but were instead consumed in general policy discussions (Calvert and Arbuthnott 2021: 199–200; 338; Johnson in House of Commons Liaison Committee 2020: q.26). The response of the UK during the autumn of 2020, which culminated in the epidemiologically disastrous relaxation during the Christmas period, was marked by complete disregard for scientific evidence. None of the measures adopted had an evidential basis and their potential impact on either health or the economy was uncharted. For instance, the role of open-air gatherings in transmitting the disease is believed to be relatively small, and the government's scientific advisers expected that their prohibition would contribute little to reducing infection rates. Indeed, numerical limit to gatherings and early closure of sociability places were already in place for months and infection rates went on climbing exponentially. The government brushed this aside by claiming, without substantiation, that "the normalisation of these behaviours has had an undoubted impact on reducing the spread of the virus", without attempting to explain which "behaviours" had what impact (HM Government 2020c: 28). When pressed by MPs to produce evidence for the necessity, proportionality and efficacy of restrictive measures, the government released a document that merely rehashed well-trodden data and tropes that were irrelevant to the current situation; and contained no evaluation of the performance of past measures or predictions regarding the performance of the measures the government purported to impose (HM Government 2020d). The tier system was reintroduced in winter 2020 without an estimate of how — or if — its earlier iteration had affected infection levels (HM Government 2020d: 13–15). Without a, perspective or retrospective, estimate on the impact of measures on either health or the economy, the government decides its policy on the basis of likelihoods, which it determines through unknown evidence, methods and procedures (see: HM Government 2020d: 21–23). Biosecurity policy can proceed against scientific basis and without any identifiable basis at all. On the first anniversary of the CVA, Parliament held a brief, solemn debate to renew it in whole, minus the few provisions the government had unilaterally decided to extinguish. The debate centred on the police powers to detain "potentially infectious persons" (Schedule 21); and to prohibit and disperse events and gatherings (Schedule 22). Members across the political spectrum challenged the government to justify their retention — especially given that the police had failed to apply detention powers lawfully and scientific reports showed that open-air gatherings could only have a negligent effect on transmission. The government made no attempt to justify its position. It did not produce scientific advise or evidence and did not respond to, or even register, MPs concerns (Hansard 2021b).

In short, government imposes measures, and Parliament legalises them, regardless of evidence. State branches *and* parties are in accord here. According to the Opposition, the repression of alcohol consumption in social settings is because “pubs and bars bring people together” and “after a few drinks people lose their inhibitions” (Ashworth in Hansard 2020d: c.201–203). In the absence of evidence and causality, policy is determined by intuition based on temperance stereotypes aimed to benevolently coerce the unfortunate classes and to control or suspend their off-work sociability.

The state not only adopted measures that its scientists predicted would be of minimal impact; it also ignored scientific suggestions for bolder measures that would have a substantial effect. The measures the government decided *not* to take offer a key to its perplexing decision-making. They would involve temporary but significant restrictions on schools, universities and workplaces, especially offices and factories. They would entail, in short, curtailment of economic activity. Scientific advice recognised the factory floor, the bus, the student hall as vectors of transmission and sought to disrupt it through brief, drastic breaks in their activity. The government’s resistance to this course of action displays its determination to ignore the causes of infection, its limited interest in curtailing it, and the reason behind this attitude: economic activity must carry on. The measures sacrifice sociability (and its commercial settings) so that the (rest of) the economy can continue unaffected. The then Health Secretary explicitly admitted that the crackdown on socialising is made in order to keep the economy going (Hancock in Hansard 2020d: c.195–200). His Shadow in the Opposition benches was more analytical. Having explained that work, schools and public transport are major vectors of infection, but must remain off limits, he wonders: “if we cannot close schools, if we cannot close workplaces, if we cannot close shops, if we cannot shut down public transport, then the only leaver we have is hospitality” (Ashworth in Hansard 2020d: c.201–203).

Thus the measures devised to counter the epidemic are premised on an antagonism between work and sociability, between economy and society, and show the determination of the state to safeguard the former by sacrificing the latter. They point to the capitalist state’s response to its existential dilemma between security and economy: economic activity, the continuation of capital accumulation is non-negotiable; security measures expand only as far as they do not infringe it. From a social perspective they outline a condition where leisure and play are banned in order for work to continue undisrupted (Wu Ming 2021). Biosecurity morphs into a regime of workfare.

Gaslighting

Biosecurity, as medical power, is undeniable, it needs no justification. Programmatically, as expressed in law, it is irresponsible — the state (of siege, exception or necessity) has powers but no duties. These qualities also mark the tactics that the British government developed in order to cope with, and overcome, the failings of its chaotic biosecurity policy. The first such tactic is to divert attention. The government diverts attention from failures by pompously releasing a promise of extraordinary future success. It was employed by the Health Secretary's promise to increase testing capacity tenfold within a month; in the announcement by the Business Secretary of the imminent arrival of 400 tons of PPE; or in the Prime Minister's promise of building a "world beating" test-and-trace system within weeks and the Health Secretary's announcement of £100 billion dedicated to this purpose under the codename "Operation Moonshot" (Farrar 2021: 143–146, 170). Each of those was issued when governmental shortcomings were coming under media or parliamentary scrutiny and deflected the discussion away from them. At its extreme, this tactic aims to divert attention through confusion, by turning perception on its head. It was employed by the Health Secretary declaring that he had, from the very start of the epidemic, placed a protective "ring of steel" around care homes — uttered at precisely the moment when the government's inertia and the ensuing devastation became apparent. And, on the day that official statistics showed Britain's excess deaths rate to be the highest in Europe, the Prime Minister declared his government's response to the epidemic "a massive success" (Woodcock 2020).

The second tactic is deflection of blame. The government admits failure, but blames it on someone else. State Secretaries have repeatedly blamed the public — especially the young — rather than their unfathomable guidelines, for the persistence and resurgence of high infection rates; blamed the failure of biosecurity policy on the, independent from government, Public Health England, which they abolished; and the Health Secretary blamed the lack of PPE on medical workers' over-consuming it (Farrar 2021: 170–171; Johnson 2020c). Accusing society for epidemiological failure is a staple for governments across Europe (France, Greece, Italy), who persistently blame for epidemiological adversities the unvaccinated and all those that deviate from their haphazard (and epidemiologically useless) rules. They have led political analysts to talk of a "guiltification of the citizen" (Andrea Miconi in Wu Ming 2021).

The third tactic is deception. The Health Secretary's account of PPE items delivered to hospitals was found to include bin bags, cleaning products and to have counted gloves individually, rather than as pairs. Similarly, it transpires that up to half the tests accounted for were not actually completed. Further, the Health Secretary asserted that asymptotic transmission was not understood in February 2020, while the opposite was the case. The government claimed that it was following recommendations by its scientific advisers in lifting the lockdown in May 2020, while their advice was to keep it (Farrar 2021: 151–153; 224). Combined, the above methods have been termed *gaslighting*: manipulation aiming to instil on its victim doubts regarding his own sanity.

The last tactic is aggression. Upon receiving a question from a member of Parliament, the Home Secretary, rather than answering, repeatedly expressed his dislike for the question and admonished his opposite number for striking a 'wrong tone' that did not rhyme with national feeling (Hansard 2020a: c.487). The tactic was adopted by the Prime Minster when facing questions by the Leader of the Opposition (Johnson in Hansard 2020c: c.567). This method reveals an authoritarian streak, innate in all national efforts against an "enemy": whoever questions any aspect of the effort or those who lead it, is condemned as a traitor; even tame political dialogue becomes akin to national sabotage.

The unjustified, irresponsible power of biosecurity is, therefore, unapologetic and intolerant to criticism. This is evident in the government's attitude towards its own rules. The PM, two Secretaries of State, including the Health Secretary, the Prime Minister's top political advisor, and two scientific advisors (one in England, one in Scotland) are known to have broken lockdown rules; and it is reported that several parties were held in 10 Downing street and in ministerial buildings throughout 2020, when social gatherings were outlawed. The Health Secretary, the person chiefly, and often solely, responsible for issuing biosecurity measures, had been breaking the rules he was issuing from the start of the pandemic and until the moment he resigned in June 2021 (Allegretti and Adams 2021; Halliday and Murphy 2020; Marsh 2021; Stewart 2020a).

Notably, in order to protect his political advisor, who has made a most provocative departure from the rules, the Prime Minster employed all four tactics outlined above and, moreover, broke governmental protocol, flaunted cabinet procedures, blamed eye-witnesses and the media for spreading false accusations (but refused to explain how they were false), and undermined the credibility and validity of his government's regulations by interpreting them so implausibly that they lost all meaning. Finally, the government relaxed some restrictions so that the adviser's conduct would, retrospectively, fall within the law (Calvert and Arbuthnott 2021: 311–316; Johnson in Liaison Committee 2020: q.5–11, 17–25, 93–94). Without offering an apology, the PM praised his advisor for following his fatherly instincts. This distils the paternalist power of biosecurity: the instinct of the benevolent pastor is the superior law.

Finally, the revelation of lockdown parties taking place in the prime minister's residence and office, threw the government into crisis in late 2021 and early 2022. It involved social outrage, collapse of the governing party's popularity in the polls, its MPs threatening to withdraw their confidence in the prime minister, an apology to the queen, and a criminal investigation into the affair. Throughout, the prime minister responded with a mix of obfuscation, denial, deflection of blame, triumphal trumpeting of his achievements in office, *sub rosa* threats to misbehaving MPs, suppression of evidence (The Guardian 2022; The Observer 2022; Townsend 2022).

In a nutshell, the rules apply to all except to those who design and impose them on everyone else. Biosecurity describes a specific ethos of power: irresponsible, intransigent, aggressive, deceptive and intolerant. Because it is caring, and mobilised to save society, it has no obligation to, and tolerates no interference from it. It has no decipherable resemblance to the ethos of democratic or rule-of-law based government.

Notes

1. The Health Protection (Coronavirus, Restrictions) (England) Regulations 2020 Sch.2, Part 3. Statutory Instrument 2020 no.350, 26 March.
2. The Health Protection (Coronavirus, Restrictions) (No.2) (England) Regulation 2020. Statutory Instrument 2020 no.684, 3 July.

7 The knowledge of biosecurity

Biosecurity measures are extraordinary not only in potency, but also in their relation to knowledge. They have been issued (and lifted) on the basis of incomplete, contradictory and even non-existent knowledge regarding the biochemical composition of the virus and, later, its variants; its propensity to mutate and the ways that this is done; the duration of its incubation; its infectiousness and ways of transmission; its mortality rate; or, early in the pandemic when testing capacity was limited, the expanse of its spread. Scientists complained that, due to lack of testing, they were flying blind in the early months of the pandemic; and that lifting many restrictive measures at once in the summer (of both 2020 and 2021) introduced too many variables and thus made causality links between infection and specific activities impossible to determine, forcing them to "having to guess" (Calvert and Arbuthnott 2021: 186, 331; Farrar 2021: 123–124, 127, 140). The state cannot even count the dead definitely: the death toll is taken in different registers with very different results (Barr, Duncan and McIntyre 2020). Worse, the extent of asymptomatic infection and transmission, widely estimated to be between a third and 80 percent of infections, means that "we do not know what we do not know" (Brown 2020).

Thus, decisions regarding whether there should be a lockdown; what should it encompass; when it should start and end; who should be quarantined and for how long; how many intensive care beds are needed; how many tests suffice; what is the appropriate length of "social distance"; access to what settings should depend on vaccination status; which vaccines should be made available to which age groups; how often should people get vaccinated; what the mortality rate is, and whether it is high enough to errand what reaction — all were determined on the basis of incomplete scientific knowledge supplemented by educated guess and intuition. Interventions are decided on the basis of forecasts on a range of scenarios and widely diverging possibilistic projections (Boyer 2021: 73–77; Caduff 2020). In short, biosecurity measures have been devised on the basis of uncertainty, even ignorance, regarding what they are trying to combat, and consequently, regarding their adequacy, effectiveness and proportionality. Drastic interventions on society, are made in the absence of secure knowledge and causal determination

DOI: 10.4324/9781003302988-8

regarding their object and their own effects. This forces us to look into the epistemology of biosecurity.

Controlling the future: prevention, precaution, pre-emption

Biosecurity intervenes in the present situation in order to remove from it an undesirable interference (the virus, the epidemic); it tries to ensure that the future situation will be identical to the past, pre-interference one. Biosecurity, then, acts on the present in order to shape the future so that the future resembles the past. It intervenes on the present in order to remove from it a threatening potentiality — a potentiality that is contained in the present and threatens to alter the future. Biosecurity seeks to shape the future by *repressing* threatening potentialities. There are three broad methods through which state power intervenes in the present in order to determine the future by selectively repressing unwanted potentialities: prevention, precaution and pre-emption. The three share strong similarities; they are, after all, of the same kind: interventions on the present aiming to avoid an outcome in the future. But there are significant differences regarding their epistemological premises.

Prevention aims to stop some identified threat from materialising. To do so, it intervenes on the causes that generate the threat, which are also identified. Schematically, prevention identifies an (actual or potential) problem; then, it identifies its causes; and it resolves, ameliorates or prevents the problem by intervening in the causes that generate it. Prevention averts the problem by neutralising its cause. Its core premise is a tight relation between cause-problem-solution; and its epistemology is one of defined and scientifically established links of determination between the three. Prevention is a knowledge-based management of problems, through intervention on their causes. It involves defined objects, methods and objectives, and definite knowledge of their relations. Accordingly, its success in managing and alleviating threats can be tested and its results measured.

Precaution, by contrast, demands intervention to avert the materialisation of threats on the basis of uncertain knowledge. It is a well-defined and debated modality, largely thanks to its incorporation in (especially environmental) jurisprudence in the form of the *precautionary principle*. The most encompassing formulation of this principle requires that epistemic "uncertainty should not be a reason for inaction in the face of serious environmental threats" (Steel 2015: 9). Precaution intervenes on the basis of doubt and suspicion, on the basis of lack of knowledge. It is premised on uncertainty: uncertainty about *what* it is trying to avert *and* its causes. Precaution expresses an ontological fear of the unknown, a suspicious, cautious stance that associates indeterminacy with danger. Precaution is rooted on fear and a demand for its avoidance. Its attitude is suspicious: it demands that things are considered dangerous until proven safe, and that they cease until their safety is established. At present, precaution refers to, and operates on, relations between things — especially chemical substances, and their interaction with the human body as a biochemical organism. This entails that, for precaution, epistemic uncertainty is removable. It can be lifted as science gains improved knowledge of substances and their interrelation. Thus, precaution is not only premised on uncertainty, but depends on it: when certainty is established, precaution is lifted. Precaution accepts that this lifting of uncertainty is possible, and demands it. Precaution then is premised on an uncertainty that it considers temporary, it is a mode of intervention that aims to its own overcoming. Finally, both precaution and prevention are suspensory: they seek to arrest development, to stop threatening and detrimental things from becoming. And, both these modalities conceptualise society as the object of the threat.

For pre-emption, society is both the object *and* the subject of the threat, its potential victim and its bearer. Pre-emption is based on a singular ontological certainty: the threat exists. Because it refers not to determinable substances, but to the social, to people and their relations, this ontological certainty is coupled with epistemological uncertainty. The threat can take any form, and strike anywhere at any time. It is irregular, even random, in its manifestations — hence statistical regularity is non-existent and evidence-based prediction unfeasible. Moreover, since the threat can take any form, so do its causes; their identification is, therefore, impossible. Thus, like precaution, pre-emption is premised on epistemic uncertainty, except now this uncertainty cannot be lifted. The lack of determination connecting the threat to its causes and the uncertainty regarding the threat's form are unredeemable. Strictly speaking, this is not uncertainty but unknowability. Thus, precluding the actualisation of the threat by intervening on its causes, whether on the basis of knowledge (prevention) or that of uncertainty (precaution), is not possible. Instead, pre-emption seeks to preclude the materialisation of threats by shaping the broader social environment so that they cannot be formed therein. It seeks to eliminate the potentiality of the threat by making the development of its vectors impossible, to shape, in other words, the overall social ecology so that certain beings cannot come to exist. As they attempt to preclude something unknowable, pre-emptive interventions are not guided by knowledge, but employ it instrumentally within an action framework determined by intuition and imagination. Moreover, since causal links between the threat, its cause, and the intervention are indeterminable, so is the effect of the intervention, it success or failure. Without a specific object of reference or test of success, pre-emptive interventions are made because they, intuitively, seem plausible or necessary. (On pre-emption, see: Boukalas 2020; Massumi 2015; Neocleous 2016: 2–15; Stampnitzky 2013: 165–200). In sum, pre-emption is a management of future potentialities. It is a creative intervention: to avert a threat, it reshapes the social environment and the subjectivities that populate it, so that the threat can find no ground to grow. Its interventions are based on absolute certainty about the existence of the threat, combined with impossibility of knowing the threat's form or causes. It is therefore guided by intuition, not knowledge. And, because it seeks to produce undefined effects on undefined objects, it is impossible to evaluate it in terms of success or failure. It is, in short, a mode of intervention, a mode of power, that is profoundly unscientific. It is intuitive, unprincipled and exercised because it must.

In mapping biosecurity across these three epistemic modalities, we notice that biosecurity interventions are based on uncertainty. This uncertainty is redeemable: despite the complexity of the pandemic as a phenomenon, its knowledge is seen as amenable to improvement and to greater completeness; and interventions can be adjusted, amended, or removed in light of improved knowledge. For many countries, these interventions tend to err to the side of caution, to opt for greater safety even if it proves excessive. In short, we are in the realm of precaution. Indeed, UK scientists seem to have been working on this premise (Farrar 2021: 109, 138); and both Scotland's First Minister and the UK Health Secretary acknowledged the precautionary principle as the guide to government actions: "it may be that we get enough efficacy from the existing vaccines against hospitalisation and death…We just don't know that yet. Hence the precautionary principle applies" (Hancock in Hansard 2021a: c.168; Sturgeon 2020).

Yet, the departure of policy from scientific evidence and projections points to unknowability as the epistemological fixture of governmental decision-making: "any attempt to estimate the specific economic impacts of precise changes to individual restrictions for a defined period of time would be subject to such wide uncertainty as to not be meaningful for precise policy making" (HM Government 2020d: 10). Having given up on "estimates" the state governs on the basis of intuition. Apart from being largely intuitive, its interventions are aimed at the broader environment. Having identified society as the generator of the threat, biosecurity suspended it: it made a decisive intervention in the social environment so that the threat could not grow in it. Moreover, the uncertainty regarding the threat makes the success or failure of interventions both infallible and unverifiable. When interventions appear fruitless or counterproductive, the state can counterfactually claim that without them it would have been worse. If omissions are perceived as endangering or detrimental, the state can claim that their effects were insignificant or that disaster was inevitable. Thus, any action is justified as long as it can claim it was taken to counter the existential threat. Finally, the vaccine, the *deus ex machina* that could resolve the biosecurity drama, is pre-emptive, both in modality and in objective. Unlike medication, vaccination does not attempt to negate the illness; it anticipates it, teases it out and manipulates its course so that it becomes harmless, so that it bears no threat. Through mass immunisation, it presents the threat, the virus, to an environment in which it cannot grow.

Announcing the first British lockdown on 23 March 2020, the Prime Minister declared to the nation that "many more families are going to lose loved ones before their time" (Johnson in Frade 2020: 12). The official opening salvo of biosecurity in the UK is striking in its categorical modality. The Prime Minister predicts the future with absolute certainty: "many more families *are going to* lose" — not "may" or "could", but "are going to". Steeped in pre-emptive epistemology, everything about the threat is uncertain, except its outcome: excessive premature death. This outcome is certain, inevitable — and, hence, the state can deny responsibility for its occurrence. Thus, when asked by parliamentarians, the Prime Minister explained that he was late in imposing the first lockdown because the disease would have spread in the UK inevitably; hence his tardiness was inconsequential (Johnson in the House of Commons Liaison Committee 2020: q. 96). In summer 2021, upon announcing the lifting of all biosecurity measures while the country was before a new wave of infections, the Prime Minister declared that "we must reconcile ourselves sadly to more deaths from Covid" (Johnson 2021). If the outcome — death by covid — is inevitable, there is no point in resisting it with restrictions. Indeed, "return to normality" for society and the economy is inevitable too — death is no reason to postpone it. Facing the imminent prospect of record infections, the government's scientific advisers counselled that the (inevitable) lifting of restrictions should happen sooner, in the summer, rather than later in the autumn. This would bring the (inevitable) rise in hospitalisations and deaths forward by a few months, thus avoiding its coincidence with the flu season which would be catastrophic for the NHS (Sample and Grover 2021). Provoking the threat to express its force early, before it can cause maximum damage, is a pre-emptive tactic. Given the inevitability of the threat, it seeks to control its timing.

Notably, inevitability, uncertain causality and, above all unknowability, are epistemic modalities pertinent to neoliberalism. While the "spontaneous order" of the market has come to absorb all social relations and thus become a "*kosmos*", due to its immense complexity the subjects that populate it are unable to grasp its overall design — this is "not limited to what the human mind can master". Moreover, as this cosmos-market has no end or purpose, it is impossible for subjects to anticipate the effects of their own actions (Hayek 2013: 38), and are unable to identify the causes of what affects them: "our adaptation to our environment does not consist only, or even chiefly, in an insight into the relations between cause and effect, but also in our actions being governed by...circumstances which we are not aware of and which yet determine the pattern of our successful actions" (Hayek 2013: 12–13). In a world he cannot know, whose causes and effects we cannot identify but only experience as arbitrary and inevitable, the neoliberal subject, in sharp contrast to its liberal progenitor, is adrift into the cosmos of the market. He is definitely "not, and will never be the master of his fate" (Hayek 2013: 507; also Gentili 2021: 100–101, 114). Neither is his state. It is busy, decisive and intervening, but its knowledge is limited, the effects of its interventions unpredictable, and its ends are not defined.

In sum, biosecurity employs an amalgam of precaution and pre-emption: precautionary epistemology embarks on pre-emptive interventions. Precaution operates through, and as, pre-emption. As the knowledge informing them improves, so will its interventions; but these interventions aim at society, and their outcomes are hard to evaluate; they are instead justified *a priory* by their professed intentions. As pre-emptive interventions come to apply on phenomena that are not only unknowable but also inevitable, they completely defy responsibility. Biosecurity is an irresponsible power, justified by its general purpose alone.

The irresponsibility of state power, expressed in Chapters 6 and 18 as the denial of responsibility by state actors, is premised on the state's conceptualisation of phenomena as unknowable and/or inevitable. However, responsibility for such act-of-god occurrences is not dissolved. In a modulation typical of the neoliberal state, responsibility is passed on to individuals. This is evident in the elevation of each person's common sense as the ultimate guide to surviving the pandemic; and in ministers putting the blame for every deterioration on the (invariably "few") individuals who do not obey their orders, break their rules, question the truthfulness of the information they broadcast, refuse the vaccines they offer, and — in anyway and for any reason — dare to protest against them.

Politicising science: the knowledge-power apparatus

British biosecurity is designed by an apparatus which comprises a forum dedicated to the acquisition of knowledge, and another that takes decisions. The first is known as SAGE (Scientific Advisory Group on Emergencies). It comprises government-appointed scientists with expertise directly related to the emergency at hand — its membership, therefore, varies in line with the specific situation. Its role is to gather the fullest, and most authoritative knowledge on the threat. In the context of the pandemic, such knowledge consists of and combines anything from the latest analyses of the properties of the virus, the ways in which it is transmitted, or the progress made to the pharmacological front; to the optimal ways for communicating measures, and the minutiae of everyday behaviour provided by digests of location and mobility data. The SAGE distils its updated knowledge into reports and advice to decision makers. The latter reside in COBRA (Cabinet Office Briefing Room A), a cabinet cluster that directs the response to emergencies. Its composition also varies according to the nature of the emergency; it invariably consists of a small number of senior ministers, top civil servants and select political advisers, and is usually chaired by the Prime Minister. Informed by scientific reports and advice, but also by considerations with political economic and social implications, COBRA decides on the measures to be taken.

Thus, when the British government claimed to be "following the science" the statement was plausible. Its plausibility was strengthened by inscrutability: both SAGE and COBRA were, at inception, secret bodies. Their existence and their role were public and official, but their workings and composition secret. Indeed, its involvement in the management of pandemic, the momentous interventions and acute public interest it entailed, informed the decision of SAGE participants to publicise their reports and advice, despite government's reluctance to such transparency.

Early disclosures revealed that almost all scientists participating in SAGE were affiliated to only two universities; and medical science was largely missing from its composition: there were no immunologists, intensive care experts or molecular virologists involved (Costello 2020). Instead, the vast majority were experts in either epidemiological modelling and behavioural psychology — two sciences dedicated to social manipulation, prediction and control. Also present were representatives of data-mining corporations which, through their participation, gained access to the sensitive, and commercially valuable, personal health records kept by the NHS (Frade 2020: 13–15).

The scientific composition of SAGE indicates that the episteme of biosecurity is one of social control. This is confirmed by a third component of the biosecurity apparatus. If SAGE is the research laboratory and COBRA the decision-making forum of the mechanism, the newfound (May 2020) Joint Biosecurity Centre (JBC) is its central nervous system. It comprises epidemiology experts under the leadership of a counterterrorism veteran. It is concerned with outlining the precise epidemiological condition and its trends in real time, in every locality, region and the country as a whole. To do so, it perpetually gathers, processes and reviews the totality of information relevant to the epidemic across the country. This information includes all location, mobility and transaction data each individual produces. Drawing from data emanating from digital payment technologies, social media websites, computers and mobile phones, it encompasses financial transactions; purchases, their place, time and type; the places a person is in during the day; transport; locational proximity to others; communications. By continuously gathering and algorithmically analysing all these, the JBC estimates the epidemiological situation at each moment and place. Its digests are codified in a colour-coded warning system with five different levels of threat, each represented by a colour (Farrar 2021: 126; Johnson in House of Commons Liaison Committee 2020: q.56–57). Thus, biosecurity decision-making is informed by two types of knowledge that inform each other: science and intelligence.

The JBC soon came under the aegis of the Health Security Agency (HSA), established in April 2021. It combines JBC intelligence with that gathered by the test-and-trace mechanism, and is also in charge of diagnostic services. The HSA integrates the mechanism of epidemiological intelligence and is therefore in charge of health protection and response to "health threats": epidemics as well as chemical, biological, nuclear and radiological incidents[1]. In the HSA, the conception of public health as a security issue acquires institutional form.

The information necessary for combating the pandemic is not limited to public health information. Far from it: it relies on the effective merging of vast and perpetually augmented datasets of personal and relational data controlled by the state and large corporations (Allsop, Bessant and Dawda 2021; Oswald, Allsopp and Bessant 2021: 16–17; Samerski 2018). It completes the move towards integrated surveillance (Lyon 2003) and comprises knowledge of all social interaction and personal conduct, of every individual, all of the time. Indeed, if the threat resides in society, if society as a practice that involves contact, proximity and interaction, is the threat; it follows that to know the threat one needs to know society: its minutest detail *and* its aggregation into general outlines and tendencies. Again, biosecurity's episteme is one of social control: it aims to know the threat, society, in order to control it. We have seen that biosecurity is medical power promulgated by police. We see now that this promulgation depends on, and is led by, intelligence (McQuade and Neocleous 2020). This intelligence is total: it perpetually encompasses all social life, in discrete specificity and in aggregate generality. The scope of biosecurity surveillance is commensurate with society; because so is its suspicion.

If science and intelligence are the two types of knowledge informing biosecurity power, it is notable how independent the latter remains from them. All knowledge is merely advisory to government: it is laid before it, but does not bind it. The claim that policy is scientifically determined (it "follows the science") is premised on the assumption of a radical separation between science and politics. Indeed, while science denotes expert knowledge — systematic, detailed, and in-depth; politics is akin to opinion, will, decision and action (Aristotle 1992; Castoriadis 2002). The problem here is the degree of separation assumed: the two fields of activity are not, never were, and cannot be secluded from each other. Politics is informed by and utilises science to achieve its objectives and even to discover the problems it needs to address. For this reason, it enhances the production of the science it needs — the history of statistics, criminology, sociology, economics, eugenics etc. testifies to this. Medical science is not exempt. In the 19th century, the requirement that the crew and cargo of harboured ships would spend forty days without coming ashore if there was illness on board, a practice that produced the word "quarantine", was anathema for merchants. Accordingly, the state, for over a century, suppressed research in contagion, the idea that viruses spread from human contact, and steered medicine to locate the origin of disease in infection, i.e. on environmental factors. By adjusting medical science, the state could liberate trade, but also justify its drastic interventions on the urban environment (Bourdelais 1998). Thus, in emphasising how it follows science, the state conceals that it also determines it.

Science denotes expertise on something specific and particular; by contrast politics is informed by, and affects, social life in its fullness — it concerns the universal (Castoriadis 1983). The demand for science-led politics can, and does, result to scientifically informed policy. Yet, such scientification of politics also *politicises science*. In guiding policy, scientists are asked to consider and respond to social considerations that are way beyond their particular expertise. From their specific base, they are asked to address the universal. Thus, medical science is required to consider — and resolve — issues foreign to it (Esposito 2021). It is asked to resolve issues pertaining to capital accumulation, legal and political principles, exploitation and inequality, and the tensions that arise between these.

To be sure, science is never truly called to assume such a role. Its invocation and its placement in a leading political role is intended to reduce a mega-political issue —one that implicates all aspects of the established social life and order— into a question of technical management. It thus serves to remove the sting of criticism against decision-making politicians; but, more importantly, it serves to neutralise the critique of a social order under duress. The tensions caused by this exploitation of science in defence of the social order are evident throughout the biosecurity saga.

Asked to assume the role of government, science is subjected to contrasting pressures emanating from society *and* from the state. Thus, in preparing for the pandemic, British scientists were *not* asked to estimate the effects that a *lockdown* would have on infections, because a lockdown was politically unthinkable (Calvert and Arbuthnott 2021: 160–161; Farrar 2021: 111). The scope of the science — and hence its answers — was not determined scientifically, but politically. It was also defined by sheer practicality: face masks were useless when they were scarce; but effective and compulsory when they became abundant (Calvert and Arbuthnott 2021: 182–336). Its proximity to political power can also lead science to subordination: in March 2020, scientific advisors were claiming that it was "too early" to consider protective measures for care homes (Calvert and Arbuthnott 2021: 161). This perceived submissiveness of scientists to politicians led to the creation of a scientific network parallel to SAGE, aiming to publicise science pure from government interference. Another parallel scientific network, the Barrington Declaration, was put together by the neoliberal American Enterprise Institute to produce science against biosecurity restrictions; it was mobilised by the UK Treasury to provide scientific advice against restrictive measures. When following science, the state can chose which science to follow. Finally, science can be little more than a gravitational crystallisation of state ideology: the prospect of a fabled "behavioural fatigue" that informed Britain's tardiness in entering lockdown was not based on any scientific theory or evidence, but on intuition stemming from expectations of how citizens of western liberal democracies would behave — intuitions shared by the government's behavioural unit (Farrar 2021: 117, 131, 136–137).

More than choosing and influencing the scientific advice it follows, the state can also short-circuit, bypass, or ignore it altogether. The decision to lift the first lockdown in summer 2020 was taken without scientific input, and SAGE was also unaware of the Treasury's scheme to subsidise restaurant bills. The trumpeting of the return to the office, and the opening of schools, cinemas and universities in autumn 2020 were decisions taken against SAGE advice. So was the tier system, which scientists considered inadequate. Further, the government's attempts to avoid a second — and, later, a third — lockdown were greeted with fury by its scientific advisers, who were becoming aware that their true role was that of scapegoat for failed policies. They publicly contradicted state policy or washed their hands off it (Calvert and Arbuthnott 2021: 321–332, 334, 349, 360, 364-365, 370, 376; Farrar 2021: 151–153, 175, 181–187).

In sum, biosecurity is a modality of power that aims to save society from the threat it represents for itself. It is a precautionary and pre-emptive power, based on the certainty and inevitability of the threat's existence, combined with uncertainty about the form and modalities of the threat. It is premised on total knowledge of society. It is benign, but also irresponsible, unaccountable and limitless. It overwhelms, highjacks and exploits the science it mobilises. Its interventions are motivated by care and aim to, partially or fully, cancel society.

Note

1. See the Agency's website: https://www.gov.uk/government/organisations/uk-health-security-agency

Part II

ECONOMIC COLLAPSE

> Today, the problem is not the improvement of living conditions in the factory, but the continuation of the life of the factory.
>
> Guido Carli, 1974 (in Agnoli 2020: 149)

We now turn to the other core area of state activity and concern, the economy, where the state is facing another crisis, a crisis without precedent in magnitude and quality. When it erupted, the economic crisis threatened the total collapse of the economy, globally. Markets, states and international directorates were seized by panic. Even the battle-hardened IMF declared this one was *not a normal crisis*. While the underlying weakness and instability of neoliberal economies — anaemic investment, slow growth, flatlined productivity and lack of reward and safety for working people — aggravated its impact, the cause of this crisis was external to the economy. Yet, it was not the pandemic *per se* that caused it; it was the state's response to the pandemic: biosecurity. In other words, the state was the author of the economic crisis. Thus, the biosecurity crisis is now joined by its twin, a twin born out of its management, that pulls state policy to the opposite direction. Given the magnitude of the crisis — during spring 2020, in European countries there was no economy to speak of — the state had to intervene not only to unblock, enhance and support the economy as it did during the financial crisis; but to stand in for it, to become the economy. The state was both the main culprit for the collapse of the economy and its saviour.

Just like the state response to the biosecurity crisis, the effort to avert economic collapse saw the mobilisation of powers that, on the eve of the crisis, few suspected the state had. They reached into areas of socio-economic relations — such as the wage — were they had not ventured for decades, and upturned the dominant neoliberal paradigm. The chapters in this Part revisit the state response to economic collapse and measure their departure from the established paradigm. As the acute phase of the crisis is successfully superseded, and the economy is entering an unstable phase of recovery and a post-pandemic economy starts to take shape, the chapters address the question of whether the crisis has resulted to a paradigm shift. They do

DOI: 10.4324/9781003302988-9

so by assessing developments and perspectives in three inter-related fields: *fiscal policy* is addressed, first at a programmatic global level in Chapter 9, and as specific policy in the UK in Chapter 10; *labour policy* is addressed in Chapters 11 and 12; *distribution policy* in Chapter 13. In each, the analysis assesses whether state policy pertains to a Keynesian (demand-side and counter-cyclical) strategy or to a neoliberal (supply-side and pro-cyclical) one. Their insights are combined in Chapter 14, to conclude that state economic policy is dual: Keynesian during crisis, but neoliberal in normal times; and, more importantly, Keynesian for capital, neoliberal for everyone else. In drawing the perspectives for the future of the economy, the chapter notes that structural shifts in the spatio-political economic architecture pose significant challenges to the continuation of neoliberal economic policy, making it unsettled and unstable.

If, in the Carli quote above, the "factory" is equated with the economy and "life in the factory" with labour, the chapters in this part try to answer which side the state prioritises. A first, important, indication is offered in the following chapter: in the context of the opposing exigencies that the twin crises place on the state, Chapter 8 deciphers which one is the state's utmost priority: "life" or "the economy"?

8 Fear vs fear

The rapid development of a biosecurity regime in response to the threat of the coronavirus marks the first phase of the pandemic. Arguably, its most extraordinary feature is the eagerness with which society accepted, welcomed and often demanded the deployment of authoritarian power that suspended its freedoms and even cancelled society as such. This attitude can be attributed to society being stunned (Klein 2007) ensuing from the perplexing nature of the threat combined with its ubiquity and lethality. While this accounts for the panic and disorientation experienced by society, it does not explain why its call for protection was answered in authoritarian terms. What enabled security to be expressed in such terms was the 20-year long conditioning of society to expect state efforts to secure it to be coercive and anti-democratic (Sanguinetti 2020). This points to a peculiar dialectic of fear in the heart of contemporary government: inculcation of society with fear is the sole platform of authority for a state that has no positive, desirable notion of a collective future to offer. And, security measures invariably take anti-social, repressive forms because the state is in fear of a society that it cannot lead.

As the pandemic entails not only a security threat, but also a monumental economic failure, it brings to the fore the limits of fear-based government. Fear cannot be switched off at will — and the state finds it hard to roll back its security measures. Having promoted and responded to the life-threatening fear of the virus, in the summer of 2020 the state discovered that its efforts to restart the economy were falling short (Helm et al 2020). Despite anxiously lifting restrictions and promoting consumerist well-being, economic activity in the UK remained considerably lower that its normal or expected levels (Bank of England 2020: 4). Despite the easing of security, the fear lingered, undermining economic recovery. This attitude persists as the biosecurity crisis completes its second year: despite the UK government imposing no restrictions against the spread of the Omicron variant in December 2021, the market remained subdued (Butler 2021). Thus, in order to resuscitate the economy the state needed not only to downplay the biosecurity threat, but to erect another threat next to it.

DOI: 10.4324/9781003302988-10

The predicament of the state was that the lockdown of society stopped the economy. The response to the biosecurity crisis caused a tremendous economic one. By offering protection, the capitalist state fulfilled its foundational duty *qua* state, but breached its foundational duty *qua* capitalist: it suspended capital accumulation. If the overall function of the neoliberal state, in particular, is to secure and enhance the market and shape society in its image, here the state did the exact opposite: it destroyed the market. To lift the suspension of society and the concomitant closure of the economy, the state needed to counter the biosecurity fear. Unable to lift it, it needed to raise another, opposite, one. The British Prime Minister started by informing the nation that "there are millions of people who are both fearful of this terrible disease, and at the same time also fearful of what this long period of enforced inactivity will do to their livelihoods" (Johnson 2020a). Soon, in terms that resonated across the western world, fear for "livelihood" was erected opposite to fear for "life": "the impact on people's jobs and livelihoods has been severe...The Government is supporting millions of families and businesses, but cannot protect every job and every business...Unemployment is rising...The Office for Budget Responsibility has published a 'reference' scenario which suggests that...unemployment would rise by more than 2 million in the second quarter of 2020...GDP could fall by 35% in the second quarter of this year — and the annual contraction could be the largest in over 300 years" (HM Government 2020c: 9–10).

Having erected this antagonistic source of fear to neuter the biosecurity one, the state must now navigate through them. Their tension necessitates a strategic response — a strategy that would synthesise the incompatible responses to the two fears. The UK set this out in its *Recovery Strategy* (HM Government 2020a). This is an odd official document that contains no policy plans but only outlines principles and programmatic thinking. Thus, the purpose of its composition and publication is not clear; ultimately, the *Recovery Strategy* is a testament to strategic paralysis: lines of thought are broadly outlined, but there is no suggestion of any (plan of) action.

The declared purpose of the government is to save both lives and livelihoods (HM Government 2020a: 15), to counter both threats without prioritising one over the other. Indeed, framing the conundrum in terms of "life" and "livelihood" allows for equanimity between the two: there cannot be one without the other. The state employs the life/livelihood vocabulary to conceal that it is facing an agonising decision between life and accumulation. Rather than overcoming or synthesising the contradiction the twin crises raise, the government simply denies it. The expressed purpose of its policy is to suppress the virus, protect the NHS, *and* keep the economy going (HM Government 2020a: 5). The drive to serve these contradictory aims at once indicates strategic confusion — or resignation.

This reconciliation between two mutually exclusive courses of action is only discursive and superficial. While never acknowledged in the *Strategy*, their tension is palpable across its text. In the absence of a clear choice, addressing their dilemma involves subtle prioritisation. The government's "overriding priority is to save lives" (HM Government 2020a: 15). This sounds like a clear choice of direction: the government opts to err towards life, to prioritise the biosecurity crisis over the economic one, to respond primarily to its duty as *state* rather than as *capitalist*. But the government's meaning is more equivocal. Full commitment to a biosecurity course is said to be counter-productive, even self-defeating. A narrow fixation on covid-19 undermines "overall health outcomes" and harms "wider health" (HM Government 2020a: 15–16). Excessive biosecurity is a danger to public health, to the good it seeks to protect. The notion that an excess of means can undermine the purpose is interesting; more so is the way in which this is said to occur. Excessive biosecurity threatens to undermine the "wider health" *not* because it has turned the NHS into a single-purpose service, nor due to the mental health harm that anti-social biosecurity measures can cause. Biosecurity undermines public health *because it harms the economy*. The economic disruption ensuing from it will cause widespread "deprivation" and this deprivation will have long-term health effects on those who suffer it (HM Government 2020a: 16). Thus, some reconciliation between the two conflicting imperatives is reached: harm to the economy results in harm to health; between the two goods, the economy is the more comprehensive. Indeed, health is conditional to the economy: "The longer this virus affects the economy, the greater the risks of long-term scarring and permanently lower economic activity, with business failures, persistently higher unemployment and lower earnings. This would damage the sustainability of the public finances and the ability to fund public services including the NHS" (HM Government 2020a: 10). Without a healthy economy there will be no public health. Health and the economy are reconciled by acknowledging the supremacy of the latter. The economy is the fundamental good and the state's primary concern.

The economy is not only primary and decisive; it also defines the axiological and epistemological parameters of state action. The state communicates the conundrum it faces as reconciling the "overriding priority…to save lives" with the need to "protect your livelihoods" (HM Government 2020a: 5). The "lives" the state is set to save are abstract; the "livelihoods" are specific: *yours*. Thus, the superiority of the economy acquires a moral attire: it prioritises concrete, embodied need to abstract universality. Further, the concern of the state is how to balance "the cost to human life" with the "cost to the economy", to "suppress the epidemic spread, while minimising the economic and social effects" (HM Government 2020a: 5). Thus, the biosecurity-*vs*-economy conundrum becomes a calculous between acceptable levels of disease and tolerable levels of economic disruption. In the same frequency, the IMF was striving to devise formulas that would relate "unit easing" with the spread of the disease; and these would inform decision-making on easing restrictions (IMF 2020c: 23–28). In other words, the state frames the entire question of the pandemic as a cost-benefit one. Whatever its priorities and courses of action are, they are determined by (and as) an economic calculus. The logic of the market defines the entire effort.

If the *Strategy* subtly indicates the state's priorities, these become more evident in practice. The declarations of the Prime Minister that the UK will be the champion and saviour of "free trade" when other European countries were considering border controls in February 2020; his urge to the citizens to continue with "business as usual" in March 2020; the adoption of a half-measures' strategy ("Contain, Delay, Research, Mitigate") aimed to let the virus spread through society until the point the NHS reaches breaking point; the tardiness in imposing, and eagerness to lift, each lockdown; the government's orchestrated effort to push home-workers back into the office in order to defend real estate prices; summer schemes encouraging people back into restaurants, estimated to have increased infections between 8 and 17 percent; and forcing students to return to halls despite warnings that this would contribute to a second, massive surge of the virus (Calvert and Arbuthnott 2021: 5, 73, 155–157, 164, 177, 343–344, 366, 398): in every count, the government would adopt biosecurity measures as little and late as possible, and only when the NHS was threatened with *visible* collapse. Its clear priority, throughout the pandemic, was to protect the market, to minimise the damage to the economy. Meanwhile, the World Bank was advising the prompt imposition of lockdowns, for when imposed early, they tend to be shorter and hence less damaging to economy (Calvert and Arbuthnott 2021: 368). Early, strict lockdowns are good for the economy: this reconciles biosecurity and economic concerns under the prominence of the economy. The capitalist state had a way out of the impasse; still, most European states ignored it: they kept their economy open for as long as their health systems' could endure.

In the UK, priorities became clear when discipline, and pretences, collapsed. After the second (November 2020) lockdown, and with infection numbers and deaths higher than ever, the government refused to impose a third lockdown. Its only concern was to keep the market open during Christmas. In late December and early January, almost a thousand people died every day. Hospitals were now *visibly* overwhelmed and patients would be treated in ambulances outside. The ambulance service could not cope with demand, abandoning patients at home. The system had collapsed, and denial and concealment efforts were overcome by the sheer magnitude of the disaster and the furious despair of those caught in it. Britain was a "plague island", new variants of the virus were emerging, and Wales, Scotland and Northern Ireland imposed lockdowns. Regardless, the government in England persisted with business as usual, and even forced schools to open (Calvert and Arbuthnott 2021: 391–395). Even if the Prime Minister had never expressed the determination to "let the bodies pile up high in their thousands" rather than introduce a third lockdown (BBC 2021), his government's policy amounted to precisely this. Saving the market was no longer the first concern; it was the only one. Among the first to realise that the real priority of the government was "to save the economy at the cost of life and health" were the medical scientists who experienced its fierce resistance to epidemiological advice behind closed doors. In order to influence the government, they too started to highlight the economic benefits of the actions they recommended (Farrar 2021: 110, 138, 184, 187).

Notably missing from the calculi and equations that the state sets out, is *the state*. Biosecurity will cause deprivation, and deprivation will cause health problems — but the government purports to do nothing to break the links of this causation. Similarly, the weakening of the economy will cause the destruction of the NHS — but the government does not suggest it will do something about it. These relations between health and the economy are fatalistic, natural and independent from intervention, from social agency. They are axiomatic — and so is the unwillingness and incapacity of the neoliberal state to intervene, to assume responsibility for them.

Similarly, the state's other declared consideration, "protecting and restoring people's livelihoods and improving people's living standards", is a misnomer. The state is prepared to do nothing for people's livelihoods and living standards as such. What it intends to do, is to strengthen the economy, for livelihoods and living standards depend on it. Strengthening the economy comprises: bringing people back to the workplace when work from home is not feasible; securing the country's "economic future" threatened by unemployment and insolvencies; maintaining the sustainability of public finances, so that the government can fund health care; maintaining financial stability so that banks maintain their lending ability; and enhancing international economic competitiveness (HM Government 2020a: 16–17). In short, the state is set to preserve economic relations precisely as they were before the epidemic; and is set to do so precisely as a proper neoliberal state should: by securing the market from "external" threats (this time the one posed by biosecurity), enhancing its freedom, and letting its effects play out naturally upon society without intervention or responsibility (Friedman 2002; Hayek 2013).

Notably, fear is not only the platform from which the state lounges its biosecurity policy and its anti-biosecurity actions; *social* opposition to biosecurity was also premised on fear: fear for the economy and "freedom" that lockdowns represent, and fear for the consequences of the vaccine to individual health and genetic outlook. This is testament to the pervasive reach of fear as a political platform: all political positions *and those against them*, must evoke it and base themselves on it. Fear vs fear.

9 This is not a normal crisis

Capitalism differs from every previous mode of production in that it instils — and depends on — constant uninterrupted motion (Marx 1992: 192; Marx 1993: 535, 719). Capital accumulation occurs through the incessant metamorphosis of capital from money to labour, to machinery, to commodities, to (more) money, and all over again. Any disruption of this perpetual transformation of capital brings accumulation to a halt. It suspends and even cancels capital's valorisation: it destroys capital (Penzin 2020: 15). The pandemic forced the capitalist state to do precisely that: to suspend the constant metamorphosis of value, to disrupt the continuity of capital.

The first wave of lockdowns brought the realisation that suspending society inescapably halts economic activity: biosecurity is an existential threat to capital accumulation. Even the International Monetary Fund (IMF), the world's most battle-hardened crisis-combating veteran, was alarmed. It contemplated a global crisis of untold magnitude. The economic crisis caused by the biosecurity "dwarfs" the 2008 global financial one, which was meant to be a "once in a century" crisis. The Fund desperately stressed that this is not a "normal crisis" (IMF 2020a: xii). It conveyed an imminent apocalypse engulfing the entire economy. The collapse in aggregate demand ensuing from biosecurity will combine with supply atrophy as supply chains are interrupted and investment plunges. From there, the crisis will culminate in a financial seizure (IMF 2020a: 2–3; also: Boyer 2021: 118; The Economist 2020l: 14). Indeed, in spring 2020, the crisis had devastated the US Treasuries market, which is the foundation of the global financial system (Tooze 2021: 107–109). Such was the expected scale of the crisis that, before it had hardly erupted, the IMF gave it pride of place amongst the giants of the genre. Alongside the Great Depression of 1929–1930 and the Great Recession of 2008–2010, the IMF adds "the Great Lockdown", scheduled to dwarf them both (IMF 2020a). In short, the biosecurity response to the pandemic "plunged the world into the worst economic crisis in the history of capital" (Harvey 2020: 99).

National economies entered this crisis with interest rates at an historic low, public debt at its highest in 75 years, private and corporate debt alarmingly elevated and higher than on the eve of the financial crisis, and chronic

DOI: 10.4324/9781003302988-11

public and private underinvestment (Blakeley 2020: 1; IMF 2020a: 27; IMF 2020b: 23). They also entered the crisis with dilapidated welfare and health systems, chronically stagnated wages, high underemployment, and levels of hunger and homelessness unseen in a century. In short, the crisis hit national economies that had not truly recovered the previous one (Boyer 2021: 42–44). Thus, the world economy was bracing for the biggest crisis ever, many national economies faced the spectrum of imminent full collapse, and entire sectors of the economy were threatened with extinction.

This is economic Armageddon. States rapidly proceeded to take drastic — truly unprecedented— measures to mitigate its immediate impact and avoid the prospect of deep, long-term scarring. In March 2020, the world's leading central banks, (US, EU, Japan and England) pledged to "do whatever it takes" to bailout corporations and prevent corporate bond markets from collapse (Blakeley 2020: 21). Optimism that once the biosecurity measures were lifted economies would automatically "bounce back" to their pre-pandemic splendour was an early paregoric but proved short-lived, for they were unfounded to the point of irrationality. They assumed that the crisis was a meteoric event, external to the economic system, failing to consider that the trends and relations prevailing in the latter were, to say the least, amplifying the impact of biosecurity restrictions. They also assumed a level of economic robustness and dynamism that simply was not there in the pre-pandemic economies of mature capitalist countries. Gradually, key economic actors realised that the economy is too weak to generate its own recovery and that the latter would be a precarious process with uncertain outcome.

In this juncture, the IMF gave the clarion call to combat the crisis. By praising actions taken by national states and admonishing against complacency, its reports urge drastic and sustained crisis-management action stretching into the foreseeable future.

The road to recovery: from counter-cyclicality to the "resilience economy"

The IMF differentiates three phases of grappling with the crisis: an "acute outbreak" phase, a "recovery" phase and one of a "new economic normality".

The first — "acute outbreak" — phase is defined by the onslaught of the biosecurity crisis. It is the phase that most countries have already experienced and many have already put behind. In this phase states should simply do whatever it takes to save their national economies. The IMF approvingly recites the colossal fiscal interventions undertaken by states across the world, the "overall speed and size of which" were "unprecedented", amounting to $12 trillion by mid-September 2020. In the advanced economies of Europe, Japan and North America, almost half of their expenditure comprised additional spending — in public health, job retention programmes and handouts to businesses — and foregone revenue ensuing from tax deferrals. The largest part, amounting to 11 percent of these countries' GDP, consisted of liquidity support: quantitative easing, loans, guarantees and capital and equity injections to the private sector. It was carried out mainly by central banks, which replicated their 2008 crisis modus operandi, albeit in a larger, faster and more decisive way (IMF 2020a: 12). It was directed mainly to large corporations, with small and medium ones receiving less than a quarter of it despite their greatest exposure to biosecurity-induced adversity (IMF 2020b: 25). Looking back at the first year of managing the acute phase of the crisis, the Fund sounds relieved and congratulatory. While the contraction has been "unprecedented in living memory", it would have been three times as large without the extraordinary support measures of national states. Thanks to the latter, medium and long term scarring was now expected to be smaller than that caused by the financial crisis (IMF 2021a: xvi).

The extraordinary fiscal intervention by the state that saved the economy, came to the cost of a dramatic rise in public debt. Across the advanced capitalist world, the deficit-to-GDP ratio increased more than five-fold in 2020–2021. It is forecast to return to its pre-crisis levels by 2026. Accordingly, the debt-to-GDP ratio exploded, by between 10 to 20 percent, and it is forecast to stay at this peak for the foreseeable future (IMF 2021b: 3–4). The attitude of the IMF towards the amassment of astronomical amounts of public debt is surprising. In autumn 2020, when most European and North American states, partly under the impression that the worst of the biosecurity crisis was over, focused their attention to the escalating debt and planned to downsize their fiscal interventions, the IMF strongly urged them to stay the course. It admonished them that the "acute" phase was not yet over and recommended that, for its duration, states should continue to provide fiscal stimulus, with the additional debt this entails, and to secure lifelines for workers and businesses so that "employee-firm relationships" are not severed due to the biosecurity crisis (IMF 2020b: 3; IMF 2021a: 17–18). This relaxed attitude to public debt seems, surprisingly, to be shared by the market: while debt is skyrocketing, the cost of serving it is drastically reduced (IMF 2021b: 2; Tooze 2021: 142–143). This is largely due to qualitative easing and the gluttonous liquidity it endows the market, combined with uncertainty regarding the future of firms and sectors: not knowing what to do with their cash, investors push it government's way.

In the second — "recovery" — phase, the economic role of the state should, according to the IMF, change dramatically. Counter-cyclical fiscal interventions should continue, but acquire a different form. Now, the maintenance of "employee-firm relationships" should stop being a state preoccupation, and accordingly the largesse towards workers should cease. Instead, the sustainability of public debt must now become the centrepiece of economic policy. In this phase, the state should be primarily concerned with reducing its deficit and gradually taming debt (IMF 2020a: 14; IMF 2020b: 3; IMF 2021a: 18–19). Typically, this entails two options — or a combination thereof: reducing public spending and/or increasing taxation. Tellingly, the

IMF contemplates only the second path. As a means to consolidate public finances, the Fund promotes rises in the taxation of the most affluent corporations and individuals and the enhancement of states' capacity to capture lost tax. For the Fund progressive taxation is more than a means to debt reduction; it is a source of pubic investment and also — explicitly — a lever for redistributing wealth downwards. It is not clear, however, if increased taxation should remain a permanent feature of the economy, or if it is limited to the recovery phase. Also, unexplained and at odds with its broader recommendations, is the Fund's persistence that taxation on capital income must *not* rise (IMF 2020b: 17; IMF 2021a: 20; IMF 2021b: 16–17). The Fund's fondness for progressive taxation is surprisingly shared by the Economist, the key collective intellectual of economic and political liberalism (Zevin 2019). The Economist (2020f: 15–17) declared its preference for progressive taxation over a new bout of austerity. The reason for this preference is taxation's redistributive effects, as well as the perception of social cohesion it conveys.

Both the accommodation of public debt and the urge to tax would have constituted heresy on the eve of the pandemic. What possibly informs the course reversal of capital's intellectual organs and directorates is a sense that capital's domination over society may have reached a perilous point. Tentatively the World Economic Forum and the IMF highlight "social unrest" as a significant factor able to derail recovery. It is likely to occur where the crisis has exposed or exacerbated pre-existing "problems" and where progress in addressing "social and political issues" has stalled. As remedy, the Fund proposes a set of policies reminiscent of the welfare state (IMF 2021a: 15; Schwab and Malleret 2020: 83–88).

Moreover, during the recovery phase, the state should not contemplate a new round of austerity. Even as the emergency needs for expenditure in public health, business support and job retention subside with the pandemic, states should continue to spend heavily. Expenditure should now take the form of robust public investment that would help compensate for the chronic reluctancy of the private sector to invest — a reluctancy expected to redouble in the wake of the crisis (IMF 2020b: ix–xi, 3, 15; IMF 2020c: 10–11; The Economist 2020g: 15). Thus, counter-cyclical policy assumes the form of "projects": state-funding of private enterprise dedicated to short, medium or long term work on infrastructure — of the physical, digital and green kind — aiming to trigger multipliers that will, in turn, stimulate private investment. While fiscal stimulus for capital continues, it now becomes selective, as the state is encouraged to facilitate a "structural transformation" of the economy. Paving the way for the new normality, the state is required to direct support to viable firms as well as those of crucial importance for the economy, while letting weak firms and those that have no place in the "new post-pandemic economy" meet their fate (IMF 2020b: xii–xiii, 14, 18, 44–46; IMF 2020c: 12; IMF 2021a: 18–19).

The structural transformation to a post-pandemic economy requires a change of state policy towards labour — or, rather, the return to the pre-pandemic policy. This means that wage subsidies to idled workers must cease and be replaced with job-search requirements (IMF 2020b: 17; IMF 2020d: 3). As "overextended job retention schemes and overly generous unemployment benefits could delay the required reallocation in labour markets" (IMF 2020b: 12–13), unemployed workers are to face a benefit system that will be meaner, less inclusive and stricter in its conditions than before the pandemic. States are urged to promote "active labour market" policies like vocational training, and to force their workforce to acquire "higher-level cognitive skills", aiming to make them capable to drive a digitalisation of businesses (IMF 2021b: 35). Instead of protecting existing "employee-firm relationships" the state must "help workers to find new jobs" by making unemployment benefit scarce, inadequate, and depended on its recipients' demonstrated eagerness to re-enter the labour market (IMF 2020b: xii–xiii).

Finally, the transitional recovery phase will give way, in an unidentified time and manner, to the "new economic normality". Its main contours are vaguely discernible in the previous phase — they are the "structural transformations" the state was meant to promote during it: a vast concentration of capital as weak businesses have collapsed while strategically important ones have flourished thanks to state support; an intensified workfare regime; and renewed focus on the management of public debt. Thus, in the new economic normality the role of the state is to manage its debts and to make welfare allowances ever meaner and less inclusive. Its fiscal role is now curtailed and persists only in obligations to long term projects the state has initiated in the recovery phase (IMF 2020b: 18–22; IMF 2021a: 19–21).

The "new economic normality" is not free from the crisis that gave it birth. The legacy of the crisis is present within it permanently. Decline in trade and private investment, disruption of global value chains, sluggish growth and productivity, and increasing inequality are all set to persist in depth of time (IMF 2020c: 8). They are structural features of the new economy. The new economy is expected to be more fragile, less innovative and more unfair (The Economist 2020g: 15).

The new economic normality will incorporate crisis not only as legacy but also as perspective. In April 2020, during the peak of the biosecurity crisis, the IMF promoted the instalment of counter-cyclical "automatic stabilisers" as a permanent structure of economic policy. There would be a "rules-based fiscal stimulus that automatically and temporarily increases public spending in response to rises in unemployment" (IMF 2020a: 41). These stabilisers would automatically trigger large fiscal countermeasures to soften the impact of "aggregate demand shocks" and build "resilience" into the economy (IMF 2020a: 29, 36–41). The Fund's suggestion indicates that it is already thinking about the next crisis. It envisions the new economy as crisis-prone; and identifies future crises as stemming, primarily, from declining demand caused by the poverty and inequality ingrained in the new economic normality. The IMF suggestion reveals increasing demand-side worries; to ameliorate them, it seeks to inscribe a "state of emergency" into the "economic constitution". Indeed, the IMF promotes a "resilience" economy, fit for weathering crises. Investment in public health enterprises, green energy and environmental infrastructures, are promoted for their high multipliers but also for their capacity to mitigate the impact of "exogenous" public health and environmental crises (IMF 2020b: 42–46; IMF 2021a: 19–21). Notably, the multipliers the IMF urges states to seek through their fiscal expenditure tend to be larger for national economies "less open to trade", as gains in demand would not leak to other countries through imports (IMF 2020b: 40, 43). Strikingly for a global institution, the "resilience economy" the IMF promotes seems designed to develop primarily within the national state envelope.

The IMF publications during the crisis seek to coordinate national state efforts into a coherent plan for coping with the crisis, recovering from it, and recasting the economy. They are a programmatic blueprint for global capitalism, outlining where it needs to go and how to get there. Seen as such, they present a number of striking features. They are marked by a curious policy mixture between Keynesian — or, in any case, countercyclical — features (mass public expenditure on job retention programmes, infrastructural projects, increased progressive taxation) and neoliberal ones (workfare, rising inequality, public debt sustainability). This mixture seems strange and unprincipled; yet, at a second glance the Fund's plan does cohere. Countercyclical measures are restricted to the first two ("acute outbreak" and, partly, "recovery") phases; they are fully absent from the "new normality", which is dominated by neoliberal elements. In other words, counter-cyclical approaches are the "crisis mode", while economic "normality" is firmly neoliberal. Countercyclical policies are tactics meant to secure the restoration of a neoliberal economy at the end of the crisis.

A final notable feature in the Fund's plan is its overall vision. The IMF advises national states to undertake herculean efforts to mitigate the crisis and lead their economies through it to a new normality that is, frankly, terrible. Marked by rampant inequality, acute exploitation, anaemic investment, low productivity, sluggish growth, weak demand and proneness to crisis, the Fund's programme describes an economy as bad as, or worse than, the pre-pandemic one. This raises the question of whether the effort is worth the outcome — and for whom. Indeed, it tends to confirm the suspicion that capital can no longer envision a different future, for society or for itself (Boukalas 2021).

As any programmatic document, the IMF's blueprint can, at most, only provide a basic grammar to help us understand the realities it addresses and the actions it envisions. If we are to grasp these in their actuality, we need to look closer into what states came up against, and what they do and plan; we need to descend from abstraction into specificity. We turn to this task by focusing to the crisis-combating policy of the UK.

10 The great mothball

During the first lockdown (April–May 2020), the UK GDP fell by 25 percent, erasing 18 years' worth of growth (HM Treasury 2020a: 4). Over the year as a whole, the UK contracted by (almost) 10 percent, its largest contraction in 300 years (HM Treasury 2021a: 1). Between March and October 2020 unemployment rose at record rates as almost 800,000 people lost their jobs, and job vacancies were down by 35 percent compared to the previous year (Chancellor of the Exchequer 2020: 9; HM Government 2020b: 38). Between April and June, sales, payments and investment fell by 30 to 40 percent (Bank of England 2020: 5–6; House of Commons Treasury Committee 2020: 8). The situation was equally grim across Europe. During the spring lockdown, the contraction of European economies was, on aggregate, triple that of the peak of the 2008–2010 financial crisis; and, for the year, they were bracing for a 7 percent recession. Unemployment rose by at least one and a half percent. The hardest hit sectors were travel, the leisure industry (tourism, cinema, theatre, music, art, sport, pubs, clubs, restaurants etc), and retail; followed by manufacture, especially in industries like electronics and automobiles, that depend on complex supply chains (IMF 2020c: 2–3; IMF 2021a: 2). In the UK, at its nadir, retail lost 41 percent in non-food sales; and leisure had fallen by around 80 percent (HM Treasury 2020a: 3). On the upside, finance, the most powerful sector of the UK economy, thrived during the crisis, with asset markets exceeding their pre-crisis capitalisation. Still, this wide divergence between valuation and real economic prospects reared "financial stability concerns" (IMF 2021a: 2) — i.e. the spectre of a bubble.

Relief

Faced with economic meltdown, states took decisive action. European governments deployed large fiscal packages to support households and firms, and eased monetary policy to avoid disruptions in finance. The aim of their intervention was to support demand and, through it, maintain supply, in order to avert a massive wave of bankruptcies of individuals, corporations and banks (IMF 2020c: 3–4). To achieve this, they strengthened unemployment benefits and subsidised wages through programmes that amount to 1.4 percent

DOI: 10.4324/9781003302988-12

of their combined GDP. Enterprises were directly supported through tax and duty deferrals, state-backed loans, and injections of equity, through programmes amounting to almost 5 percent of GDP (IMF 2020c: 5–6). Among European states, the UK was the most fiscally active, with a contribution approaching 10 percent of its GDP. However, its intervention was weighed towards corporations and the part of expenditure for the labour market was smaller than in France, Italy or the Netherlands (IMF 2020c: 6, 10).

Specifically, the UK funded one-off grants of up to £10,000 for small businesses, and up to £25,000 for businesses in the leisure sector. Large businesses were helped to access loans of up to £200 million; and through the Corporate Financing Facility, the Bank of England would buy short term debt from big companies. Small and medium size enterprises (SMEs) were offered access to up to £5m in state-backed loans. By December 2020, these were picked up by more than 80,000 enterprises to an overall cost of almost £20 billion. A "bounce-back loan scheme", fully guaranteed by the state, allowed access to loans between £2,000 and £50,000 with a 2.5 percent interest rate counting from the second year. The uptake for these loans was tremendous: by December, almost 1.5 million businesses had accessed them, to a total cost of more than £43 billion. There was also a scheme offering to lend up to £5 million of public money to promising start-ups, as long as they could raise the same amount from private lenders. The uptake here has been modest, with less than a thousand businesses taking less than £1 billion (House of Commons Treasury Committee 2020: 30; HM Treasury 2020c). To further relieve pressures, the state waved the onerous business rates and slashed VAT — from 20 to 5 percent — for the leisure sector until September 2022. It also contributed 50 percent towards individuals' restaurant bills during August 2020. As a tonic to overall demand, the UK Treasury cut stamp duty on land tax until October 2021. Alongside this prolonged suspension of stamp duty, the government introduced a mortgage guarantee scheme meant to encourage banks to lend against very low deposits. The government, in other words, opted to turn the private consumption ensuing from house purchases into a motor for economic activity. In doing so, it invited the risk of a house prices bubble (HM Government 2020b: 39; HM Treasury 2020b: 10–13; HM Treasury 2021a: 41, 46; House of Commons Treasury Committee 2020: 17). Overall, during the first year of the crisis, the government had provided approximately £100 billion to businesses in grants, loans and tax holidays (HM Treasury 2021: 16).

In the labour front, the UK increased unemployment benefits — which still remained amongst the lowest in Europe — by £20 per week until October 2021. It also introduced the Coronavirus Job Retention Scheme. This allowed private sector employers, regardless of their exposure to biosecurity restrictions, to furlough any number of their workers. The state covered 80 percent of the salary of each inert worker up to £2,500 per month. In the first year of the crisis 40 percent of workers became furloughed, and more than 11 million jobs were depended on the government's scheme, to a cost of almost £54 billion (Bank of England 2020: 7; HM Government 2020: 39; HM Treasury 2021a: 16).

Concerned with the prospect of rampant unemployment among the young, the government expanded trainee schemes; doubled the number of "work coaches", i.e. of unemployment office clerks that help claimants find a job; tripled apprenticeship positions, for which it covers 95 percent of their remuneration; and, moreover, pays employers up to £2,000 for every apprentice they take on (HM Treasury 2020b: 9–10; HM Treasury 2021b: 121–122).

The overall expenditure of the UK government in support of the economy in 2020 and 2021 amounts to £407 billion (HM Treasury 2021a: 9, 17). During the first lockdown, in spring 2020, government spending comprised 56 percent of the entire economy (Resolution Foundation 2020: 2).

The effort of the state was a resounding success. Simply put, it averted a certain and complete collapse of the economy. Across Europe, state intervention is estimated to have saved 4 GDP points, 15 percent of employment, 25 percent of value added, and to have averted bankruptcies and the accumulation of bad debt at the hands of financial institutions (IMF 2020c: 11, 13, 38). As the first year of the crisis drew to a close, prospects for the economy were looking up. Most of the world's advanced economies, including the UK, are scheduled to recover quickly, exceeding their pre-crisis GDP levels in 2022; industrial production and merchandise volumes have recovered globally (IMF 2021a: 1); and the collapse of the labour market did not materialise: UK unemployment rate is set to rise only by one percentage point and peak at just below 5 percent (HM Treasury 2021b: 169). Instead of Armageddon, biosecurity seems to have been only a sharp, temporary shock.

Nonetheless, mid-term prospects are not fully optimistic. Once it recovers its pre-pandemic level, GDP is set to stay there, resuming its sluggish growth of 2 percent or less (HM Treasury 2021a: 92; HM Treasury 2021b: 169; IMF 2021a: 8). Similarly, unemployment, which rose despite a million economically active people leaving the UK as it exited the EU, is not expected to return to pre-pandemic levels in the foreseeable future. Worse: the market that emerges from the pandemic is saddled with onerous levels debt, and servicing it will be a permanent drag to growth, investment and productivity. The predicament of small and medium enterprises is especially preoccupying. They account for approximately half of economic output and provide the great bulk of employment. The support they received from the state was limited and comprised only of loans, as the liquidity of the central bank's bond-buying schemes could not reach them. They were utterly depended on these loans; yet, they had difficulty accessing them, forcing many to go under. Those that survived will have greater difficulty servicing their debts, for their margins are extremely narrow and they are not able to negotiate repayment terms. The worry is that a slow-burn wave of bankruptcies could be lying ahead and, with it, prolonged pressure on employment figures (Blakeley 2020: x; House of Commons Treasury

Committee 2020: 31–32; IMF 2020c: 32–39; The Economist 2020g: 15; Resolution Foundation 2020: 9–10, 32). It is, in short, possible that the economy is exiting biosecurity only to enter stagnation. As an explosion in energy prices is driving up inflation, in early 2022, the economic "recovery" appears to consist of stagflation.

Finally, as the state entered this crisis with empty coffers, the entirety of its colossal expenditure was financed through borrowing, resulting to an astronomical increase of public debt. In the UK, borrowing has exceeded £300 billion, more than double its peak during the financial crisis (Chancellor for the Exchequer 2020: 18; HM Treasury 2021b: 174; Resolution Foundation 2020: 1). The UK public deficit jumped by more than 11 percent in 2020 and, while it is expected to rapidly decline from 2022 onwards, it is not forecast to reach pre-pandemic levels in the foreseeable future (2026). In line with galloping deficit, the debt-to-GDP ratio leapt from 85.2 percent in 2019 to 103.7 in 2020. This ratio is expected to drop drastically from 2024 onwards, during a period when GDP remains almost flat; but will not recover its pre-pandemic levels in the foreseeable future (IMF 2021a: 140; HM Treasury 2021b: 34, 37, 173). Yet, in an expression of lenders' approval of state efforts to save the economy, the cost of servicing government debt has been falling and is expected to remain at historic lows, despite the elevated levels of debt and borrowing (HM Treasury 2021b: 29; Resolution Foundation 2020: 21).

Despite the relaxed attitude of the markets, the UK government raised alarm over public debt as soon as early 2021. The reasons for concern it gave seem, oddly, to testify to the sustainability of the debt and advocate for a relaxed approach (HM Treasury 2021a: 25–26). Betraying an obsession with financial discipline, the Treasury catalogues the devastating effects of all manners of risks, dangers and uncertainties without assessing their likelihood. Uncharacteristically for a Department that cannot devise a mid-term strategy or even do its own forecasting, the Treasury is far-sighted regarding fiscal discipline, elevating the sustainability of debt to a moral duty towards future generations (HM Treasury 2021b: 34).

The UK is not alone in prematurely departing from IMF guidelines for fiscal policy relaxation. The President of the European Commission Ursula von der Leyen and the German Minister for Economic Affairs Peter Altmaier made clear that repaying the debt amassed during the pandemic will be paramount for the EU, which is determined to avoid another debt crisis by all means. The EU strategy entails a return to austerity policy that will bind many generations of citizens in the future (Minakakis 2020: 150–151).

While this promotion of fiscal discipline reinstates neoliberal dogma, there is an important shift in meaning here. For the Treasury, strict discipline is an iron rule in "normal times" — *only*. The UK, following the EU, Germany, Canada and Australia, institutes an "escape clause" that allows it to temporarily take "more active fiscal policy" when the economy receives "a shock" (HM Treasury 2021b: 34, 150–153). In other words, while economic normality is governed by prudent fiscal policy, crises will be dealt with counter-cyclical measures. Essentially, the government elevates its practice during the biosecurity crisis into a rule. Notably, both the magnitude of the "shock" needed to trigger a shift in fiscal modalities, and the expanse of state intervention in combating it, are open-ended. Thus, the fiscal "constitution" of the UK now provides for the "exception" that would neutralise fiscal rules and allow the government to take unrestricted action in the context of economic emergency. This means that a staunch neoliberal state finds neoliberal dogma to be inadequate for governing the economy during a severe crisis. It also means that the prospect of such crisis is inscribed into the framework of economic policy; and this, in turn, means that it is acknowledged as a structural feature of the economy.

If suspending fiscal discipline marked the crisis period, recovery appears to be marked by another departure from the neoliberal dogma: public investment.

Recovery

In line with IMF recommendations, the UK will sustain public spending and investment at relatively high levels during the recovery period. Overall state spending is set to increase at a yearly rate of 3.8 percent until 2026, representing its highest increase in 15 years (Chancellor of the Exchequer 2020: 2; HM Treasury 2021b: 11). The lion's share (almost 40 percent) of spending increases is directed to the Department for Health, while Education, Defence, Transport, and Business also receive sizeable funds. Still, with the exception of the last two, these funds represent only a modest percentage rise to their budget (HM Treasury 2021b: 40). Across departments, the bulk of the expenditure will be directed to infrastructure projects; rises to operational budgets range from modest to negative (HM Treasury 2021b: 41–42).

The emphasis on infrastructure entails that, despite headline rises, the uplift to services might not be tangible. Characteristically, while local government is set to receive a considerable rise in funds, very little will be directed towards the delivery of services to citizens. Its biggest tickets are dedicated to strengthening local governments' cybersecurity; and enhancing their capacity for procurement and commercial activity (HM Treasury 2021b: 109). Thus, further advancing neoliberal strategy, local governments are forced to become "entrepreneurial" and the provision of services to citizens will depend on their success in that role.

Similarly, in Health, funds will be mainly consumed in buildings: upgrading hospitals and building new ones. Other sizeable expenditures go to diagnostics and digital technology. This is contrasted with a rather paltry provision for the care sector: it is set to receive £5.4 billion over three years;

in the same period the receipts from a special Health and Social Care levy are expected to exceed £56 billion (HM Treasury 2021b: 94–95, 175).

The Health Department budget points to another feature of infrastructure spending: it is not directed to the workforce but to private capital. Thus, through the NHS, the state is set to hand out enormous sums of public money to the private sector — construction, medical industries, IT and logistics. The government's plans and funds do not involve hiring and better remunerating healthcare staff. Similarly, a large rise in R&D funding, which is scheduled to reach almost 2.5 percent of GDP by 2027, will be focused on quantum computing, artificial intelligence, bioinformatics and aerospace. It will provide a boon to the future profitability of the IT and aerospace sectors, and is explicitly meant to compensate for anaemic private investment in R&D (HM Treasury 2021b: 53–54).

The last great beneficiary of public expenditure is security. Capital expenditure in Defence is set to grow by almost 7 percent annually for the foreseeable future (albeit its operational budget is set to shrink: budget rises are, again, dedicated to procurement and infrastructure, not staff). Similarly, the ever-increasing funding for the intelligence apparatus is set to continue — its budget is among the fastest rising in the public sector. It is mainly directed towards enhancing cybersecurity and integrating police forces under its control within the counterterrorism structure (HM Treasury 2021b: 128–129). Strengthening security is a response to the "global context". Tellingly, the latter is perceived as unmistakably hostile: "challenging, competitive and uncertain" (Chancellor of the Exchequer 2020: 51). While the preferred means of engagement with the world remain those of free trade, strengthened security is now seen as vital. Alongside Defence and Intelligence, the Justice Department emerges as the third pillar of the security endeavour. The significant increase in its budget is almost fully consumed by "the biggest prison building programme in over a century". Indeed, the government shows a peculiar understanding of "criminal justice" as a metabolism where more police officers bring more criminals to court, which expediently delivers them to prison (HM Treasury 2021b: 51). Absent from this mechanical process is any notion of justice.

Firmly at the bottom of the expenditure list lies the much advertised "green industrial revolution". Spending on environmental policy will receive just under £30 billion until 2025. Most of it is directed towards renewing the car fleet and reducing houses' energy consumption. With regards to energy production, the only sizeable investment is in nuclear (HM Treasury 2021b: 69–73). Even these modest arrangements seem precarious: the government has already pulled out from some of its own green policy commitments and the associated expenditure (Harvey 2021).

If the rise in state expenditure, focused as it is on capital spending, is effectively an avenue for transferring public money to private capital, how this is done becomes a significant question. Public funds will be channelled to private companies through a newly established national infrastructure bank. Its purse will be a, rather modest, £12 billion (HM Treasury 2021: 58). Pointing to deregulation, a "Project Speed" taskforce will see to the reduction of the time needed to develop and deliver infrastructure projects by overhauling the procurement, planning and environmental rules that govern the process (Chancellor of the Exchequer 2020: 4, 6, 34, 49). Crucially, decisions on infrastructure spending will no longer be primarily guided by cost-benefit analysis. They will be "first and foremost based on whether they deliver on policy objectives" (Chancellor of the Exchequer 2020: 49). This shift is significant. The state announces that market rationality is no longer the dominant criterion for investment spending; the key factor is political: "policy objectives". The state acknowledges public expenditure as a political tool, and declares its intention to use it. This carries tremendous ideological consequence: the state declares that politics and the economy are not separate, smashing the core of the liberal and neoliberal dogma. Further, this is an open declaration that rule-based processes are obsolete, hence the government can distribute public money to private enterprise as it likes, without objective criteria. In practice, this means that the state can directly select which specific capitals to "partner". For capitalists, this means that the flourishing and even survival of specific businesses and sectors comes to depend on the whims of ministers, leading to a scramble to secure ministers' favour or control over them. Thus, to survive and prosper, businesses and sectors must align with the state's "policy objectives"; even better, they must determine what these objectives are. In short, the selection of capital favourites according to "policy objectives" requires capitalists to "capture" state personnel and to determine state policy. The end result will be a feudalised state, where specific capitals and sectors establish their fiefs within the state and fight against other capitals to define state policy and, thus, access public treasure. While decisionist in appearance, this politicised and arbitrary procurement regime is in fact a byzantine one. In its context corruption is systemic and indispensable.

To conclude on investment spending, we note that it is not radical. If its total scheduled increase does materialise, it will bring public sector investment to, roughly, its 2011 level, and total expenditure in par with 2015 (HM Treasury 2021b: 43). Worse: these increases are lower than what they were scheduled to be before the pandemic (Emerson, Stockton and Zaranko 2021). While the wave of state expenditure represents a departure from austerity, the latter is not reversed: the budget for most Departments will still be more than 30 percent lower than it was in 2010; and, by 2025 most Departments will be re-entering the orbit of real-term cuts (Resolution Foundation 2021b: 23, 27).

Finally, none of the state's newfound largess is directed towards labour. Accompanying the announcement of rising state expenditure was an imposition of a freeze in public sector wages. The freeze officially lasted for a year — it is set to expire in April 2022. Yet, its political significance is unmistaken: within an orgy of state spending, there is nothing for workers. Indeed, in the context of rising state expenditure, the wage freeze appears dissonant. The Treasury justified it as an act of justice to private sector workers who have suffered redundancies and wage cuts during the pandemic (Sunak 2020: col.828). This justification is not convincing, for public and private sector wages are converging (Ferguson and Francis-Devine 2021: 6–7). It is, however, close to admitting that, through a "race to the bottom" tactic, the state is actively engaging in wage suppression. Even lifting the pay freeze is unlikely result to pay rises. The "de-freezing" will take three years to reach every employee, will be contingent on departmental budgets, and will certainly remain "affordable" (HM Treasury 2021b: 44; Resolution Foundation 2021b: 25). Thus, as a combined result of the crisis and state policy, wages are forecast to be an average £1,200 per worker lower compared with pre-crisis expectations. Indeed, workers earnings are expected to still be lower in 2026 than they were in 2008. Factoring in rises in taxation and national insurance contributions, household incomes are set to experience their most prolonged decline since the mid-1970s (The Resolution Foundation 2020: 1, 11–12; The Economist 2021b: 25–26). This decline is further — and drastically — accentuated by the rise, in 2022 of energy bills by 50 percent; and by rising inflation, which is set to nominally exceed seven percent, but is much greater for goods that address basic needs (Aratani 2022; Inman 2022a; Monroe 2022).

The economic recovery policy is defined by rising expenditure and the state's reluctance to accrue debt. Hence, increased taxation is inevitably its third pillar. UK tax revenue is set to reach 40 percent of GDP by 2027 (HM Treasury 2021b: 31, 34). The pace of its increase is particularly fast and will amount to a rise of approximately £3,000 per household between 2019 and 2025 (Resolution Foundation 2021b: 36). National Insurance contributions are set to rise in step with inflation. On top of these rises is a yearly Health and Social Care levy (HM Treasury 2021b: 141–142). Combined, they result to a more than 4 percent rise in National Insurance. This is a flat tax, paid by workers and their employers. The hit for some of the latter will be partly offset by generous tax-relief measures (HM Treasury 2021b: 143–144); for the workers, there is no relief.

Further, scheduled for 2023 is a rise in the highest rate of corporation tax from 19 to 25 percent — a rate that the government is keen to advertise as the lowest in the G7. It is ameliorated by a super-deduction (130 percent) for money allocated to new plants and machinery, a measure aiming to encourage private investment. From there on, there is no increase in income, wealth or inheritance tax, not even for the highest earners; and income from rent — real estate, assets and dividends — also remains untouchable (Wood 2021). Notably, an advertised initiative to tackle tax avoidance appears vague, is not matched by any rise to the budget of the tax collector (HM Revenue and Customs), and is scheduled to contribute £2.2 billion over five years. It is, in short, insignificant (HM Treasury 2021a: 51–52; HM Treasury 2021b: 123).

The appearance of a taxation drive is further undermined by the introduction of freeports. These are the government's fixed idea for economic recovery, and their appeal is that they will benefit business with "generous tax reliefs", allow employers to slash their contribution to National Insurance, and afford them customs benefits and "wider government support" (HM Treasury 2021a: 58; HM Treasury 2021b: 75). Freeports are indeed tax havens within the main territory of the state; fiefs within which capital is exempt from national tax and labour law.

Overall, the UK is set to accrue its largest tax-base in 70 years (Wright, Smyth and Aldrick 2021) at the cost of middle and lower income earners. If more states interpret the IMF call for progressive taxation in similar terms, there is no need to puzzle over a supposed Keynesian resurgence. Similarly, in the US a mass increase in taxation is scheduled. It will partly reverse the corporation tax cuts introduced by the previous administration; and reduce taxation of middle and lower incomes, while increasing it for the top earners. Still, taxation on capital gains is set to remain untouched. This not only allows the greatest part of top earners' income to remain off-limits, but also offers them a way out of income tax increases altogether, as they can divert their income to shares (The Economist 2021a: 34–35).

Thus, less than two years since the biosecurity crisis erupted, the broad contours of UK economic policy are already decipherable. It can be summed up as a big state, high tax, low wage economy. High tax is predominately paid by working people to fund increased state expenditure directed towards private capital in the form of procurement and infrastructure projects. This is combined with repressed wages and continuing starvation of public services. As for the "big state", it is only reluctantly and temporarily so. Its core approach is a "small state" one, of minimum intervention in the economy, and keeping a tight leash on public finances is its primary duty. It does, however, acknowledge crisis as a structural element of the economy, and is prepared to proceed to large scale interventions in response. We see, in other words, the outline of a dual economic policy emerging. Dual in the sense that its modalities differ drastically between norm and exception; and also dual in the sense that its effects in relation to capital and labour are diametrically opposite.

Mothball

There are two ways in which economic orders die — i.e. expire through discontinuity. The first, best outlined by Marx (1977) to account for the transition from feudalism to capitalism and, from there, to communism, is when the development of the forces of production overwhelms the relations of production. It amounts to *explosion*. It is a situation where the dynamics of the economy accelerate, intensify and expand to a such a degree that the existing economic relations, practices and structures can no longer contain them, and are smashed under their pressure.

The other way, describing the demise of countless ancient civilisations, amounts to *implosion*. Here, the dynamics of economic activity atrophy to such a degree that they can no longer sustain the existing economic relations and structures. This is precisely the spectrum that biosecurity raised: catastrophic — implosive — atrophy, as businesses that were not allowed to operate would shred their workers who would have nothing to spend, and the withdrawal of their demand would cause supply to cease. It is indeed impressive that an entire "form of life" can crumble, while its material infrastructure remains immaculate. In our recent experience, the infrastructure for air-travel, for instance, or retail — airplanes, trucks, airports, shops, supporting technologies, legal frameworks and personnel — all remained intact; but without activity to animate them, these industries collapsed (2&3Dorm 2020: 87). In short, by suspending economic activity, the biosecurity crisis raised the immediate prospect of complete economic implosion.

Facing this existential threat, the state stepped in to replicate the missing dynamic, so that the emptied economic relations and structures could be sustained. The relief measures for companies and sectors threatened with extinction and the extraordinary assumption of wage payments by the state, aimed to maintain the demand for products, services, real estate etc. This would, in turn, maintain supply activity and keep the economy moving. Thus, the state replicated the economy, as if it were continuing while society, and hence the economy too, were suspended. The state tried to install a virtual economy without society, and guaranteed its reproduction as a virtual reality. It cocooned the economy, tried to preserve it like a sleeping beauty, so that when the biosecurity crisis was resolved it could emerge as it was at the moment of its suspension, as if nothing had happened. State policy was designed to bracket out the event of the epidemic and mothball the economy so that, in the course of time, it could re-emerge intact. State policy aimed to suspend time on the present moment. While time is suspended, the state effectively *becomes* the economy. It assumes the role of general director and protagonist actor, a role that it contemplates playing for the foreseeable future, as an economy bereft of dynamism — investment, employment, productivity, demand — is set to be in need of resuscitation over the long haul.

This is as far as the play goes. Beyond emergency response and the fabled recovery, the state cannot envision an economic future. The state's intervention was meant to support the economy during the time of its suspension, with measures designed to last for three to six months. They were extended to last three times as much, as a result of both the persistence of the biosecurity crisis *and* the absence of ideas regarding the overall management and direction of the economy. Official statements and "plans" came almost as thick and fast as biosecurity measures, and they were as partial, contradictory, and confused as the latter, neither designed nor capable to operate for more than a few weeks. The furthest state economic policy could stretch was the realisation that the economy emerging from the biosecurity crisis would not be that of the moment of its mothballing, but a sickly creature depended on the state for its existence. Crucially, the purpose of state intervention in this "recovery" phase is the same as before: to preserve the economy as is, to avert its collapse, until it can sustain itself again. In essence, *there is no difference between the crisis and the recovery* — only the means of state intervention shift: from direct handouts to channelling money for infrastructure projects.

In every measurable sense the mothballing effort of the state appears to be successful. In the UK, as well as most of Europe and North America, the big macroeconomic volumes are set to emerge from the crisis almost unscathed. Gross Domestic Product is set to recover its gigantic losses fully and quickly; unemployment will register a relatively modest rise; borrowing and debt will eventually be tamed; and long term scarring will be limited. Notably, all these indicators are set to be much healthier than predicted during the course of the crisis, and the prospect of complete catastrophe is fully averted.

Still, nothing can be preserved intact — certainly not complex, dynamic sets of relations that involve everyone in society, like the economy is. The attempt of the state to mothball the economy — rather than abandon it to its fate or change it — speaks volumes regarding the state's intentions in the economic and social field; but this attempt had failed from the moment of its conception. For, by its very existence, an action necessarily impacts its object even when it tries to preserve it — hence, preservation is an impossible, self-cancelling endeavour. The state's mothballing then, was in fact an attempt to avoid collapse, and to control the direction and secure the outcome of change, to shape the form of the new economic "normality".

The modality of the state's intervention is notable. The "whatever it takes" approach, comprising mass creation of fiat money, expansive borrowing and free-form handouts to businesses, is certainly a drastic diversion from established neoliberal economic dogma. Yet, it was, strictly speaking, nothing new: since the 2008 financial crisis, it had entered the repertoire of the neoliberal state in the event of emergency. A more significant departure from neoliberalism appears to be the persistence of countercyclical policy. The quasi-permanent character it seems to be acquiring sits uncomfortably with orthodox economists. More importantly, the rewriting of the economic rulebook so that it allows for unrestrained fiscal interference during crisis not only acknowledges crisis as a permanent, structural feature of the economy; it also betrays a lack of trust to the market to overcome its crises by itself, by its own innate "laws", without "external" intervention. The core of the neoliberal doctrine is in tatters. The true scandal, however, were the job retention schemes: the substitution of the employer by the state in the wage relation is an unprecedented move that undermines the conceptual basis of capitalist social relations.

Nonetheless, these countercyclical elements are inscribed into a policy that aims to an end-state, a new economy, that is the same as the old one.

Countercyclical policies are employed to achieve a neoliberal end. The change the state seeks to dictate is merely a return to pre-crisis neoliberal arrangements, their entrenchment and intensification. The state seeks to control change in order to pre-empt its outcome — and it seeks to pre-empt its outcome in order to negate change.

It is too early to conclude the discussion of economic policy and its overall character with any certainty: the crisis has not played out for long enough. The analysis shall return to these issues — especially those of economic strategy and Keynesian vs neoliberal tendencies therein — after a discussion of state policy from a class perspective has shed its light on them.

11 Sacrificial labour

Throughout the pandemic, and across the endless spectrum of prohibitions and regulations, the only uncontested reason to exit the household was work (Chapter 6). Rather, going to work was not a question of license but of obligation. This obligation was imposed sequentially on different categories of workers, who found themselves classed in innovative ways according to the exigencies of biosecurity and accumulation.

First to be forced to go to work were the "essential workers". This newfound category comprises medical workers, care workers and pharmacists; those who maintain the public order (police, intelligence); those necessary for the smooth operation of the social metabolism (farmers, transport and supermarket workers, couriers, refuse collectors); and the auxiliaries who enable all the above to reach their workplace (public transport workers, teachers, child carers, taxi drivers). Through their work, these workers alleviated the danger faced by everyone else. But no one alleviated the danger *they* faced. For months, they were forced to work with inadequate or non-existing protective equipment, in environments were social distancing was not possible and lacked adequate ventilation and disinfection. They were decimated; even parliamentarians expressed alarm by the number of deaths amongst health care personnel, care workers, police officers and transport workers, and attributed them to state neglect of their safety (Joint Committee on Human Rights 2020: 6; Asquith 2021). Forced to expose themselves to the virus, essential workers also became its conductors, spreading the disease to their families, colleagues and the people they met in the course of their duties. This was most pronounced in care homes. While the government knew that the main source of epidemic spread in care homes where the workers who were contractually bound to move from one care home to the other, it did nothing to change working relations in the sector (HM Government 2020c: 34). Ergo, care homes became the site with the highest transmission and death rates (Asquith 2021).

In summer 2020, as soon as the pandemic showed slight signs of retreat, a new hastily curved category of workers were put under obligation to return to the workplace: those "who cannot possibly work from home": factory

DOI: 10.4324/9781003302988-13

and construction workers, many of whom had been working *in situ* under the lockdown anyway. The government did "actively encourage" these workers to go to back to work; but did not mandate any improvement of the health and safety conditions in the workplace or in the way to and from it (Frade 2020: 12–13). Employers correctly decoded the government's "active encouragement" call: they pressured their workers to return or remain at the workplace, even when sick, under threat of dismissal (Savage, Wall and Trapper 2021).

The call to return to work was issued as the government's scientific advisers declared that a third of social contacts are made in the workplace, and are prolonged and relatively intense. The government was fully aware that the workplace is a high-transmission environment. Still, it forced most workplaces open and did not impose any requirements on businesses to make their sites and practices safer (HM Government 2020: 29–30). Even the people that the government acknowledges as "clinically extremely vulnerable" to covid-19 were forced to the workplace if their employer would not allow them to work from home. The government simply issued them with "the best advice on protecting themselves" (HM Government 2020: 33), transferring the responsibility for surviving on them. As a consequence, throughout the pandemic workplaces remained the second highest site of disease transmission (Asquith 2021); and machinery, process and plant operators, sewing machinists and retail assistants joined the nurses, care home workers, retail assistants and bus drivers in the ranks of the most numerous victims of the disease. These workers are three times more likely to have died from the disease than their better remunerated counterparts in other lines of work (Barr and Booth 2021). There is indeed a strong correlation between income, wealth and surviving the pandemic (IMF 2021b: 30); the state is a key factor in this.

By being the prime victims of the disease, low paid workers became its prime conductors. Manual and precarious workers often have to travel on public transport and work in close proximity to their colleagues, facing a high risk of infection. The working poor and those not entitled to sick pay had to continue working even when ill. And, in their households, density of space is pronounced. In short, much more than health and epidemiological measures *strictu sensu*, the question of transmission, and therefore of the epidemic as such, resides in the "hidden abode of production" (Marx 1990: 279) and in the, equally obscured, abode of reproduction (Global Labour Journal Editorial Board 2020: 74–75). Thus, in the UK, places with large working class populations —big cities like Liverpool or small towns like Merthyr Tydfil — were hardest hit by infections and their death rate was double that of affluent areas. Their residents' work is conductive to the spread of the disease, and the scarcity of their resources make them unable to withhold their labour (Hinsliff 2020a; IFS 2021). More than a technical, medical issue, the epidemic is a social one: a class issue. It spreads through exploitation and poverty.

The state set off to systematically deny the workplace massacre it orchestrated. The official policy, devised and promulgated by Public Health England, the Department for Education and the Health and Safety Executive (the inspectorate for workplace health and safety standards) was to leave workplace outbreaks unreported. Industrial units were requested to contact their local health authorities *only* if they have "reasonable evidence" that covid cases have been caused by occupational exposure. Even then, the authorities advised employers not to report unless the situation got so bad that they have to close down a plant or they get "significant interest" from local media. The ensuing underreporting of contractions in the workplace and associated deaths is estimated, with a high degree of uncertainty, to be of a magnitude of 1 to 8 (Department for Education 2021; Health and Safety Executive 2020–2021; Martin 2021; Newsham 2020). Thus, throughout the pandemic companies could, and did, force their workers into busy workplaces without adequate protective measures. They did so with impunity. Of the almost 100,000 cases that, despite the state-imposed omertà, were referred to the Health and Safety Executive between March 2020 and January 2021, less than a hundred resulted to administrative measures against the firm, and none led to prosecution for breaching safety laws (Wall 2021a).

Exploitation and inequality were shown to be key motors of epidemic spread in the case of Leicester and the *Boohoo* garments factory situated there. A precarious, mainly migrant, workforce which was paid below the minimum wage and worked without a contract, was terrorised by its employer to continue coming to work, even when sick, in a factory devoid of any protective equipment, upon penalty of dismissal. Despite complaints, the factory was not inspected by the Health and Safety Executive. The inevitable outbreak in the factory enveloped the entire town, forcing a localised lockdown that lasted for four months (Labour Behind the Label 2020). Crestfallen Parliamentarians expressed concern with the "abuse and exploitation" of workers in the garment industry. Labour conditions in the *Boohoo* factory, which continued to operate as normal during lockdown, were seen as the key factor for the acute spike in infections in Leicester. Parliamentarians pointed that, neither before nor during the pandemic, had the government done anything to address the underpayment of wages, lack of employment contracts, and disregard for workers' health and safety that mark working relations in the garments industry and amount to "human rights abuses and violations of work and employment regulations by businesses" (Joint Committee on Human Rights 2020: 11).

While manual, blue collar and precarious workers continued working as if the pandemic did not exist, their proletarianised formerly middle class counterparts were not fully spared either. In autumn 2020, amidst fear that working remotely would force a dip in prices for business real estate, the Prime Minister issued a call to office workers to "go back to work"; sectors of the press close to the government and the rentier interests it represents, completed the PM's message: "or lose your job" (Rayner 2020). The state not only lead employers' efforts to keep people working as usual; it also forced its own workers to do so. The treatment of public health workers has been discussed already. That of teachers was similar, with the government persistently attempting to force them back into classrooms that it, equally persistently, neglected to adjust to health exigencies (Weale and Duncan 2021). Similarly, nursery workers were left to work without PPE or protective infrastructure in environments were distancing is impossible, and were not given priority for vaccination. Consequently, within only two months (December 2020 and January 2021), ten percent of them contracted the disease (Berry 2021). The Department for Transport's bullied its workers to remain in the office throughout the pandemic — which resulted to almost its entire workforce in Swansea becoming infected and spreading the disease across the town (Wall 2021b).

In its labour policy throughout the pandemic, the state was juggling a seemingly impossible act: it forced some people to home confinement, while simultaneously forcing others to work, to face the danger it forcefully protected others from facing. This unfolded sequentially, as the state forced into the workplace the same people it had previously forced out of it (Leoni and Alkamar 2020: 42). This paradox points to another, deeper one: that of the person as a schizoid subjectivity which is protected and secured as a biological entity but as embodied labour power is neglected and exposed to the same threat that commands its protection *qua* biological unit. The outcome of this policy is equally paradoxical: the worker — the labour power part of the schizoid subjectivity — becomes the victim and conductor of the threat to the biological part of the split. This scission is the form that the tension between biosecurity and capital accumulation takes in the realm of labour policy. In these terms, the bias of state policy towards accumulation is clear. Its policies cohere only in forcing labour to continue for as much, and as cheaply, as possible. Across Europe, workers were effectively a sacrifice to the Moloch of capital accumulation (Frade 2020: 13; Wu Ming 2021). The sacrifice was performed by the hostile policy of the state flanked by the iron grip of necessity that grips workers (including those of the proletarianised former middle class) during the neoliberal era. The class that saved society from the disease was left to face its full force systematically unprotected.

Fixated on age groups and underlying conditions, the techno-scientific medical discourse that dominates the discussion of the pandemic represents these social inequalities as biological ones — and by this token it tends to render them unproblematic natural facts. However, none of this — the naturalisation of their predicament; the clash of health and accumulation exigencies; the subjectivity split between "human" and "worker"; the sacrificial role forced upon the latter; or the state's involvement in forcing it — escaped the notice of workers themselves. Starting with Italy, the first European country to face the pandemic, a wave of workers' unrest spread together with the pandemic and the state's labour policy. In Brazil, Cameroon, Chile, China, France, Italy and the US a wave of wildcat strikes and riots erupted, culminating with the first world-wide strike in history, that of the workers in the behemoth of exploitation known as *Amazon*. The reluctance of workers to strike due to fears of losing their employment was overcome by the immediate threat to their lives if they continued working (Antithesis 2020: 31; Global Labour Journal Editorial Board 2020: 79; Wu Ming 2021). Strangely, its sacrifice seems to reinvigorate a moribund working class rather than kill it.

12 Workfare

In its strict sense, the term "workfare" refers to the policy that makes access to unemployment benefits conditional on the recipient's enrolment in the skill-enhancement schemes she is requested to: training and re-training programmes, apprenticeships, work placements and trials, etc. Her prompt and satisfactory involvement in such schemes is a requirement for her receiving benefits. In other words, workfare makes access to benefits conditional on the worker's demonstrated willingness to enter and remain in the labour market (Jessop 2002: 152–161). This shift in the accessibility of unemployment benefits, from unconditional to conditional, appears to be a rather technical and innocuous one. It is, however, emblematic of the neoliberal strategy in the key terrain of its application, that of class dynamics.

Workfare denotes the absolution of the capitalist state from its commitment to secure employment for all who want it — and from its subsequent obligation to compensate those who want but cannot find it. In legal terms, it reconfigures the right to work, so that the latter no longer imposes a duty on the state to help provide employment to its citizens. Workfare is, in other words, a departure from the commitments that the welfare state made to workers. While the responsibility of the state towards labour is withdrawn, that towards capital is expanded. Workfare points to a commitment of the state to provide capital with skilled and disciplined labour, impervious to any arbitrary and detrimental conditions placed on it. This neoliberal state is committed to maintain, at public expense, a pool of labour force that is fit for exploitation, absolving capital from the cost of the reproduction of the labour force.

Thus, workfare denotes the core attitude of capital towards labour. Capital needs labour to be available — active or in reserve — and ready for exploitation: disciplined, skilled, docile, up to date with the trends in production and the needs of accumulation. But it does not wish to be burdened with the costs of labour's reproduction — it outsources them to the state. This attitude is constitutive of neoliberalism. In opposition to Keynesianism, neoliberalism conceptualises labour, its employment and reproduction, as a cost of production rather than a source of demand (Jessop 2002: 152). The repression of this cost is the core of the neoliberal strategy (Boukalas 2014: 28–32).

DOI: 10.4324/9781003302988-14

Thus, the apparently innocuous shift that workfare represents is a key aspect of the transformation of the state, from a Keynesian-welfare state to a neoliberal-workfare one. This transformation, and workfare *per se*, emanates from the core of neoliberal strategy: the suppression of the cost of labour. The term "workfare" then can — and possibly should — apply to all neoliberal attempts to suppress the cost of labour. It would then come to apply to the suppression of wages and pensions; the decimation of social, health and education services; the weakening of workers' rights; the flexibilisation of employment conditions; the erasure of collective bargaining; the expansion of the working day, week and life.

Pandemic workfarism

Biosecurity resulted to a rise in unemployment — a rise much more modest that anticipated but expected to be persistent. Unemployment is set to remain permanently higher than its pre-pandemic levels, and rise further if fears of a slow-burn wave of bankruptcies does come to pass (chapter 10). Markedly absent from the state's engagement with this prospect are roarings for "whatever it takes". Indeed, unemployment policy lacks both impetus and imagination. It is filed along the well-trodden tracks of workfare.

For the state, rising unemployment is not something unthinkable, like a disruption of accumulation, but an unremarkable natural fact. In June 2020 the British Prime Minister matched the inevitable loss of "loved ones" with inevitable loss of jobs: "we also know that the jobs that many people had in January are also not coming back" (Johnson 2020b). Along with death, unemployment is a certainty of life. Once again, the state surrenders to inevitability and absolves itself from responsibility. Oddly, the statement was uttered at a moment when the state's wage subsidies programme was protecting, according to the Bank of England, four in every five jobs under risk (Elliott 2020). The declaration of inevitability came precisely at the moment when the state was proving the absence of inevitability. The invocation of inevitability is a tacit declaration that the state will do nothing about unemployment. *Labour policy is not 'counter-cyclical'*. Indeed, the Prime Minister understands rising unemployment in positive terms, as an opportunity for people to acquire much needed new skills. Accordingly, the government response to unemployment is to promote apprenticeships, which will help people to get back into the job market and find work. The Prime Minister dreams of making Britain an "apprenticeships' nation" (House of Commons Liaison Committee 2020: q. 64).

The workfare drive of the "apprenticeships' nation" is relentless. It comprises a variety of schemes that deliver (especially young) workers and unemployed people to employers and subsidise the latter for hiring them. Thus, a Kickstart Scheme funds six-month placements for people aged 16–24. Employers receive from the state between £1,000 and £2,000 for each apprentice they hire, and 95 percent of the apprentice's salary is also paid by the state. Further, unemployed people, in order to receive their benefit payments, are obliged to enrol in a mushrooming variety of training programmes, like SWAPS (Sector-based Work Academy Programme) and Skills Bootcamps. These programmes are solely dedicated to the convenience and benefit of the employer. There are no provisions for the worker or tangible benefits for her other than the prospect of finding "real" employment once her enrolment is successfully over. The workfare drive is especially notable in two Departments: Work and Pensions, and Education. The former seems to have no other purpose but to strengthen workfare through reskilling programmes and the multiplication of "work coaches". Notably, its main idea for helping those in need is to offer "free, high-quality debt advice". The Department for Education is dedicating increasing sums to "skills". While its overall budget rise is set to be 8 percent over the next four years, the segment dedicated to re-training and apprenticeships is set to grow by 26 percent. Indeed, "improving the skills pipeline" and "supporting" people to work is the top priority for the Department (HM Government 2020c: 40; HM Treasury 2021b: 60, 97–98, 121–122; House of Commons Treasury Committee 2020: 22). Thus, the Departments once responsible for welfare and education are turning into workfare departments. This means that (young) people are treated as economic matter. And, as with all workfare programmes, none of these will create a single job. Workfare is not concerned with creating employment but *employability*, with forging a workforce ready (able and willing) to serve the needs of employers. Workfare is designed to benefit capital, not workers.

As for employed workers, biosecurity has hit their earnings. These had been rapidly declining between 2008 and 2013, and only modestly recovered between then and 2020. They received a new blow during the pandemic period, and are not expected to return to their 2007 levels in the foreseeable future (Resolution Foundation 2020b: 11–12). A pool of idled workforce, skilled and disciplined by workfare schemes into a "reserve army of labour" in itself puts downward pressure on wages and the overall social cost of labour (Marx 1990: 762–870). This "natural" suppression of wages was further enhanced by the state management of the economic crisis. Its unconditional offerings to capital allowed the latter to directly attack an unprotected workforce. Under threat of redundancy, the pandemic period was an orgy of firing and rehiring workers to do the same work with worse remuneration and conditions. This practice was pioneered by firms that have received vast sums of public money, as the state was handing it out without conditions to the recipients; indeed, the government overtly defended this practice by blocking parliamentarians' attempts to regulate it (Walker 2021b). It is estimated that almost 10 percent of workers succumbed to employers' blackmail (Brown 2021; House of Commons Liaison Committee 2020: q.99–100).

Further, the state engages in wage suppression directly. The Treasury imposed a pause in pay rises for public sector workers for the 2021–2022 financial year (HM Treasury 2020b: 21), which represents a real-terms pay cut equal to the rate of inflation. In this manner, the government reconnects with its austerity policy, which between 2010 and 2018 froze public sector wages or capped them to 1 percent (Ferguson and Francis-Devine 2021: 12–16). The 2021–2022 freeze is piled upon a decade of real-term cuts. Its lifting will not improve the situation: rising inflation in basic goods and rising taxation of workers income will result to a new retreat of workers income that will last for the foreseeable future. Indeed, real wages, across sectors, are expected to fall, making this decade the worse for wages since the 1930s. Consequently, household incomes are declining: the crisis is set to reduce them by more than 2.5 percent in depth of time (Resolution Foundation 2021a: 9, 12–13).

By suppressing the wages of its workers, the state sends a clear message to private employers: it will not "distort" the labour market, but maintain the conditions in which they can continue suppressing their "costs of production". Finally, in a masterstroke of cynicism, in March 2021 the Department of Health and Social Care announced that frontline NHS staff will be exempt from the pay freeze. They received a pay rise of 1 percent (Ferguson and Francis-Devine 2021: 9–10). This was still a real-term pay cut, but its importance lies is elsewhere: in the symbolic humiliation of the sector of the workforce that, especially during the pandemic, enjoyed the greatest popular support. By thus insulting NHS staff, the Treasury raised a moralistic outcry that focused attention on a single sector, leaving the broader wage-repression move uncontested.

Finally, in early 2022, wage repression policy broke the confines of the public sector to envelop all working people. As inflation becomes a persistent macroeconomic feature, the Governor of the Bank of England strongly admonishes against wage rises, for the latter would cause an inflationary spiral (Andrew Bailey in Chan 2022). Thus, the state uses the inflation that devastates whatever is left of workers income to repress their wages. Wage suppression policy is now explicit and presented as a necessity. The state's wage suppression policy is bearing (strange) fruits. During the "recovery", Britain's labour is experiencing *simultaneously* a 'recruitment crisis' as there are not enough workers to fill vacancies, *and* a drastic fall in workers' pay, especially in the public sector (Office for National Statistics 2022). In the labour market, the state is clearly engaging in counter-cyclical policy —the question is to whose benefit and to whose detriment. It seems that the neoliberal state is perfectly capable of counter-cyclical policies as long as they suppress the cost of labour.

The social wage is subject to similar treatment. During the pandemic, the government offered a £20 weekly rise to Universal Credit payments, the UK's unemployment and income support scheme. The increase was seen as a necessary top up for a system inadequate in every sense. Eligibility is onerously restricted, payments are typically slow to reach recipients and invariably meagre. Universal Credit is a ticket to debt, homelessness and prostitution (House of Commons Work and Pensions Committee 2021b). Even after the

£20 rise, unemployed and poor people in Britain had less disposable income than virtually in any other northern European or North American country: less than half of that of their Irish counterparts, less than a quarter of their Dutch ones (House of Commons Treasury Committee 2020: 28). The Universal Credit top-up is estimated to have prevented a rise in poverty that would have resulted from the spring 2020 lockdown (IMF 2020b: 12). Regardless, in October 2021, the government axed it. As a result of the £20 cut, almost a million people are expected to fall into poverty within a year, a trend estimated to accelerate in depth of time (House of Commons Work and Pensions Committee 2021a; Westwater 2021). Further, while the state promptly tore its fiscal rulebook regarding handouts and contracts to capital, it maintains an absolute cap on welfare expenditure. The cap is arbitrarily set by the Treasury and is not adjustable to inflation, at a time when inflation is rising considerably and eats into people's disposable income (HM Treasury 2021b: 11, 33). Further, unemployed workers are set to face an increasingly mean regime of sanctions. They are only allowed to seek work in their "preferred sector" for a month. Upon the month's expiry, they are forced to seek employment, and accept a job, in any sector that would have them — regardless of their skills, experience or physical attributes; and certainly regardless of their aspirations. Failure to thus become infinitely flexible signals the termination of their benefits (Butler 2022a; Department for Work and Pensions 2022). There is also a renewed commitment to curtailing access to disability benefits by making the selection process more onerous (HM Treasury 2021b: 139). As a result of the onerous and exclusionary character of workfare, in the "recovery" phase, Britain is seeing a simultaneous fall in *both* unemployment and in the size of the economically active population (Office for National Statistics 2022). A large transfer of idled workforce has occurred, from unemployment to 'economic inactivity', as workers give up looking for work. Forced to economic non-existence, they cease to be a cost for the state. This forceful reduction of the workforce amounts to state-induced sabotage of the economy. But this is of no consequence as long as the cost of labour is being suppressed.

If the purpose of benefit sanctions is to lead unemployed people into work, even by force of compulsion, they have failed. They are as likely to force people to stop claiming benefits while remaining unemployed. This is officially known to the state since, at least, the heyday of its austerity drive (National Audit Office 2016). Still, the government persists with intensifying sanctions, and is fiercely protecting from publicity recent investigations into sanctions' effects (Butler 2022b). Far from any considerations with "labour market efficiency" this strand of workfare is an article of faith for the neoliberal state. Its immediate purpose is to get unemployed people off the state's books. In this manner the state withdraws from any responsibility towards its citizens' sustenance, and places relevant blame on them for breaking the conditions of the "contract" governing benefit provision — a contract, of course, unilaterally authored by the state (Handler 2004;

Macleavy 2010). The deeper purpose of workfare is to make the unconditional surrender to the requirements of accumulation an absolute condition for survival. Workfare is punishment inflicted on the poor.

Further, the government imposes a freeze on the Local Housing Allowance, the scheme that subsidises the rent for those on the lowest income. Thus, the government reconnects with its long-standing policy (dating from 2011) to impose yearly real-term cuts on housing benefits — a policy it had briefly interrupted during the height of the pandemic. The housing benefit freeze begun in April 2021, when an estimated half a million tenants were in rent arrears. In tandem, the government lifted the moratorium on evictions due to the pandemic — and the UK is bracing for a wave of evictions and a rise in homelessness (Jayanetti 2021). To complete the move, the government removed the lifeline for homeless youth (HM Treasury 2021: 46).

The final element of the social wage is public services. While the state has embarked in a spectacular increase in public expenditure, this mainly consists of capital spending on infrastructure. Regarding the everyday running of services, there is a significant rise for Health and Education, but a flatlining of expenditure in virtually all other government Departments. This constitutes a departure from the government's pre-pandemic plans; compared to them, it represents a decrease in expenditure of more than £15 billion by 2025 (Resolution Foundation 2021a: 42–49). Notably, there is no provision for a rise in central government payments to local authorities. These are responsible for the delivery of most public services to citizens and, after a decade of cuts, are on the verge of bankruptcy and forced to stop providing services or outsource them to private companies. As a response, they contemplate rising Council Tax — a flat tax that disproportionately affects the poor.

In sharp contrast to the generous and unconditional way the state treats capital, it treats those depended on wages and the social wage in a mean, punitive manner. It is questionable whether there is economic sense in this; but it displays commitment to offer nothing but discipline and punishment to the unemployed, making their survival next to impossible; to keep those who are in work perilously close to poverty; and to make the life of the poor miserable and agonising in every way. It displays, in other words, full adherence to the dogma that society's basic needs are a cost of production to be repressed to a minimum. Emblematic of the neoliberal state's drive to devalue life is the resistance the government offered to calls to extent free school meals over the Christmas 2020 holiday. This would have cost a pittance, and it would prevent hundreds of thousands of children from going hungry. The government reluctantly cave in under public outcry, led by a campaigning footballer (Hinsliff 2020b). Again, the issue functioned like a lightning rod, concentrating moral anathema on the most extreme aspect of a policy that, by this token, was largely absolved from criticism on the whole.

The vicious treatment of (employed and unemployed) workers in the UK is contrasted by developments in the US, which seems to be promoting a pro-labour policy. The American Jobs plan is, thus far, the only articulated vision of state intervention that would lift the prospects of workers. It is notable, however, that it does not decisively break with workfare. The improvement in labour conditions is limited to the creation of jobs through vast state handouts to private capital; the legal requirement that employees would not repress workers' attempts to unionise; and their liability for discriminating between workers along gender and, especially, racial lines (White House 2021a). Missing is any commitment to augment welfare services and enhance access to them; and wage increases are hoped to result from rising productivity, achieved through the retraining of the labour force.

Workers' devaluation is also evident at work. The key issue raised by the biosecurity crisis was that of sick pay. To counter the possibility that workers would go to the workplace whilst ill, and drive up infections, the government made statutory sick pay available from the first day of illness, rather than the fourth as it used, rather absurdly, to be. Moreover, the state subsidised employers' sick-leave payments to workers. Yet, while employers receive a partial relief from the sick pay duty, employees do not rip any benefit from the new arrangement. Sick pay continues to amount to less than £96 per week. It is the lowest among OECD countries (exempting South Korea and the US, where workers do not have such right), and it is virtually impossible to survive on. Moreover, the two million workers that are paid less than £120 per week remain excluded from sick pay entitlements (House of Commons Treasury Committee 2020: 28–29; Resolution Foundation 2020: 4–9). The mean treatment of workers in illness was instrumental in forcing them to work whilst ill. It was a key driver of infection spread, and contributed to the disproportionate suffering of poorer workers from the disease (Schwab and Malleret 2020: 99). The state is fully aware of this, and resisted all calls to rectify it.

The major developments in the realm of work during the pandemic concern its duration. France expanded the length of the working day, reduced paid leave and overtime pay, and froze wages (D'Eramo 2020: 27; Leoni and Alkamar 2020: 60). Greece instituted a 10-hour working day. Across the world, a new model of work has emerged: home-working. Apart from virtually eliminating sick-days, working from home has extended working time, undermined holidays, and increased the length of working day by an hour on average. Workers were absolved from their daily commute but, facing intensified exploitation through high-end machinery, complain of being overworked and exhausted. Employers, quite illiterately, see in the extension of the working day and the elimination of absence through sickness an increase in "productivity" —while it is in fact an extension of surplus labour time (Marx 1990: 340–344). As surplus time means surplus value, "hybrid work", an alternation between office and home-work, is set to become permanent. In this context, the architects of the "working from home" infrastructure assume the role of universal (meta-)managers, issuing advice to employers on the optimal conditioning of their workforce for "extreme flexibility" (Microsoft undated; The Economist 2020n: 19–21).

The lifting of the spatial boundary between work and leisure (office and home), results to a lifting of their temporal boundary: working hours expand until bedtime and are interjected with "leisure activities". For employers, this raises a need to monitor workers' activity in their new workplace, their home (The Economist 2020n: 21). Home-work surveillance gear is the next big seller for the IT sector. Employers buy in large numbers, and force their employees to use, webcam and AI systems that monitor the worker's activity: her posture before the computer screen, the amount of emails she sends, her key-strokes, etc., and feed the information to her boss. They monitor her time of inertia and absence from the screen, and alert her to return "to work" or face consequences. At their most advanced, electronic sensors monitor all sensual responses of the worker — eye movement, muscle contractions, breathing — and compare them to a model of responses appropriate for the task the worker is meant to be executing (Connolly 2020; Tiltrecordings 2020). On this basis, algorithms decide the level of remuneration, promotion and demotion of each worker, as well as the termination of their employment (Crispin 2021). In other words, home-work introduces the *telescreen*, the device installed in people's once private space to monitor their psychological responses and innate dispositions (Orwell 2021). Total intelligence advances: from monitoring every *trans*action (Boukalas 2020) to monitoring every *re*action; it traverses all aspects of existence from the omni-social and relational to the intimate and molecular. As biosecurity imposes extreme privatisation by erasing the public; the "extreme flexibilisation" of work also erases the private.

Thus, workfare expands to work. The new model of labour imposed by biosecurity signifies the conflation of the spaces for production and reproduction — the merging of the home with the office. Through this conflation the requirements and operation of production invade and colonise the space of reproduction (Chapter 6). The same occurs with time. Leisure is pushed at the interstices of a diffused working day that encompasses all waking time. The occupation of reproductive space and time by production is imposed, policed and defined by surveillance — perpetual and molecular. The home has turned into an office, and the office into a prison.

13 Pandemic distribution

During the time of its suspension, and the suspension of its time, the economy presented some observable trends. None of them were new. Still, the pandemic suspension aggrandised them, gave them new impetus and made them more pronounced. It also made more decipherable the key role of the state in promoting them. Combined, the trends discussed in this chapter outline some key perspectives for the post-pandemic economy in the near future.

Concentration

Economic crises tend to result to capital concentration and the present one will do so to a superlative degree (Blakeley 2020: 21). During the pandemic, a few people made a lot of money. Some of them did so *because* of the pandemic — or, more precisely, because of biosecurity.

The large pharmaceutical companies were mobilised in the biosecurity effort and, by developing vaccines, they were instrumental to its successful conclusion. In doing so, they secured considerable profit. Thus, Pfizer expects $36 billion revenue from its vaccine for 2021, contributing to a 134 percent overall revenue rise; in its most conservative estimates, profits will be in excess of $8 billion, making its vaccine "the most lucrative medicine ever produced" (Kollewe 2021c). For Moderna, a young biomedical company, its vaccine will represent a jump in revenue from $60 million pre-pandemic to $16 billion in 2021 and $8 billion in profit (Corporate Watch 2021; Isidore 2021; Kollewe 2021a).

It is natural that pharmaceutical companies would make large profits in the context of a pandemic. This course of nature was greatly aided by state action. Pressurised by pharmaceutical companies, states across Europe and North America refrained from intervening in the pricing of the vaccines. Thus, vaccine prices were set be the companies alone (Corporate Europe Observatory 2020; Lerner 2020; Public Eye 2021). This is perplexing, first, because reduced prices would have benefited poorer countries and hence led to a faster decline of the pandemic globally. And second, because the vaccines were largely developed by public funding. Total public expenditure for vaccine research is estimated at $12 billion; and it enabled the early stages of research that were more risky from an entrepreneurial point of view. The Moderna vaccine

DOI: 10.4324/9781003302988-15

in particular, the most expensively priced, was funded exclusively by public money (Mazzucato 2021). The bemusement is lifted if we consider that this is a neoliberal state, for which the demands of pharmaceutical companies for strong property rights protection and freedom of pricing are hardwired into its health policy (Waitzkin 2016: 137–139). Thus, Canada, the EU, UK and US, as well as the Gates Foundation, vehemently opposed suggestions from developing countries to lift intellectual property protections for covid vaccines, even when some developers (Moderna and Oxford University) raised no objection to their patents becoming public (Tooze 2021: 245). The property and profits of pharmaceutical companies reflect their contribution to the biosecurity effort, but also their bargaining power in its context, as the resumption of economic activity depended on them. They also reflect the willingness of the state to protect and promote their interests and to do so as a matter of principle, regardless of the wishes of individual vaccine developers.

The other major beneficiary of the crisis was IT, the products of which substituted for society and doubled as the intelligence apparatus of biosecurity. Thus, between March and September 2020, Microsoft's founder saw his wealth increase by $20 billion as his company's products pioneered the surveillance intercom systems for homebound offices. The founders of Google added almost $160 billion to their fortunes, and the co-founder of the electronic surveillance company Oracle saw his wealth increase by 50 percent. Similarly, the fortune of Facebook's founder increased by 80 percent in ten months. Finally, with physical consumption sites shut, the giants of e-commerce saw a tidal rise of their fortunes. The owner of LVMH doubled his wealth, and that of the Zara group owner rose by 50 percent. Similarly, the founder of Amazon saw his wealth increase by $70 billion, or 66 percent (Neatte 2020). While reflecting big increases in profit, these breath-taking evaluations of wealth are due to valorisations in the stock exchange, where asset prices are in steep incline way ahead of the rest of the economy, setting the scene for a bubble (Tooze 2021: 129–130).

The rocketing of profits and valuations of IT capital is due to the crucial role that software plaid as a substitute for activities (work, education, shopping, communicating) that could no longer take place physically. It also played a crucial role in governmental manipulation and surveillance during the biosecurity effort: from "nudging" people to epidemiologically optimise their behaviours, to producing real-time knowledge of the epidemiological environment and sanctioning potential bearers of the disease. Thus, both society during the pandemic and the biosecurity effort were entirely dependent on advanced IT (Boyer 2021: 23; Storeng and de Bengy Puyvallée 2021). This dependency is symptomatic of a deeper attitude towards that sector: a faith in the production of hi-tec "solutions" to the "problems" created by the existing social, economic and political arrangements. Thus, IT effectuates a crucial political and ideological task, as it naturalises social arrangements, develops a cult of technique, and thus reduces the question of change to one of technical adjustment (Morozov 2020).

Another sector was enriched not because of the pandemic, but in advance of recovery expectations. This is the "green economy" sector, a compound of, especially, energy, chemicals and transportation industries that is currently molten and dynamic, comprising a multitude of upstart and relatively small businesses mushrooming around state subsidies. The founder of one of its flagships, Tesla, tripled his fortune during the first months of the pandemic (Neatte 2020). This example can be seen as an encapsulation of some key traits of the fledging green economy: Tesla is, after all, a car manufacturer. It produces a commodity emblematic of industrial capitalism, liberal ideology and associated everyday practices, relations and attitudes that span leisure, work and urban planning. Thus, the green economy seems to represent a deep continuity of capitalism dressed in green livery. It is a variation on established relations, and even its green credentials appear doubtful — in the case of car manufacturing for instance, it remains a stubborn fact that the "green" automobiles are powered by lithium. Crucially, the new green economy is not less exploitative than the dirty old one. Tesla and the e-commerce companies mentioned above, kept forcing their workers to continue working throughout the pandemic, under hazardous conditions and for reduced pay (Agustin et al 2020; Sainato 2021). The green economy is, essentially, a way to capitalise on the environmental crisis. It opens a new field for accumulation and keeps capitalist relations intact; any benefits to the environment will be merely collateral. In the green economy capital turns the crisis it imposes on the environment into a driving force for accumulation. In other words, *accumulation is now motored by the devastation it necessarily causes.*

The turn to a green economy has resulted to a drastic rise in energy prices. The price of gas, which is a stabiliser for renewable energy production, more than doubled within a month (August 2021) and rose by 900 percent in the course of 2021, drove abrupt rises in other energy sources, and resulted to a 50 percent rise in household energy bills[1]. Energy is a universal commodity, incorporated in every product and service; thus, rising energy prices cause inflationary pressure in the overall economy, repress overall demand and thus drag heavily on growth. The causes of this sudden price-hike remain uncertain. The release of demand for energy pend up during the pandemic seems a plausible factor; but their specific trigger appears to be a sudden thrust by China and the EU to curtail the production of non-renewable energy sources at a moment when renewable ones are far from fulfilling energy needs (Tooze 2021: 191). Thus, the inaugural act of the state's "green economy" policy results to accentuated hardship for wage earners, uncertainty for businesses, and to a serious undermining of the prospects for a post-pandemic economic recovery.

The anticipated growth of the green economy is not the only redistributive effect of state policy. The latter is set to have a lasting impact on sectors that struggled during the pandemic, from manufacturing to retail and hospitality. There, a bout of concentration is due, with state policy benefiting the larger players to the detriment of the smaller ones. State relief for small and medium size businesses has been inadequate to compensate for the loss they made.

The relief these businesses received came in the form of loans, rather than grants. Thus, smaller companies are burdened with debt, which curtails their growth and makes insolvency a distinct possibility in the medium term (Chapter 10). By contrast, while they did take a hit, large enterprises received most of their relief money in the form of, often bespoke, grants; are able to restructure their debt as their negotiating power towards lenders and the state is greater; and they have easier access to liquidity and benefit directly from quantitative easing. In short, the modality of the relief offered by the state ensures that the recovery — survival and growth — prospects for big capital are significantly greater than those for smaller capital. The former will occupy the space evacuated by the shrinkage of the latter, resulting to concentration across most sectors.

Finally, where there is large and sudden transfer of value between sectors of the economy; between small and large players therein; between the public purse and private ones; and between the economic present and future, the financial sector thrives (Makortoff 2021; Neatte and Jolly 2020). Its most eponymous player, Warren Buffet, enjoyed a 26 percent increase in his fortune between March 2020 and the end of that year (Neatte 2020). Again, the state has been a catalyst. Pointing to a counter-cyclical policy regarding the stock exchange, the overall effect of the interventions by the US Federal Reserve was to put $7 trillion of wealth at the hands of equity investors at the moment when the real economy would have brought the opposite result. Exactly like in the 2008 crisis, the central bank action as lender of last resort was to socialise losses and privatise gains (Brenner 2020: 17–19).

The overall outcome is a sudden concentration of wealth, unparalleled in magnitude and pace. During the biosecurity crisis, the world's 2,755 billionaires saw their collective wealth increase by 62 percent, to exceed $13 trillion — a figure larger than the GDP of Germany, India, Italy and Japan combined (Therborn 2021: 25). More impressively, this massive redistribution of social wealth occurred whilst the economy was mothballed. It points to wealth creation being divorced from economic activity as we know it (Frade 2020: 3). In the context of a de-coupling of wealth-acquisition from investment and production, the state's rescue interventions redistributed wealth upwards trough a virtual economy (Brenner 2020: 20–21). This is a spectacular economy whose purpose and function is the concentration of wealth — not its production. The state is indeed attempting to maintain the economy as is: concentrating wealth without creating it, through extraction (Boukalas 2021; Brenner 2020: 21–22).

Corruption

The cost of the twin crises to the public purse is enormous: in Britain alone it has exceeded £400 billion. It involves a massive transfer of funds from the public to the private sector. Here, the state is directly involved in redistribution: the latter does not occur as a policy effect, but through procurement of services and products.

The main areas of biosecurity expenditure in the UK were the testing and contact tracing programme and PPE procurement, which between them costed almost £60 billion. Virtually all related contracts (98.9 percent) were awarded through emergency procedures, without any form of competition (Transparency International (UK) 2021: 19–20).

The government's test-and-trace programme was outsourced to private firms, with US-based Serco and Deloitte dominating its delivery. The rationale and criteria for selecting two companies specialising, respectively, in security and logistics are not set out publicly. Neither is the selection of private contractors, which was undertaken by an ad hoc public entity ("NHS Test and Trace"), conjured up for that purpose. Its head, Baroness Harding, was appointed by a "tap on the back" from the Health Secretary with prime-ministerial approval. She did not have any public health expertise, but is a Conservative member of the House of Lords, and former CEO of an IT company —a background she transferred into the public sector where she was appointed, by the previous Health Secretary, to head "NHS Improvement", another ad hoc entity charged with modernising and privatising the IT infrastructure of the NHS. It is unclear why the state created this dubious structure to deliver a crucial social service and handle a significant amount of public wealth, when the relative infrastructure was already there: test-and-trace could have been run by a well-rehearsed collaboration between local NHS Trusts and local authorities. The government, without explanation, opted for a centralised and privatised programme, raising concerns of a stealth privatisation of the NHS and its utilisation as a distributor of public money into private hands (Garside and Neate 2020).

The scheme was a failure. It was found to have made no measurable difference to the progress of the pandemic. To achieve nothing, the programme consumed, within a year, £37 billion in more than 400 contracts with more than 200 suppliers, and employed 2,500 consultants for whom the average daily pay was £1,100 and the highest exceeded £6,500 (House of Commons Public Accounts Committee 2021: 4–6). Not unreasonably, a former chief civil servant characterised the scheme as the "most wasteful and inept public spending programme of all time" (Nick MacPherson, cited in Rawnsley 2021a; Gregory 2021).

Regarding PPE procurement, of the £18 billion directed to it between March and August 2020, less than £200 million were awarded through a competitive process. Here, the government instituted a "high priority lane" for contracts to be awarded to "VIP" suppliers. These suppliers were over ten times more likely to secure a contract than their "non-VIP" counterparts (National Audit Office 2020; Transparency International (UK) 2021: 22). Many of these companies, ranging from dog food producers to jewellers, were irrelevant to PPE production; but they were Conservative party donors or owned by people with ties to government ministers (Good Law Project 2021b; Pegg and Conn 2020). Indeed, the very existence of a "VIP lane" was only known to government ministers and top Whitehall officials and their contacts in the world of business. Through the VIP lane the government bypassed established associations of businesses specialising in protective equipment and testing, whose offers were ignored (Calvert and Arbuthnott 2021: 99–101). Similarly, contracts were awarded on the recommendation of politicians, bypassing organisations of relevant expertise like the Royal College of Nursing or the British Medical Association. In sum, most PPE contracts were awarded to companies with limited track record on supplying relevant goods, including companies that were created on the spot for this purpose, to the expense of companies established in the field (Transparency International (UK) 2021: 9, 22–24).

In early 2022, the High Court found the operation of the "high priority lane" to be illegal (High Court 2022; Good Law Project 2022). To be able to reach this verdict, the court had first to establish the relevant facts. That was not straightforward, for the government insisted on keeping the majority of contracts awarded through the "lane" secret. Thus, in order to adjudicate on facts, the court had first to force their publicity. It did so by finding governmental secrecy on the issue unlawful in a judicial review case brought by civil society organisations and members of Parliament (Good Law Project 2021a; High Court 2021a).

The secrecy covering government contracts spreads beyond the VIP lane machinations. It is estimated to envelop a fourth of public health expenditure during the pandemic (Transparency International (UK) 2021: 27–28). The practice of distributing service and procurement contracts through administrative bodies that the government conjures up and places under the leadership of arbitrarily selected persons, appears to have been typical during the pandemic. It has made the identification of specific awards impossible, and has been brought under judicial scrutiny (Good Law Project 2021c; Transparency International (UK) 2021: 6, 29–30).

The arbitrary, dilettante, clique-based, secretive and often absurd, ineffective and unlawful regime of awarding contracts expands to epidemiological surveillance and propaganda operations (Good Law Project 2021c; High Court 2021b). Further, it seems to encompass all manner of government initiatives and actions (Rawnsley 2021b). From a former Prime Minister lobbying the Chancellor of the Exchequer so that the shadow-finance firm he represented could access state-backed loans (Walker 2021a); to the Business Secretary issuing an unlawful planning decision that saved a party donor £45 million in tax (Syal and Stewart 2020); and from the Health Secretary awarding, before the pandemic, NHS contracts to a firm owned by his sister (Rawlinson 2021); to the former Mayor of London, and current Prime Minister, awarding City Hall sponsorship to his friend (Lydall and Sleigh 2021); or to the persistence of the Prime Minister to keep the names of those who paid for the refurbishment of his official residence secret (Allegretti and Syal 2021) — cronyism is a key modality of state-market relations. It denotes that, rather than a public affair, the state has become a private mechanism operated by cliques that siphons public wealth into select private hands.

Destitution

Arguably, the most crucial redistribution of wealth is that between capital and labour. There is a strong inverted correlation between wealth and economic loss during the pandemic. The poorer someone is, the more likely to have suffered economically from the biosecurity measures. This resulted to an acute rise in inequality during the pandemic, even in comparison to its already heightened pre-pandemic levels (IMF 2021b: 31; Schwab and Malleret 2020: 79–82). Again, the state was pivotal in effectuating it. Its generosity towards capital is matched by its meanness towards society.

While crucial in adverting unemployment from reaching unprecedented levels, the government's furlough scheme only covered 80 percent of a worker's salary. Furloughed workers, saw their wage cut by a fifth. This was unsustainable for the large fraction of workers in part-time occupations and those working on, or near, minimum salary; and it was precisely these low-paid workers who were more likely to have been furloughed or to have lost their jobs (Brewer et al, 2021: 18; Marmot et al, 2020: 35). At the same time, faced with pressures on their businesses, employers increased the rate of exploitation under cover of lockdown: the number of jobs paying less than the legal minimum rose fivefold in England in the first months of the pandemic, to reach 2 million (Marmot et al, 2020: 35).

The result is a dramatic rise of poverty. The rate of low income families who find it difficult to cope financially exploded during the pandemic: from approximately 15 to almost 80 percent (Marmot et al, 2020: 29). Similarly, the number of people officially into poverty increased by almost 45 percent, and so did the number of households classed as "destitute". Extreme poverty — households facing hunger — rose by 2 percent to reach 14 percent (Marmot et al, 2020: 42–43; NIESR 2021). Indeed, the number of people who rely on foodbanks in order to eat increased dramatically and came to include people who were previously considered of "middle-income" (Buther 2020).

Worse than the actuality of workers' earnings is their prospects. Here, the government's wage suppression policy is taking effect. Average earnings will be permanently lower as a result of the pandemic. They dipped by approximately 3 percent during the pandemic, and are not expected to recover, in real terms, their 2019 level before 2026. By then pay growth will have been suspended for almost 20 years, marking two "dreadful" decades for living standards (Brewer et al 2021: 7, 21–22). Inequality, as imprinted in the Gini coefficient, is set to rise throughout the 2020–2024 period (Brewer et al 2021: 7). Wage repression, combined with tax increases and rising inflation, is set to cause, in 2023, the largest yearly fall in living standards ever recorded (Office for Budget Responsibility 2022: 8–9). It is the last act in a prolonged drama that has started over 12 years ago (for large parts of society it started over 40 years ago) — a drama of ever intensifying poverty that engulfs ever wider sectors of society. For the British and most European societies, economic recovery comes in the shape of a *cost of living crisis* (Partington and Kirk 2022; Tooze 2022).

The state is not idly observing the rise in inequality and poverty; it exacerbates it. The government's decision to reverse the £20 weekly increase in welfare benefits will bring welfare benefits to its lowest real-term value since 1991. It will represent a 22 percent cut in earnings for 18 million of the poorest people. As 54 percent of citizens at the lowest income quintile already need to borrow to cover the costs of food and housing, the benefit cut will cause a severe poverty crisis. People on the edge of the poverty threshold will fall into poverty, and the level of deep and persistent poverty is already rising (Brewer et al 2021: 5–6, 26–27, 43–49; The Resolution Foundation 2020: 17; Social Metrics Commission 2020: 2–12). Further, the government also imposes flat taxes that disproportionately effect lower earners (Chapter 10). As for the shock to household finances caused by the explosion of energy prices, the only relief the government offers is to spread half of the additional cost over a length of time, in anticipation of wholesale prices eventually declining. Unlike most of its European counterparts, the UK government refuses to slash the value added tax it imposes on energy consumption. It is, however, in accord with European governments in taxing as lightly as possible the astronomical profits that energy companies make from the rising prices (Inman 2022b; Sgaravatti, Tagliapietra and Zachmann 2022). As for the broader rise in inflation, the only intervention the state is willing to make is to suppress wages (Chapter 12).

In conclusion, redistributive policies transfer wealth from labour to capital, and from small capital to big. Redistribution within capital is an exercise of turning public wealth into private on the basis of executive fiat, and presents a tendency to clientelism. In the shape of the green economy, it aims to instil dynamism in the accumulation process by championing select capitals within a still amorphous sector that comprises any business that can present itself as "green". The green economy will be forged by state handouts to select capitals. Beyond it, state policy is instrumental for a transfer of wealth from: (a) the public purse to private capital; (b) within the private economy, from certain sectors to others; (c) within each sector, from small companies to large ones; (d) within each company, from the workers to the owners; and (e) across the board, from the future to the present. Crucially, for many, the economic recovery is nothing but the agonising prolongation and intensification of the "crisis" — a perennial crisis that seems to have always been there and to remain so permanently, for it is now the normal mode of their economy.

Note

1. This situation is set to be gravely exacerbated as, in the time of writing, Russia, a major energy producer, is invading Ukraine.

14 Towards a dual economy: Welfare for capital, workfare for everyone else

Significant changes occurred to the economy whilst it was mothballed. Businesses — and entire sectors — have either gone bankrupt or accrued crippling amounts of depth; work, consumption and leisure habits shifted; and the rulebook of fiscal policy is rewritten. This chapter attempts an early charting of the economy that emerges from the biosecurity crisis. It tries to decipher some of its trends and the general direction of economic policy. It thus outlines the emergence of the commodification of data as a green field for accumulation; the implications that lack of reserves has for economic resilience and for the just-in-time production model; and the prospects for the organisation of the economy in a global context. These tendencies are in turn partly absorbed into a discussion that concerns the broader socio-political regime of accumulation. Finally, the chapter tries to decipher whether state policy signals a continuation of neoliberal strategy or a shift to a Keynesian one — more accurately, it tries to decipher the meaning of the sudden shift to countercyclical economic intervention. Needless to say that this is an attempt to chart a terrain that is molten. Even if boldly expressed for purposes of clarity, the conclusions drawn cannot be more than tentative.

From the commodification of leisure to the exploitation of data

A first legacy of biosecurity will be a massive round of capital concentration. This will result from the bankruptcy of many small and medium size enterprises, either as a direct result of the biosecurity measures or of the debt these companies have accrued (Chapters 10, 13). At the same time, the digitalisation of economic activity that the pandemic drove to a climax heightens the capital threshold a company will need to initiate operations. Thus, the space evacuated by extinguished small companies is less likely to be occupied by their peers and more likely to be captured by large enterprises. Indeed, digitalisation is a decipherable trend, one that pre-dated the crisis but was greatly accelerated by it. In contrast to struggling traditional industrial and post-industrial sectors, what emerges triumphant from the pandemic, performing profits that by far outstrip the average, is a digital

DOI: 10.4324/9781003302988-16

"platform capitalism" based on expansive extraction, collection, analysis and marketisation of enormous volumes of data, personal and relational. In essence, the omni-surveillance of society becomes a driving motor of accumulation (Boyer 2021: 153–158). This, in turn, means that the self, its expressions and its relations, becomes a (most lucrative) commodity.

A decisive trend of the pre-pandemic economy was an exponential growth of world money. As a long term legacy of the abandonment of the gold standard, there has been an ever-increasing excess of money in the circuit of capital that, decades before the biosecurity crisis, could not be absorbed by investment in production (Harvey 2020). Instead, throughout the neoliberal era, excess money is directed towards real estate and, more importantly, intangibles: financial assets and IT: communication, information and computation technologies including, eventually, the commodification of data. Thus, from production, accumulation had turned to rent, speculation and extraction; the heart of the economy was not tangible commodities but what Debord (1994) would call *images*. The biosecurity crisis is set to strengthen this trend further: if nowt else, the massive new bout of quantitative easing undertaken in its context will significantly add to the gluttony of money in the capital circuit.

Production models and the question of reserves

An acute problem revealed by the pandemic is that of reserves: there are none. Every disruption in the supply chains implies immediate halting of production, for production units typically hold no stocks of necessary parts. Similarly, the temporary closure of a company would immediately cause it to face insolvency — for, no matter how healthy its business, it typically lacks the cash reserves that would allow it to cover expenses beyond a few days or weeks. Hence, through rent moratoria, tax deferrals and wage subsidies, the state stepped in to substitute for non-existing cash reserves. The absence of reserves also contributed to epidemic spread: For workers without savings, missing a few days' work could mean hunger and exposure to the appetites of loan sharks; hence they would continue working — with or without safety measures; with or without symptoms. An old, forgotten adage rung true during the pandemic: *Proletarians are those who have no reserves* (Bordiga 1949). Finally, lack of reserves undermined the biosecurity effort: there was no testing capacity, not nearly enough ventilators and intensive care beds, and PPE stockpiles could only last for days. In short, the accumulation circuit, and indeed the socio-economic system as a whole, was deprived of reserves.

Shielding the economy from exogenous disruption would seem to require the build-up of "excess": cash reserves for companies; savings for workers; excess productive capacity; "redundancies" in the health system; and warehousing. These would imply a temporal disjunction — a delay — between inception of production and valorisation through sale. Such a build-up of reserves would enhance the resilience of the economy, but at the cost of a slowdown in turnover time for capital in all its forms.

Regarding production processes, a build-up of reserves in the form of warehousing would involve a retreat of just-in-time production and an associated decline of complex, extended supply chains. There appears to be a growing realisation among capitalists that the just-in-time model can guarantee reduced costs only under conditions of certainty and predictability. Expanded value chains, and the concentration of supply in a few countries, like China and India, are increasingly seen as unstable (Boyer 2021: 148, 231–232). Beyond the acute phase of the crisis, the early stages of the economic recovery are undermined by supply malfunctions. Currently, supply chains present weaknesses across production and distribution; encompass most sectors; and result to relative scarcity in several types of goods including food and energy. In response, a tendency towards shrinking them seems to crystallise, as political actors, especially in the US and the EU, turn to protectionist measures that will "repatriate" supply chains (The Economist 2021d: 6–7).

The just-in-time model, however, and the expanded supply chains it involves, enhances efficiency, reduces turnover times, and allows capital to exploit differences in labour cost across countries. Thus, whatever the merits of a departure from it for the resilience of the economy as a whole, it is unlikely that any specific corporation, however dominant, would voluntarily depart from it. Even for a partial switch to occur, the state will have to intervene, to incentivise and even coerce capital. Indeed, state efforts to domesticate production of goods deemed to be of strategic importance is starting to become decipherable (Boyer 2021: 23; Schwab and Malleret 2020: 108). Crucially, the notion of "strategic goods" can expand ad infinitum, until we reach a fully protectionist national economy. Indeed, the IMF notes with horror that protectionist measures have emerged, especially with regards to technology; while World Economic Forum analysts see protectionism as *fait accompli* (IMF 2021a: 15; Schwab and Malleret 2020: 112–113). The country most advanced down this path is the US, which has produced a comprehensive plan to repatriate industrial and energy production, as well as construction and R&D, by placing legal requirements that generous federal handouts will only be directed towards US-based corporations and by restructuring the (national and global) tax system so that US corporations are deterred from investing abroad (White House 2021a).

The protectionist turn regarding advanced technology may prove consequential for the overall modality of accumulation. It involves securing access to an astonishing range of commodities, from rare earth to semiconductors and systems-architecture knowhow (Ni 2021). It already feeds into a "cold" military standoff between China and the USA focused on Taiwan, the global epicentre of semiconductor production. Such intense antagonism could implicate and upset not only supply chains but the entire regime of economic governance. Further, this antagonism could dramatically affect the accumulation regime, i.e. the broad socio-economic environment that accumulation needs. The IT sector, in alliance with finance, had thus far been best served by, and demanding, an accumulation regime based on a sense of relative abundance of resources (especially energy and money), economic optimism, extended lines of trade in a "borderless" world, tight fiscal policy, and market deregulation. The China-US antagonism over semiconductors means that now the optimum regime for IT sector accumulation is provided not by this expansive arrangement, but by its opposite, an intensive one. It involves maximising the surplus value extracted from labour, reducing production costs per unit, and rising prices combined with flat growth. It is historically associated with protectionist measures and increased state expenditure, directed especially towards contracts and subsidies. This accumulation regime is crisis-prone: the combination of flat growth and rising prices it aims for can result to stagflation; and, as it is based on intensified exploitation and deprivation of workers and the extinction of small capital, it sets the conditions for economic and social crisis. For this reason, it can only be advanced through fear. It necessitates a perception of scarcity — traditionally in energy; now in core IT components — and the anticipation of imminent crisis (Nitzan and Bichler 2009: 334–397). As the increasingly important IT sector subscribes to this intensive accumulation regime, the expansive one loses one of its pillars and collapses, leaving fear-based accumulation as the only viable one. Indeed, economists are contemplating the possibility of stagflation, as the chronic slow growth that marks the neoliberal era is now combined with rising inflation (The Economist 2021e: 69–70). With greater certainty, they predict that scarcity will define the economy for the foreseeable future (The Economist 2021f: 70–71).

De-globalisation and national economy

Accumulation occurs somewhere. Thus, an account of the perspectives for the economy must address the question of its arrangement in political space. The issue can be schematically put in terms of globalisation, national economy and their institutional architectures.

The processes of global economic integration had been, since its apogee in the 1990s, in relative decline long before the pandemic. International trade had ceased to be the main driver of global economic growth for more than a decade: between 2003 and 2018 international trade was decelerating in volume growth and declining in value. Similarly, international capital flows have been in prolonged decline. These trends have intensified during the crisis (Boyer 2021: 149–152; IMF 2021a: 141–142; The Economist 2020h: 7). This has forced analysts to consider a reversal of globalisation as a long term feature in an economic space marked by the resurgence of national economies and regionalisation, i.e. economic integration within regional blocs relatively closed to each other (Schwab and Malleret 2020: 112–113; The Economist 2021d: 4,12).

More importantly, free trade seems to have ceased to be the "supreme economic value" in political terms (Therborn 2021: 24). Despite the emphasis on flows (of capital and goods), the key element for globalisation were the contact-points, the endpoints of flows, for it is there where capital is valorised. It is not a disruption in the flows, in trade, that upsets globalisation, but the redrawing of contact-points architecture, a redrawing that shortens the flows and brings them partly within the national envelope. As such, flows are abstract, directionless and, ultimately, in-significant; it is the contact-points that engender, specify, actualise and render them meaningful. Thus, rather than international trade flows, which occur in most eras, globalisation is specified by the development of an architecture of contact points. This architecture is a political work. Thus, globalisation refers to the development of a global architecture of contact points; the development of political institutions —the World Bank, IMF, WTO, EU, G7, G20 etc — that develop and manage this architecture, the practices within it and the rules that govern it; and, the predominance of these supranational political institutions over those rooted at the national scale (Jessop 2002: 177–215). It is precisely here, at its constitutive institutional element, that globalisation seems troubled.

Since the start of the century, western countries (especially the US) have decoupled their security policy and associated political economy from processes of transnational integration, and secluded them within the national folder (Boukalas 2014: 214). Beyond the realm of security, since the collapse of the Doha round in 2001 (and again in 2008), processes of capitalist integration have ground to a halt (Waitzkin 2016: 140–141). While the WTO is in prolonged strategic impasse, the key funder of capitalist integration, the IMF, is caught in strategic confusion as it registers the impossibility of the present socio-economic arrangements to either continue or change. It appears, in short, that the Washington consensus of global integration in a neoliberal context has collapsed, and is replaced by nothing. Tensions between China and the US have resulted to a deadlock over key appointments in transnational directorates, most notably the Appellate Body of the WTO which cannot function, leaving international trade without a dispute resolution mechanism (IMF 2021a: 20; The Economist 2021d: 4–5). Even amongst advanced capitalist countries, there are problems of coordination and strategy. The G7 failed, for two consecutive years, to reach even a rudimentary agreement, and did not even care to conceal its failure (Mallet 2019). The EU, the most advanced bloc of transnational economic and social integration, lost Britain, one of its key members, in a first reversal of its hitherto inexorable expansion. Finally, NATO, the exemplary transnational alliance, was declared "brain dead" by the President of France (BBC 2019), pointing to its strategic paralysis. To top developments in both economic and security registers, the US and China are entering the orbit of a trade war; and Easter Europe is now the theatre of a military standoff. In short, virtually all institutions of transnational cooperation have lost strategic direction and, with it, the capacity to coordinate the processes they were designed to promote. Insofar as globalisation is a strategy expressed through institutional architecture, on the eve of the pandemic it was stagnant and showed signs of disintegration (Boukalas 2021). The pandemic exacerbated this predicament.

The biosecurity crisis exposed the degree to which the economy relies on global production chains and migrant labour (Global Labour Journal Editorial Board 2020: 76). Moreover, the pandemic shows that health is a global relation, as its persistence in one region of the world exposes the entire planet to contagion — which, in turn, imperils the smooth operation of the economy. In short, the pandemic exposed public health and the economy as interconnected relations of global expanse. Yet, biosecurity responses were strictly national. Facing a reality of interconnectedness, states closed their borders, protecting their societies from interdependency risks by secluding them from the "outside". Even astutely liberal states presiding over open economies (Australia, New Zealand, US) resorted to this tactic; others, like Britain, who were slow in adapting it were criticised for their tardiness. Moreover, national might marked the processes of procurement of health equipment, with states hijacking each other's deliveries, employing their intelligence agencies to the task, outbidding "rivals", blocking vaccine exports, etc. In short, the default state response to the pandemic was marked by hostility and aggression that sometimes verged on piracy. Perhaps the most impressive feature of this response is that it was not challenged on either political, moral or legal grounds. In effect, every sense of international collaboration and order collapsed; it was replaced by national necessity and might; and this was accepted as normal.

Moreover, the biosecurity response showed a further weakening of transnational governance institutions. The reputation of the World Health Organisation is fatally undermined as the Organisation is caught in the crosshair of China-US friction. The EU saw its member states abandoning any sense of cooperation precisely at the moment when their prospects before the pandemic were more intertwined than ever. Italy, the first European country to experience the full force of the pandemic, was left to cope by itself. Its EU partners refused to send even a morsel of medical aid and promptly shut their borders to it — to a country with which they claim strong bonds of solidarity that makes territorial borders superfluous. EU countries did not refrain from pilfering each other's supplies; while several, especially eastern, EU countries broke ranks from the block's faltering vaccination policy to procure vaccines from China and Russia.

Notably however, the EU response to the *economic* crisis is significantly different. After more than a year of resistance by northern states, the EU finally decided to issue joint bonds. These will amount to 390 billion euros, will be distributed to member states over the course of six years, and will be matched by a similar amount in the form of loans (European Commission 2021). Compared, in proportion, with the funds that the US and the UK have made available, this is meagre — indeed, the combined amount of grants and loans is significantly shorter than the shortfall in private investment caused by the biosecurity crisis (Tooze 2021: 186–187, 281). The funding is subject to EU approval of spending plans submitted by each member state, and which must prioritise the development of IT and the green economy. While the loans will be repaid by each state, the grants derive from collective debt issued by the EU as a whole. Funding, then, is small; through it, the EU dictates policy on member states; and the part of it that is loaned is likely to be repaid by a new round of austerity measures each state will force on its society. While all these are typical traits of EU government, something novel *has* happened: the EU has issued common debt. This exceptional move is strictly connected to the extraordinary circumstances in which it took place. But, it does set a precedent and, given the abundance of impeding exceptional circumstances, it may prove to be the first time of many. In short, while the prospect of renewed austerity, exploitation and pauperisation is engulfing EU societies in continuity with established policy; the ordoliberal dogma against collateralising debt is breached — leaving the bloc without a steadfast doctrine to guide its economic policy.

Beyond the pandemic, the key question is whether economic globalisation can continue alongside political nationalism, or whether there will be increased resort to relative autarky within a national framework (Global Labour Journal Editorial Board 2020: 77). It seems possible — more possible than it has been at any moment during the last 70 years — that the economic crisis ensuing from the pandemic could signal a retreat from processes of globalisation. It certainly strengthens existing tendencies to protectionism, industry repatriation, the selection of strategic sectors and national champions, and the development of industries and policies of national autarky (Leoni and Alkamar 2020: 59). The trend already encompasses military industries, as well as those concerned with health, medicine and IT; and it is not implausible that it will expand to encompass virtually the entire economy — food, minerals, spectacle, garments etc — and result to a national security economy.

An entrenchment to the national envelope will be detrimental to capital, as it will curtail its capacity to locate and exploit cheap labour across jurisdictions. A re-nationalisation of production processes could entail a significant strengthening of labour: if it is not combined with continuous inflow of migrant labour, economic nationalisation would lead to labour becoming finite and scarce —and therefore expensive, forcing a rise in wages. Moreover, in the context of a relatively enclosed economy, the wage represents a source of demand for capital operating within it. Thus, the recurrence of protectionism, the halting of globalisation and the nationalisation of the economic envelope could result to the eclipse of neoliberalism as the dominant organisation of capitalism.

The pressures on globalisation were already pronounced before the pandemic. The latter intensified them and promoted the national state as the predominant shell of political economy. This predominance, however, is not established. It is barely nascent and faces considerable challenges. The first, is the inherent tendency of capital to expand until it encompasses and integrates the planet and humanity into a global market (Marx 1848). The second, more tangible one, is the interest of dominant capital in its unfettered operation across a smooth, flattened global terrain and its access to all the labour therein. Thus, both the interest of dominant capital and the logic of capitalism bring the "nation-first" attitude to political economy under pressure. In short, capitalist integration is in crisis, but a return to the national context does not seem a sustainable remedy. The tension is, essentially, one between accumulation and its political underpinnings. While the horizon of capitalist *economy* remains global; the terrain of *political* economy seems to return to the national fold. The direct, and possibly most important, effect of this tension is a re-politicisation of the economy, which is no longer perceived as a natural or inescapable process, but as a politically determined one.

Goodbye neoliberalism...

Production models, accumulation regimes and the spatial integration of the economy, are issues of economic strategy. For almost a century, the latter has been dominated by two alternating paradigms of socio-economic organisation of capitalist societies: a Keynesian and a neoliberal one. Economic globalisation, its political underpinnings, and spatially dispersed just-in-time production lines are hallmarks of a neoliberal strategy; the tight integration within national and regional closures, is akin to a Keynesian one.

Overall, the state's response to the economic crisis constitutes a drastic departure from the predominant neoliberal paradigm of political economy. Gigantic state support schemes can in no way be understood as pertaining to a neoliberal macroeconomy founded on the theory of market automatism (Boyer 2021: 33). Throughout the pandemic, the state became the guarantor of wages and revenues: incomes, of workers and entrepreneurs, were socialised under its aegis. This constitutes a complete reversal of neoliberal orthodoxy. It is not the first time that such a reversal occurs: a monumental state intervention had recently saved the US financial sector from collapse and the euro from extinction. In the current crisis state intervention reached apotheosis: it was responsible for cancelling the economy; for mothballing it during the biosecurity crisis; and for revitalising it after it (Boyer 2021: 167, 171).

Neoliberal orthodoxy sidelines fiscal policy as a way to manage the business circle, for it sees it as inviting socio-political pressures. Instead, it limits economic policy to creating the conditions for economic efficiency by keeping inflation stable and low — and restricts the means for attaining this to the raising and lowering of short-term interest rates (The Economist 2020l: 13–14). Instead, the state effort to prevent the imminent collapse of the economy consisted of unlimited issuing of fiat money, and a titanic fiscal intervention, which — incredibly — directly substituted for missing wages and earnings. In other words, to avert collapse, the neoliberal state undertook measures that are of markedly Keynesian provenance. There has been a hiatus from fiscal discipline and from the quest to subdue inflation, the two key neoliberal levers that discipline — and define — economic policy. The state's relaxed approach to rising inflation emanates from its anticipation that the economy will not heat up, as investment is set to remain anaemic, productivity flatlined and wages and labour costs repressed. Efforts, in the EU and the UK, to bring public debt at the forefront of the agenda seem dogmatic and willed, as not even financial markets are preoccupied by it. They rhyme, however, with the IMF's staged approach, the long view of which leads back to debt reduction. In short, the two key neoliberal economic tropes — repressed inflation and restricted debt — lost their absolute validity, making unclear what, if anything, currently guides economic policy.

The confusion is palpable amongst economists in the leading directorates of capitalist integration. There, neoliberal orthodoxy is said to have reached its limits, especially as interests rates have stuck, for almost 20 years, close to zero, and therefore the margins for lowering them have vanished; and debt remains persistently high, making raising interest rates impossible. Thus, the only neoliberal macroeconomic method of action is neutralised. Moreover, in the context of the 2008 financial crisis and the long recovery from it, neoliberal theory could not make sense of persistently low inflation *combined with* underemployment. This epistemic aporia leads to strategic paralysis (The Economist 2020l: 13–14).

To overcome the limits of neoliberal orthodoxy, economists are engaging in a creative programmatic cacophony. A school of thought, based in the IMF, thinks that the problem with inflation is that it is *too low*, and, in quasi-Keynesian terms, exhorts the state to use its budget as fiscal lever to enhance growth. Another school, containing many central bankers, calls for reduced taxation *and* increased public spending that would be financed by high borrowing and deficits over the long term (The Economist 2020l: 14–15). Both these approaches converge on the need for high state expenditure; they defer on how it is going to be paid for: through taxation or borrowing. The former bears the hallmarks of a Keynesian approach; the latter seeks to increase the dependency of the state on the financial sector (Streeck 2014). Finally, beyond dominant institutions, some economists highlight inequality as the root-cause of economic weakness and instability. Noting that fiscal stimuli are, as such, more likely to increase than ameliorate inequality, they propose a strengthening of the position of labour through employment law, the nourishment of unions and collective bargaining, and the strengthening of the safety net for the unemployed (The Economist 2020l: 15–16).

Signalling defeatism in the capitalist camp, at the start of the pandemic (and somewhat prematurely), key economic actors, including the founder-director of the World Economic Forum, saw "radical reforms" and a "period of massive redistribution from the rich to the poor and from capital to labour" as *fait accompli* (Schwab and Malleret 2020: 78, 83).

The role of the state in the "free economy" is reassessed, departing from neoliberal dogma. The abhorrence towards protectionism and a bounded national economy has subsided. State intervention in the economy is, for the first time, discovered to not weaken the free market, but to preserve it (The Economist 2020c: 22; The Economist 2020d: 56). Central banks are now the "marketmaker[s] of last resort". During the lockdown in spring 2020, the Federal Reserve's intervention was estimated at $23.5 trillion, the largest in its history. There is no sense that this is an emergency modality. Such interventions are perpetual since 2008, they have established customary protocols to intervene in a "bewildering array" of financial markets through a wide range of instruments (The Economist 2020m: 57–59). Overall, it is predicted that we are heading for a bigger, more intervening state, with more economic powers, responsibilities and "the taxes to pay for them". This is a *welcomed* development. For, only governments "can coerce and mobilise vast resources rapidly" and thus "only they" can offset economic collapse (The Economist 2020b: 9). This, then, is the new role of the state: to constantly rescue an economy in recurring crisis.

...and welcome back

Thus, neoliberal orthodoxy was jettisoned in order to rescue capitalist accumulation, and the rescue effort consisted of counter-cyclical interventions. Such a derailment, however, is not beyond the pale for neoliberal political economy: as leading neoliberal economist Robert Lucas announced, "in a foxhole, we are all Keynesians" (in Elliott 2021). Yet, this "novel notion" that the state has to preserve firms, jobs and workers' income at any cost entails "a danger": it may become entrenched. Ironically, the more successful the rescue effort, the more pronounced this danger becomes (The Economist 2020c: 24). Capital is keen to jettison the strategy that brought it unprecedented wealth and power, but strictly when it faces a "foxhole" moment. Indeed, recalling the strategic ordinances of the IMF, deviation from neoliberalism must only be temporary and employed in order to reinstate neoliberal macroeconomics, not overcome it. Thus, any detection of a radical shift in economic policy should be guarded: the employment of counter-cyclical tactics is aimed to preserve the neoliberal economic order. The problem here is that crisis, and the emergency economics it entails, has become a perennial feature of neoliberal accumulation. Crisis recurs perpetually and, importantly, this is acknowledged by key economic actors, from capitalists to central bankers. The upshot is that we are heading for *a dual macroeconomic constitution*, one which provides for regularly occurring emergencies and their management beyond and against neoliberal orthodoxy, and the reinstatement of the latter in periods of economic recovery and normality.

Crucially, however, it is not certain that the counter-cyclical policies employed to combat the crisis really diverge from the core of neoliberal strategy — which consists of conceptualising labour as a cost of production, a cost that must be minimised. The return of public expenditure is set to benefit capital, rather than labour.

The nature of "big" state expenditure is evident in the public health sector, which, due to its volume and its political sensitivity, is the most important element of the welfare state. *Prima facie*, the UK seems to be staging an emphatic return to welfare policy: the funding for the health service is set to rise considerably in the next few years, so that by 2025 it will be, approximately, 17 percent larger than it was in 2019 (HM Treasury 2021b: 40). However, this expenditure is only a fraction of what is deemed necessary (The Lancet Commissions 2021); and very little of it will be received by its personnel. NHS workers will be receiving a significant real wage cut; and planned recruitment is anaemic (Campbell 2021b). Instead, additional expenditure, dedicated as it is on buildings, diagnostics and IT, will be appropriated by private capital. This points to an increase of the ten percent share of the Health budget currently appropriated by private companies; and its expansion: from logistics, surgery and diagnostics' services, NHS commodification will now envelop patient's data (Campbell 2021a; Garside and Neate 2020; Hyde 2021). Finally, legislation currently under consideration in parliament will model the NHS on the US system (Pollock and Roderick 2021) — which is the most expensive for the public purse, the most restrictive in terms of access, and the most profitable for private companies. This is precisely the neoliberal strategy for health. It demands a sustained and ever-increasing, public expenditure to support for-profit private involvement, the profitability of which is guaranteed by state subsidies. The aim is that the state would fund public health systems but not offer relevant services (Waitzkin 2016: 90–91, 114–115). Thus, what appears as (increased) welfare expenditure, transpires to be a lever for private appropriation of public funds.

The boldest drive towards public expenditure — and boldest attempt to break with neoliberal policy — comes from the US. The Biden administration plans to dedicate $3 trillion dollars to projects of a distinctly Keynesian flavour: infrastructure construction and development, combined with strengthening of the position and bargaining power of labour. Yet, while impressive in headline numbers, these spending plans are not as potent as they first seem. They have already been curtailed by Congress, are set to be distributed over an 8–10 year period, and will be shared across "projects" covering anything from roads to childcare (Garrison and King 2021; Tooze 2021: 299–300; The Economist, 2021c: 44). Moreover, half these funds are directed to infrastructure — they are essentially a new round of handouts to private enterprise; and their labour-strengthening aspects have been watered down by Congress. In short, while a return to the status quo ante of economic relations and practices seems impossible, any new arrangements are to be brought about by the actors and trends that dominated economic relations pre-pandemic (Boyer 2021: 70). Thus, a paradigm shift cannot acquire escape velocity.

Instead of using welfare and public investment budgets as a lever, a more direct way to aid capital is the crisis *as such*. Capital's greatest achievement during the financial crisis was to have its profitability guaranteed by the state. The war cry "we will do whatever it takes", first uttered by the European Central Bank during the 2012 euro crisis, was repeated by finance ministers and central bankers throughout the biosecurity crisis. By May 2020, Congress had already fleshed out this resolve, in the shape of $3 trillion dedicated to supporting US corporations, especially the largest ones, through schemes involving loan guarantees and direct acquisition of assets; the UK Treasury spent over £320 billion in similar schemes; and both these sums were dwarfed by the quantitative easing efforts of central banks (Brenner 2020: 13–15; Boyer 2021: 101; HM Treasury 2020b: 14). These mass subsidies to capital are unconditional. The state does not require recipient companies to maintain their workforce, enhance their environmental credentials, or reinvest a part of the funds; nor does it prohibit them from spending the subsidies in directors' bonuses or shares' buy-backs (Brenner 2020: 14). Ergo, much of the relief money was spent in the spectacular economy of the stock exchange: while the economy was still suspended, share prices reached record heights (Quiggin 2020: 42). In a nutshell: the state — governments and central banks — signal to the corporate world that they will always be bailed out of trouble, and enriched in the process. This points to a fundamental transformation of capitalism: the political power of capital removes the risk once associated with entrepreneurship and saddles society with it (Blakeley 2020: xiv).

Using welfare institutions to siphon public funds to private hands, and offering unconditional support to capital are mainstays of the neoliberal repertoire. What was truly novel during this crisis were the job retention schemes advanced across Europe. Still, in paying the wages of idled workers, these schemes subsidise their employers: the state covers their wage costs. Through increased taxation, repressed wages, and a declining social wage (Chapters 10, 12), these wages will be eventually repaid by the workers. Further, the EU, despite breaching its dogma against collateralising debt, continues to demand deregulation of working relations and suppression of wages and the living wage. It demands, in other words, a deepening of the workfarist character of the economy (Boyer 2021: 215–218). Its member states oblige. During the pandemic, France expanded, for the first time in its history, the working week; and Greece expanded the working day to 10 hours and dismantled labour law leaving all relations to be determined by individual contract (Papanikolopoulos and Katsoridas 2021). Similarly, the UK entrenched employers' right to fire and rehire workers as they please (Partington and Topping 2021; Walker 2021a). In short, this "countercyclical" policy seems rather peculiar: unlike its Keynesian variants, it tends to redistribute power and wealth upwards.

Finally, the intensification of workfare is backed by an authoritarian hardening of the state. Western states advance nationalist discourses, rule by decree, and restrict civil liberties to vanishing point (Global Labour Journal Editorial Board 2020: 80). The UK is set to pass legislation that makes public protest subject to Home Office approval, effectively cancelling this right; Greece has already done so (Papanikolopoulos and Katsoridas 2021). In France, police violence against protestors has intensified to a degree unsuited to the status of a citizen of a republic (Chrisafis 2019). While brutal police violence has been a tradition in the US, there we also see the systematic cultivation of *faci*; the move seems to be replicated in the UK (chapter 19). This authoritarian hardening is the most unequivocal indication regarding the nature of economic policy. A state aiming to bring new social arrangements guided by social justice and marked by downward redistribution of wealth and power would expect to enjoy popular support. It would, therefore, not rush to authoritarian practices. A neoliberal state aiming to intensify exploitation, inequality and injustice, *would* — especially if it anticipates that its plans could cross the limit of social tolerance.

Thus, next to the committed, virtually institutionalised, limitless support of the state to capital, stands the full repertoire of workfarism: suppressed wages, declining and privatised public services, deregulation of working relations, expanded and intensified exploitation, and an arsenal of state violence. What is emerging is a dual political economy. Its duality consists of an alternation between crisis and recovery modes; and of a differential treatment that profoundly marks the entire social order: welfare for capital, workfare for everyone else.

Prospects — and their dangers

It is too soon to conclude the discussion of economic policy with any certainty — the crisis has not played out long enough, neither in its economic aspects nor its, slower burning, political ones. Early signs point to a resumption and intensification of neoliberal policy flanked by force. The adoption of counter-cyclical measures is intended to be limited to moments of "exception", employed in response to acute crisis of the neoliberal economy. It resembles what Carl Schmitt (2014) would call a "commissarial dictatorship": a temporary suspension of the (neoliberal economic) *norm* in order to save the (neoliberal economic) *order*. Crucially, the effects of countercyclical measures are not countercyclical at all; they enhance the trends of the "normal" neoliberal economy: concentration of capital, upward distribution of wealth, suppression of labour costs. Rather than a return to Keynesianism, what emerges from the crisis is a *dual economy* — dual both in terms of its modulation (normality vs emergency) but, more importantly, in terms of its social effect: welfare for large, dominant capital; workfare for everyone who has to work in order to live.

This dual economy outlines a transformation of capitalism, which was already underway long before the crisis and is galvanised by it. *Capitalist despotism* denotes the form of capitalism marked by vast capital concentration and consolidation under the aegis of high finance. In this form, capital depends on the state, which it fully controls, to continue its accumulation, which is based on extraction rather than production and is therefore socially parasitic and static, rather than dynamic and productive (Boukalas 2021).

These economic prospects contain three dangers. The first is that of a new financial crisis similar to the 2008 one. States never sought to reverse, or even ameliorate, the core condition that generated the 2008 financial crisis, i.e. deprivation leading to anaemic demand which, in turn, had to be stimulated by an abundance of credit and debt (Boukalas 2021). In 2019, private — household and corporate — debt had reached a peak after climbing for two decades. It was calculated to almost 150 percent of global GDP. Corporate speculative grade debt, a key indicator of corporate distress, was approximately 50 percent of the total corporate debt in four leading economies: China, Italy, UK and US. Piling up on this alarming situation, the first year of the pandemic saw an unprecedented round of corporate borrowing. As a result, corporate liquidity pressures and solvency risks have emerged, risks that are disproportionately more severe for small and medium size businesses (IMF 2020b: 23; 2020c: 31). In the face of underlying conditions much worse than those on the eve of the financial crisis, EU and US regulators *relaxed* the macro-prudential requirements imposed in its wake, lifting the requirements for banks to hold buffer capital as insurance against financial turmoil (IMF 2020c: 5). At the same time, the UK is blowing a new housing bubble (Ryan-Collins 2021; The Observer 2021). Under these conditions, a financial crash of considerable magnitude is better described as impeding rather than merely possible, and prolonged stagflation becomes a likely prospect (Roubini 2021).

The second danger is more remote, but also more grave. It is that the people may have enjoyed the emergency economic policy employed during the pandemic. It is understandable that people would like the idea of having the bulk of their income guaranteed when they cannot work, and to get breaks from tax and rent when they cannot pay them. People may, in other words, take the false signs of a Keynesian realignment seriously and demand its realisation. Notably, public perceptions regarding downward redistribution policies have favourably changed during the pandemic (IMF 2021b: 41). National states and transnational directorates would find it hard to resist such demands through argument and reason — for it is them that instigated relevant policies, and the latter proved effective. However, with the labour movement incapacitated, there are no social forces to promote such demands. A return to the folder of a national economy could strengthen the power of labour, but the state has already undercut its ability to struggle. Without social forces to animate them, an articulation of such demands is left to enlightened economists, and its promulgation would be made by the state — and, hence, on capital's terms. A more certain legacy of the biosecurity crisis lies in the realm of perception. After 40 years of unquestioned rule, the *There Is No Alternative* dogma exploded within a week. The response to the economic crisis created a fissure in the creed of the strict separation between politics and the economy. It revealed the political character of the economy, making it hard for governments to convincingly relapse to the ideological tropes of an economy governed by natural laws that admits no interference to its functions (Blakeley 2020: 75–76). The crisis has brought to consciousness that the economy is *political*. It can, and sometimes must, change.

The third danger is abstract, but existential. It arises when change fails to come. Capitalism is, by its constitution, a dynamic system — the most dynamic system humanity has known (Marx and Engels 2015). It constantly changes society and its material world — and, by doing so, it itself constantly changes. *Static* ("despotic") and *capitalism* are contradictory terms. Their cohabitation in a single regime can only be transitional. Soon one, capitalism or despotism, will be eclipsed — or both.

Part III

THE STATE TO COME

> It's about a guy who falls off a skyscraper.
> On his way down, past each floor, he keeps telling himself:
> *so far so good*
> *so far so good*
> *so far so good.*
> But it's not how you fall that matters; it's how you land.
>
> Mathieu Kassovitz (1995)

The analysis of the state's engagement with the biosecurity and the economic crisis informs the outline of the state-form that emerges from the twin crises in the chapters that follow.

The term *state-form* denotes the socio-historically specific articulation between the logic, strategy, institutionality and power of the state, as well as the ways the state relates to society. The *socially and historically specific* character of the state-form is crucial for an analysis of the state that wants to avoid being abstract to the point of absurdity (Chapter 1). By addressing the state in its socio-historical specificity, the notion of the state-form enables a less abstract, and more fruitful, analysis of *specific* states in specific periods. Thus, the analysis can expand from a single state to address all states that share the same form — in our case North Atlantic neoliberal states. By this token, state-form analysis invites comparisons (and comparative studies), first between different states of the same form; and, second, between states of different forms.

To capture the emerging state-form, the remaining chapters address the key features of the state that can be deciphered from the pandemic experience. First, Chapter 15 addresses the "logic" of the state. "Logic" is a structural element of the state; it refers to the deeply set ontological premises about the social world and the state's role in it. The chapter notes the biopolitical character of biosecurity, including its conception of the body; highlights the capitalist character of biopolitics; and suggests that the latter is overcome by *threat governmentality* — a novel state logic that is a continuation of biopolitics by

DOI: 10.4324/9781003302988-17

means of its reversal. Next, Chapter 16 addresses the modality of state power; and Chapter 17 discusses the relation of the state to law. In doing so, it continues the assessment of the modality of state power, addresses the institutionality of the state, and opens the account of the state's relation to society. State-society relations are further discussed in Chapter 18 that focuses on the relation of responsibility between the state and society. Chapter 19 draws from all proceeding analysis to complete the outline of the state-form. It completes the account of state power, institutionality and state-society relations, and deciphers the key structural and strategic contours of the state — and their (mis)alignment. Chapter 20, deciphers some potential dangers that social resistance represents for the emerging state-form. The postscript — Chapter 21 — draws a peculiar insight into our contemporary state by comparing its crisis-response to that of the Athenian democracy.

The following chapters try to outline a state-form that has yet to crystallise. Indeed, the twin crises have not yet fully played out — a lot less has the state that emerges from them congealed. More than contingent, the state-form outlined here is *molten*. This is an account of a state that does not (yet) exist. The chapters that follow draw from the pandemic experience to capture its more pronounced features, its deepest trends and their articulation. They attempt to outline *the state to come.*

15 Biopolitics and threat governmentality

Biosecurity is biopolitical. *Biopolitics* refers to a logic of government oriented towards life, aiming to enhance the potential of life's innate faculties — to "increase, protect and regulate life" (Muhle 2014: 79). Biopolitical power is "the set of mechanisms through which the basic biological features of the human species became the object of a political strategy, of a general strategy of power" (Foucault 2007: 1). The object of this power is the welfare of the governed, their health, wealth and longevity. Thus, biopolitics signals the inscription of life — its qualities, expressions and duration — into relations of political power (Esposito 2008: 28, 36).

Concerned with life faculties, this biopower is centred on the human body. Yet, it sees the body not as an enclosed anatomic mechanism, but as specimen of a genre, of a species. The body is an open entity, impacted by its environment and influential to it. This means that biopolitics is primarily concerned not with any individual body, but with their interrelations: their aggregation into a *population*, a living body composed of living bodies (Adorno 2014: 98). Biopolitics makes the population the object of political power and aims to enhance it, to "improve the condition of the population, to increase its wealth, its longevity and its health" (Foucault 2007: 105). Thus, the life that concerns biopolitics is *relational* (Boukalas 2012: 289–290); it is the totality of social relations.

Biopolitics operates through a compound of state mechanisms and techniques that organise the circulation of the population — of "men and things" — within a physical, juridical and political infrastructure, while "eliminating its dangerous elements" (Foucault 2007: 17–21, 325). In short, biopolitical power operates as *security*. It operates on exchange and circulation (of people, products, money, diseases), attempting to selectively facilitate or cancel certain potentials inherent in them (Foucault 2007: 18, 20–21, 319–326; 335–339; 351–354).

Life is not only the object of biopolitical power; it is also its *method*. Biopolitics governs not by antagonising life processes, but by imitating, anticipating and manipulating them (Muhle 2014: 87–93). In contrast to absolutist *raison d'etat*, whose purpose is to shape a violent and anarchic "state of nature" into a pacified hierarchical social order (Hobbes 2008), biopolitics

DOI: 10.4324/9781003302988-18

finds order *in* nature: in its innate laws and processes. Accordingly, it seeks to discover the immanent regularities of the population and its behaviours. Government then consists in optimising, encouraging and enhancing some, while correcting, disciplining or excluding others (Opitz 2012: 98).

To govern life according to its natural propensities and potentialities, biopolitics needs a thorough knowledge thereof. Accordingly, it employs a formidable arsenal of knowledge-extraction and organisation in surveillance, statistics, biology, sociology, epidemiology and demographics (Lemke 2012: 173–177; Opitz 2012: 98). Indeed, the population is nothing but the total of relevant knowledges, it is a construct of biopolitical science. To enable government in accord with life, biopolitical knowledge needs to envelop its aspects, from the most intimate and trivial to their aggregations into general "laws", and to be constantly updated (Boukalas 2012: 290; Foucault 2007: 349–350). It needs to identify patterns, regularities, norms, tendencies, proclivities, mutations, contingencies and anomalies as they emerge in dynamic interaction. In short, bio-power is surveillant and analytical, and *totally* so: its horizon encompasses the entirety of the population's condition and prospects.

Biopolitics governs life, through life — but not *for* life. Its purpose is the *economy*. Its object, the population, is seen as "essentially and fundamentally a productive force...on condition, of course, that it is effectively trained, divided up, distributed and fixed by disciplinary mechanisms" (Foucault 2007: 69). Its objective is to nurture those natural faculties of the population that make it productive, while restricting and erasing those that do not. Biopower seeks to shape the population's nature in order to improve its usefulness for the economy (Lemke 2012: 170; Opitz 2012: 98). In essence, *biopolitics is the management of labour power*, of the innate human faculty to *create*, harnessed for the benefit of the economy (Virno 2015: 159, 166).

Thus, the "final end" of biopolitics is the economy. Politics, however, cannot reach that end. The economy is seen as a natural entity, governed by innate laws that do not allow for political interference. Biopolitics is, then, a self-limiting form of government. It is founded on a drastic separation between political power and its referent object: it governs *for* the economy, but cannot govern *the* economy (Foucault 2008: 8–10, 22). Instead, it intervenes on the population, and shapes it to benefit the economy. While the population is the object of biopolitics, the economy is its *reason* and the source of its legitimacy (Boukalas 2012: 290; Foucault 2007: 349–354; Foucault 2008: 30–32, 84; Opitz 2012: 98). And, the set of knowledges — of the economy and the population — that inform biopolitical government is called *political economy*.

The separation of politics from the economy; the elevation of the latter to "final end" of politics; its seclusion from political intervention; the urge to govern in line with nature; the knowledge of the latter by means of political economy...biopolitics is a *liberal* governmentality (Foucault 2008: 78).

Biopolitical pandemic

Biosecurity testifies to the biopolitical character of state power. Its confessed objective is to “save lives”. It is concerned with the life properties of the virus; those of the human body; those of the population; and, above all, with the interaction between them. It intervenes on its object not by trying to negate its properties, but by adjusting, manipulating and anticipating them, so that some of its relational potentialities are encouraged while others are prevented from actualising; and by anticipating and preparing for the possible actualisation of unwanted potentialities.

This management of life’s potentialities is premised on knowledge: ever-advancing knowledge of the life-properties of the virus; of its interaction with the human body; and of the conduct of the latter, individually and within mega-body of the population. Biosecurity gathers this knowledge by monitoring life in all its expressions, from the singular/molecular to the general/aggregate, through viral testing, mass surveillance of behaviour, and their analytical digestion into patterns.

In every epidemic the danger lies in contagion, in the relations and admixtures of the three types of life: the virus, the body and the population. Accordingly, the heavy artillery of biosecurity concentrates on the management of the relations between the three. Here, at one end of the spectrum, “herd immunity” represents the true (if dogmatic) liberal biopolitical stance: every man for himself and devil take the hindmost. It is a *laissez faire* approach, aiming to let nature take its course unhindered, by allowing unlimited interplay between the three life-forms. At the other end of the biosecurity spectrum, quarantine constitutes a drastic separation of the virus from the body, and of the body from the population. In both approaches — and in all intermediate ones — security is focused on the proximity and contact among the individual bodies that comprise the population and are, *per se*, suspect virus-bearers. Biosecurity is concerned with, intervenes on and recasts the circulation “of men and things”, of people and viruses. Vaccination too is exemplary of biopower. It does not try to prevent or negate the disease, the contact between virus and human life; it imitates it. It aims to secure the health of the population by provoking the disease on individual bodies, albeit in a weakened, and therefore controlled and safe, state (Foucault 2007: 59; Muhle 2014: 89).

These practices — vaccination, quarantine, herd immunity — make evident that biosecurity aims to protect life by governing (through) life: by selectively enhancing and hindering its potentialities through imitation, anticipation and manipulation; in one word, through *control.* Notably, vaccination, herd immunity and lockdown, are interventions in the social environment aiming to reshape it so that the disease cannot grow in it. Biosecurity, then is biopolitical; and biopolitics is a modality of power that is typically *pre-emptive.*

Thus far, biosecurity appears to be a textbook case of biopolitics without adding to or altering it in any significant way. True, some key types of intervention (e.g. the manic issuing of regulations; the sequestering of quarantined bodies in space and time) are closer to disciplinary power than to biopolitics (Foucault 1995: 195–228; Foucault 2007: 340). But — leaving aside that no modality of power is ever true to its pure type — these disciplinary practices are employed in and by an effort that is in conception, logic, concern and method, biopolitical. But this is not all. Biosecurity poses an obvious — and fundamental — problem for biopolitics.

In the pandemic, "life" and "livelihood" remained interdependent *and* became incompatible with one another. Thus, the pandemic caused a scission between biopolitical means and ends, between life and the economy, and even set them against each other. This scission is the heart of our biosecurity experience — and recasts the textbook account of its biopolitics. Starting with the knowledge that biosecurity extracts and utilises, it is notable that most of it is knowledge of conduct directly related to the economy: trends in public transport use or online consumption, for instance. This knowledge is overlaid on, and combined with, the knowledge more typical to political economy: the rate of unemployment, of private and public debt, GDP, etc. This "bio-economic" knowledge informs, and strives to address, the grand calculous that defines the biosecurity effort: the determination of the affordable loss of life *versus* the acceptable cost to the economy. The overall concern of the state is to optimise these two volumes — economic cost; loss of life — and, more importantly, their ratio. Based on knowledge of both the epidemic and the economic situation and trends, including its own anticipated effects on them, the state sets out a calculous of the risk to life that can be acceptable at every juncture so that the damage to the economy is limited — or reversely, of the acceptable damage to the economy so that risk to life is restricted. This grand calculous can be boiled down to "how many healthy people does it take to make an economy run?" (McQuade and Neocleous 2020: 3). Across this calculous, different classes of life are assigned to different degrees of optimal and acceptable risk. A different calculous then operates. It concerns what lives must be saved, what lives are worth saving, and what lives can be risked, endangered or sacrificed. This calculous is overdetermined by the broader — life vs economy — one. Some lives can be endangered or sacrificed in order to save other lives, but also in order to protect the economy, to maintain the "circulation of men and things". Also: the classification of life, from unriskable to disposable, is based mostly on a determination of each life's value to the economy (Chapter 6). At the end, life is requested to take "personal responsibility" for itself. Indicating an entropic tendency of biopolitics, life is left to fend for itself, to face its dangers by its own means.

The body of biosecurity

Biosecurity, in both its (defining) biopolitical and (auxiliary) disciplinarian aspects, comes to apply on the human body. The body is the object that biosecurity sets out to protect. But, the body is — equally and simultaneously — the habitat, vessel and vehicle of the virus; it is the threat incarnate. Thus, it is the cardinal locus of the biosecurity struggle. It becomes the laboratory on which treatments and vaccines are tested and applied, the terrain of combat between the disease and the cure. The body is treated with concern: care and suspicion in equal measure.

At a first remote, biosecurity sees the body as an enclosed, integral unit of life. It is constitutionally vulnerable — and hence in need of security (Gros 2019: 135). Its vital integrity is paramount, to be maintained by all means. Hence, even the hardest quarantine rules contain *force majeure* escape clauses, allowing the individual to break restrictions when her bodily integrity is under threat: by fire, earthquake or (depressingly often) an abusive partner.

At a second remote, the body is seen as a metabolism. To maintain its vital integrity, it needs water, food, air and medicines. Hence, under lockdown supermarkets and pharmacies remain open and people are allowed to visit them, and exercise in open air is also permitted. While its metabolic function relates the body to its environment, it does so in a very specific sense. Acknowledging the body's metabolic needs and functions is at the same time the reduction of the body to (its) metabolism. The opening to the environment does not acknowledge any need, or faculty, for sociability: for contact with other bodies, for play, mourning, celebrating or protesting. Indeed, social contact is precisely where the threat — the threat to the body as vital integrity — lies. Biosecurity reduces the body to metabolism. It does not attach to it any social, sentimental, sensual, moral or political value. It conceptualises such attributes as conditional to vital integrity at best; as enemies to it at worst.

The metabolic body causes over-consumption of spaghetti and toilet paper. It is a body certain that it can do nothing to affect its fate: it cannot influence the conditions of its life and environment. It clings to its metabolism precisely because it is the only thing it can, to some extent, influence, within a universe that is firmly beyond its agency. The metabolic body is an entity of life. But life is what happens through and *to* it — it can only preserve and endure it. The reduction of the body to metabolism is its reduction to (animate) matter. This body is not a person, let alone a citizen, an entity defined by its capability for initiative, desire, will or creativity. It is a biological unit: capable of, depended on, and determined by specific biological functions. Ζόων.

The denial of the body's social faculties is not complete. There is one social function the body must continue to perform: it must work. It should continue to actualise its labour power within the given framework of socio-economic arrangements, relations and conditions. It must, in short, continue to work for the economy: on someone else's terms, for someone else's profit, within an overall arrangement it cannot influence. When forced to stop working, it must strive to maintain its capacity to work, its labour power, intact. It needs to do so — to work and maintain its labour power — even when ill. For, if it stops, it has no means to maintain its metabolism and its vital integrity. Work is therefore an integral part of the body's metabolic functions: it is their precondition. If the conception of the body as metabolism and as vital integrity did not already outline the political character of biosecurity, its conceptualisation as labour-force does. The body is a unit in, and for, a capitalist social arrangement. Labour in exchange for metabolism. Ζόων εργατικόν: a beast of burden.

Finally, the body provides a unique signature, captured by biometric techniques and allowing the identification of activities in their spatio-temporal matrix. Biosecurity thus reduces the human subject to a transmitter of information (Gros 2019: 136–137; Samerski 2018; Situations Collective 2020: 18). More than relating the body to its social environment, it treats the body as a datum in this environment, an environment composed of data. The body's only acknowledged social function, labour, is thoroughly monitored and measured: from the molecular level of individual productivity, to the mega aggregate of the (national, regional or global) Gross Domestic Product. The body, as the bearer of biosecurity attributes — i.e. as object and subject of threat; as vital integrity; as metabolism; as labour-force — is the object of constant manipulation and observation: the target of behaviourism and surveillance. It is, essentially, of interest not as such, but as an abstraction: an atom in demographic aggregates and their trends and dynamics.

Asserting the insignificance of the body as a specificity, *its face is erased.* The protective mask de-faces the body — but protects it and protects the other bodies from it. The defacement is therefore obligatory in the space of interaction among abstracted bodies. Each is insignificant in itself; they are abstracted conduits and objects of threat. Thus, the body loses its specificity and its materiality; it is disembodied. It evaporates into a cloud of data that represent the movement of a threat. The inscription of the evaporated body into a network of interactions makes it fully determinable. Its interactions are predetermined, observable and controlled. As data, the body can be modelled, forecast and adjusted through surveillance and intervention. Above all, it can — and is — commodified: the datalised disembodied body is the new commodity and the new horizon for capitalist accumulation (Zuboff 2019).

At every count, biosecurity reduces life to matter: determined, measurable, predictable and, hence, exploitable and marketable. What it denies is life as force: as eruption, initiative, feeling, indeterminacy and change. It denies life's capacity to overcome determinations and to define its environment rather than simply populate it. In modernity, the understanding of life is defined by the dynamic tension between two conceptual poles, one of which sees life as *organic matter* set in a state of equilibrium with its environment and fixated with its self-preservation and growth through reactive assimilation, adaptation and resilience. The other sees life as a *creative faculty*, a normative force that deviates from existing norms and establishes new ones, a transgressive force in dynamic relations with its environment, a force defined by its capacity to create everything including itself (Muhle 2014: 84–86). In biosecurity the second conceptual pole is erased, making life univocally understood and treated as passive matter. The unpredictable, creative force that makes history stems from sociability and is now erased with it.

The reduction of life from constitutive agency to constituted matter is the conception at the heart of biopolitics. Indeed, the lexicon of the "body" (rather than subject, citizen, person, etc) as the social and material unit; of the "population" (rather than people, society, etc) as the aggregate field of interaction; and of "identity" and "subjectivity" (rather than psyche, self, ego, personality) as the mode of insertion of the former into the latter, is a biopolitical lexicon: it is how biopolitics sees and organises the world it governs. Bodies, identities and populations are abstracted, atomised, passive and determined. They are the objects — never the subjects — of political power. Thus, curiously absent from modern epi*demics* and pan*demics* is the *demos*.

Biopolitics, capitalism, thanatopolitics

Biosecurity turns the human body into a beast of burden, a labouring metabolism, reducing its innate creative faculty into productivity. Further, it abstracts the body into a vapour of relational and behavioural data, which it commodifies. In both counts — as labour force and as generator of data, the body is a source of capital accumulation. Life becomes capital. Further, biosecurity turned the planet into a laboratory for biotechnology. The latter produces vaccines that manipulate life in order to secure life; and turns the human lives it can save into a source of capitalisation and profit. These mutations of life offer a new insight into biopolitics: it is capitalist. We saw that biopolitics is a modality of power striving to make society — the "population" — capable of serving the economy. We saw that it ultimately amounts to a management of labour power, of the innate human faculty to create. We must now add: *the motivating spirit and purpose of biopolitics is the accumulation of capital.*

Biopolitics is a liberal governmentality; liberalism is the ideology of the capitalist class. It is a malleable one, for it reflects the interests of capital at every given circumstance. It can endorse democracy, empire or dictatorship as long as they guarantee the unfettered operation of capital — the "free market" — and the subjugation of society to it (Bonefeld 2017a; Cristi 1998). Yet, even when the class jettisons liberalism in favour of non-liberal regimes, from corporatism to fascism; and even when there is no capitalist class to speak of but bureaucrats and mandarins (Prozorov 2016), biopolitics persists because so does capital accumulation. Biopolitics overall effort, i.e. the "strengthening" of the population-as-labour force, is at the same time the inscription of this power to capitalist relations of exploitation. Biopolitics ensues from the violent disruption of pre-capitalist conditions of life: it is the management of the newly dispossessed and urbanised masses of people, proletarianised by the private appropriation of their common property by capitalists (McQuade and Neocleous 2020: 3–4). It is concerned with forging this mass of people into a productive labour force, and hence centres on their conditions of existence and reproduction: health, hygiene (of the physical and the moral kind), housing, movement, alimentation, their *living* wage. In other words, the "birth of biopolitics" is the corollary of the "primitive accumulation" that kick starts capital accumulation — the two are necessarily coupled (Nigro 2014). As "primitive accumulation" is not a singular event, but a re-occurring phase of capital accumulation (Harvey 2003: 142–154), accumulation and biopolitics are not twined only at birth, but perpetually. Crucially, the biopolitical imaginary of life's enhancement, optimisation and growth is identical to the imaginary of the ever-growing and expanding capital. They are identical because they are one.

As a great industrialist exclaimed when popular rebellion in Italy threatened the continuation of capitalist accumulation: "today, the problem is not the improvement of living conditions in the factory, but the continuation of the life of the factory" (Guido Carli 1974 in Agnoli 2020: 149). "Life *in*" the factory is of concern only inasmuch as it affects the "life *of*" the factory, with all the social relations that the factory signifies and encapsulates. This is "the problem" today too. The life *of* the factory — the life of capitalism — is not a consideration that only arises in crisis situations; it is always the ultimate concern of biopolitics.

In short, biopolitics manages life strictly in order to make it amenable to capitalist accumulation: to produce individual life as "human capital", and collective life — the "population" — as labour force. It is concerned with life's capacity to produce for capital, and to reproduce itself for it.

As life is absorbed by the circuits of accumulation, it becomes a particular form of capital: labour force. As capital, it acquires a measurable value. Its value varies according to its — actual or potential — usefulness for capital and its amenability to exploitation by it. As neoliberal accumulation regimes usher prolonged stagnation of productivity and growth, biopolitics is altered. The developmental urge that marked biopolitics in classical liberalism vanishes, and all that remains is a stringent adherence to human-economic accounting. Whether a life is worth living or not is determined by a cost-benefit calculous between its continuation and its dissolution (Bröckling 2012: 256).

The "stringent adherence to human-economic accounting" is operative in biosecurity. Indeed, the calculous of the cost and benefit of continuing life over the cost/benefit of ending life has determined the response to the pandemic. Capital-life of lower value could — and was — risked in order to enhance the prospects of capital-life of higher value to survive. "Lower-skilled" workers (of blue and white collars, in public and private sectors), i.e. lives that bear lower capital input and therefore represent smaller investment and produce lower output, were made to work throughout the pandemic and face its dangers unprotected. This was necessary in order to help "high-skilled" workers — lives who embody larger investment, are harder to replace and tend to produce higher returns — and above all their bosses, to emerge from the pandemic unscathed. Simply put, biosecurity sacrifices the life *in* the factory in order to secure the life *of* the factory.

The life-value accounting that informs biosecurity reached its apogee in care homes, often sealing the fate of their residents and workers. Care homes were the setting hardest hit in terms of death toll. State policy turned them into a death trap, even if the danger to them was obvious and easy to alleviate. Instead, they were sabotaged by being forced to admit untested patients expediently rejected from hospitals. The protection they were given was so incomplete and late in arriving, that its offering can be seen as reluctant. Their residents were effectively made right-less; and the ban on inspections and visits from doctors and relatives turned care homes into death camps, secluded from outside contact (Chapter 5). This is not surprising. Care home residents, whether elderly or disabled, are not economically active. They are not productive — they cannot provide surplus value for someone else — and their consumption is limited and not autonomous. For the capitalist economy they are surplus population. Accordingly, the workers that care for these people who, in capital's logic, should not be there, are the most undermined and devalued workforce (Amnesty International 2020: 13; Harding 2021: 123–125; Hayes 2017). The treatment of care homes exposes biopolitics and biosecurity as unequivocally capitalist. The value of life biopolitics seeks to foster, stimulate, enhance, manage and control; the value of life biosecurity seeks to protect and save, is the market value ascribed to it.

"Under conditions of capitalist exploitation, to be declared healthy means nothing other than to be declared 'fit to work'". The unproductive can be sacrificed. The nursing home-turned-morgue is a material condensation of the orientation of state power towards the needs of capital (McQuade and Neocleous 2020: 8–9). The treatment of care homes is the treatment of life-capital that is spent — of life that does not incorporate capital any longer. It brings to the fore the biopolitical treatment of disposable life, and reveals biopolitics corollary: *thanatopolitics*, the politics of life's negation (Breu 2012). Indeed, the treatment of care homes is foretold in the programmatic texts of neoliberal biopolitics: "The good hunter or defender of the community, the fertile mother and perhaps even the wise old man may be more important than most babies and most of the aged". Pretending to overlook the misogynist idiosyncrasy of this statement, we note that life's value resides in its productive and reproductive capacity. Reconnecting with the utilitarian liberal tradition, neoliberal vitalism openly declares: "The requirement for preserving the maximum number of lives is not that all individual lives are regarded as equally important" (Hayek 1988: 132). Biopolitics connects neoliberalism to the utilitarian liberal tradition. All along it jettisons the liberal demand for (and pretence to) equality. The life/death calculous is one of utility: utility for the "community" i.e. for the "spontaneous order" of the market.

The life that refuses to be inscribed in the economy, that resists its transformation to economic value despite biopolitical efforts to make it such, the life that escapes capitalist valorisation and exploitation, is exterminated: the destruction of rebelling slaves and colonised people; the genocidal war against native American and Australian peoples; the communards; those systematically starved in concentration camps or eugenically prevented from being born to "defective" parents... (Losurdo 2014; 2015) — we may add those left to die in care homes and "death wards" because they no longer embody life-capital. To those that are unable to become exploitable labour power, to those who refuse to do so, to those that in any way stand in the way of capitalist accumulation, biopolitics shows its other face: necropolitics (Mbebe 2003).

Biosecurity is necropolitical. The British Prime Minister displayed acute capitalist logic in declaring lockdowns unacceptable, once he realised that the majority of the pandemic's victims were elderly, non-productive people. He would rather see their "bodies pile up high" than disrupt the economy with another lockdown (BBC 2021; Cummings in House of Commons Science and Technology Committee 2021: q.115, 170). Triaging protocols against the elderly; their abandonment in death wards; the refusals to take them into hospital or send an ambulance for them — all point to the typical liberal-capitalist way of killing: through exclusion from resources, starting with the means of sustenance.

Biopolitics is the capitalist way of government — and the logic of capital animates and defines biosecurity's concern with life. Biosecurity has been an economic operation throughout.

Threat governmentality

Biopolitics is concerned with, and productive of, life. For biosecurity, *life is a threat*. Life bears its own negation. This attitude is not merely a negative configuration of biopolitics into thanatopolitics — it is not simply the politics of life turned upside-down into politics of death. It is a radical mutation of the object of biopolitics: of life, the population, its conduct and relations; in one word, of society. Rather, it is a *radical mutation of biopolitics*, of the way it sees the world and acts on it. Life/society and its potentialities are a threat: biopolitics is no longer in ontological and operative accord with its object; it is in an antagonistic relation to it. For lack of a better term, I propose to call this mutation *threat governmentality* — to denote the shift from a biopolitical management of life to the management of threat (Boukalas 2020).

Biosecurity sees life as a threat to life. Virus-life constitutes a threat to the life of the body; more importantly, the life of the individual body is a threat to the life of the collective body of the population — and *vice versa*. Society then becomes a relation between mutually threatening individuals, which threaten and are threatened by their collective life. The threat is commensurate and coextensive with society; society *is* threat.

The threat is an undeniable and inescapable property of life, social and individual. For biosecurity, people who have tested negative for the virus are not considered less threatening. They may be "false negatives"; or they may have caught the disease since the moment they were tested. As counterterrorism taught us, "the absence of evidence is not evidence of absence" (Rumsfeld 2002). This dogma resonates in biosecurity and its assumption of the threat posed by the apparently innocent: asymptomatic individuals and children (Chapter 3). The absence of threat is inconceivable. Healthy people are equally threatening with those infected. The assumption is that they will catch the disease in the immediate or remote future. This makes them already threatening *now*. And, even when infections finally subside, the emergence of a new variant, and a new virus, is certain. Thus, "scanning the future for risks" is now the main role of the state — for the future is pregnant with catastrophic threats: man-made, natural and extra-terrestrial (The Economist 2020j; 2020k). The threat is, after all, always *in potentia*; it only exists as a futurity (Massumi 2015: 27, 30, 175). But its potentiality, its futurity, acts upon the present and determines it.

Threat governmentality is, then, a modality of power founded on the ontological certainty of the threat: on the certainty that the individual and society not only face, but that they also are — in their potentiality — a threat. Whereas biopolitics sees life as labour power, i.e. as innately endowed with creative potential; threat governmentality sees the individual and society as threat-power, as innately endowed with destructive potential. And, whereas biopolitics seeks to manage life's innate creative potential so that it becomes "productive" i.e. exploitable by capital; threat governmentality tries to deny life's threatening potentiality the conditions of its actualisation. Whereas biopolitics manipulates life's potentiality, threat governmentality aims to erase it.

The aforementioned quote from the "war on terror" Secretary, and its resonance with biosecurity, indicate that threat governmentality predates the pandemic. Indeed, the first ontological conceptualisation of life and society as a threatening potentiality was forged in the context of counterterrorism and defined that endeavour (Boukalas 2019; 2020). Biosecurity, however, made threat governmentality biomatic for virtually every person in every society. While most people can, and are, absolutely certain that (at least) their closest friends and relatives do not pose a terrorist threat to them; no one can afford such certainty regarding the virus; worse, no one can be certain that himself is not a lethal threat to those he loves. Biosecurity has made people know, experience and manage themselves as a threat.

The interchangeability between things as different as terrorism and disease points to another feature of threat governmentality. Its object and foundation, the threat, is amorphous. As such, it can take any form: illness, terrorism, environmental destruction, economic crisis, war...(Boukalas 2014: 51–56, 155; Massumi 2015: 103, 223; Neocleous 2016: 2–4). The threat's shape-shifting is not surprising: if society *per se* is threat, so is every one of its expressions. The pluriprotence of the threat combined with its futurity, make it present in all parts of society at all time: truly omni-*present* (Boukalas 2020: 17–18).

Finally, its ever-emergent character and the pluriprotence of its form, make the threat unknowable. Indeed, terrorist attacks, pandemics and big economic crises are atypical (Boyer 2021: 48–49). The threat is vested in radical uncertainty regarding its causes, forms and consequences. The only certainty about it is its existence (Neocleous 2015; Stampnitzky 2013: 184–200). The omniscience of social life that forms the basis of biopolitical interventions, in threat governmentality becomes an accessory that supports, and is often ignored by, decisive action based on intuition, imagination, gut feeling and, indeed, common sense.

For threat governmentality the threat is an ontological condition of the social becoming. Its ontological certainty regarding the existence of the threat is coupled with radical epistemological uncertainty regarding its forms, causes and effects (Chapter 7). Premised on this peculiar dissonance between ontological certainty and epistemological uncertainty, the interventions of threat governmentality are primarily guided not by science but by intuition. Still, they are decisive. They seek to arrest the potentiality of the threat before it is formed. They do so by pre-emptively erasing the ontogenic conditions of the threat, by changing the social environment that could generate it. Threat governmentality is not a biopolitical management of species-life; it is an onto-power that aims to determine what "species" will come to comprise the social (Massumi 2015: 40–41, 86).

The existential core of the threat is fear — a sentiment peculiar in that it exists as a futurity: no one fears what has already happened, but what will or may. There cannot be fear without a perceived threat; and there certainly is no threat without fear. Fear is the platform on which threat governmentality is launched. It is the last remaining platform of state authority and legitimacy. Indeed, since the start of the 21st century, our political "leaders" do not offer a vision of the future to which they purport to lead us; they do not even promise incrementally improved versions of the present conditions we live in. They do not lead us anywhere, but demand that we keep acknowledging their authority, for if we don't, we shall be prey to a pandemonium of spectacular threats: the Taliban, ISIS, the Russians, North Korea's bomb, China, the virus, economic Armageddon. The state governs through fear — it *can only* govern through fear — because it has no future to offer (Boukalas 2021). Having lost its future perspective, and with it the ability to lead, the state relapses to the role of protector. Its sole source of authority is the protection of its "population" from quasi-natural, external and domestic threats, including those they pose for one another. Overall, the protector-state protects the existing social order from danger and change — from the danger of change. Its authority is present-oriented: it seeks to preserve what is, to perpetuate the present into the future, to render the present eternal. Its authority is based on fear: fear of violence, catastrophe and change — fear of change-as-catastrophe.

Biosecurity saw an extraordinary uptake of this fear-based governmentality by society. We recall: people demanding that their freedoms are immediately suspended so that they are protected from the virus. The more tardy or reluctant the state was to curtail their freedoms, the more we started doing so ourselves. We "nudged" the state to rush into authoritarian measures. We claimed our freedom to not have freedoms but only security. At the other end of lockdown, when restrictions were lifted, we were too scared to step out. Similarly, in order to be articulated, social opposition to biosecurity measures also raised the spectre of fear: biosecurity is a threat to liberty, to jobs and livelihoods; and vaccines threaten mutations, health complications and death. Society subscribes to threat governmentality: it can do nothing *without* being afraid, and can do nothing *but* being afraid — of threats.

Soon, the state discovered a key problem with governing through fear: you cannot lift it, you cannot remove or scale it down — neither wilfully nor rationally. Fear cannot be un-feared. Having scared the people stiff, you must provide the security you made them demand, in perpetuity. Thus, in order to really lift the lockdown, the state resorted to promoting another fear: the threat of economic collapse, imminent and catastrophic (Chapter 8). In order to act, the state needs to raise the spectre of threat and impeding catastrophe; in order to change course of action, the state needs to outbid the fear it has raised with another. Policy shifts by replacing one threat with another: terrorism, financial crisis, epidemic, economic catastrophe, environmental Armageddon, World War III. All the state does is combat each threat as it emerges. Threat-determined policy is always urgent, undeniable and necessary. It is always already justified. The threat both dictates the action and provides its legitimacy. There is the possibility that different threats and fears clash and demand mutually excluding remedies. This, after all, constitutes the present crisis — a crisis of threat-government. Yet, our current experience also shows that political antagonism is reduced to conflict between fears. The full prospect — and limit — of threat governmentality now becomes apparent: in order to act and legitimise its actions, the state is forced to identify or produce ever more spectacular threats. *To remain governable, society will become unviable.* From saviour and securer from the threat, the state will itself become the threat; from manager of fear, it will become its author.

Threat governmentality emerged as a shift of the biopolitical object of government: from labour power to threat power. Whereas biopolitics sees individuals and society as innately creative — and, hence, exploitable; threat governmentality sees them as innately destructive — and therefore dangerous. Obviously this is a deeply ideological perspective: mystifying and nonsensical. People (as monads and collectively) are always both destructive and creative. Destruction and creation are not two different faculties, but one and the same. What changed is not society's potentialities, but *the state's perception* of them. Meaning that what has changed is *the state.*

Biopolitics pertains to the liberal state, which seeks to forge society so that the market is free to operate according to its nature. For neoliberalism, by contrast, the market is not a natural entity, but a moral imperative and, for that reason, a political project (Friedman 2002; Hayek 2013). Crucially, the market is constantly under threat and in need of security (Harvey 2005: 64–86; Jessop 2016: 205–207; Mirowski 2009: 417–455). It is under threat from — and needs to be secured against — society: popular pressures and struggles, and a democratic state that could succumb to them (Hayek 1993; 2013; also: Bonefeld 2017a; Cristi 1998). Moreover, whereas for classical liberalism the relation that defines the market — and society — is exchange; for neoliberalism the predominant market relation is *competition* (Euken 1942; Hayek 2013; also: Bröckling 2012: 257). Neoliberalism conceives the market-society, its moral and political imperative, as a terrain of danger, a minefield where every participant is, for every other, a threat: *homo homini lupus.*

Finally, the imaginary of ceaseless growth in wealth premised on an ever-expanding mastery of nature — including human nature — that marks liberalism has been fatally undermined by neoliberalism. The latter has set up an accumulation regime which is based on extraction rather than production, and aims to concentrate wealth rather than grow it. It has resulted to our familiar reality of grotesque inequality, rampant pauperisation and extensive exploitation of humans and nature. "The economy has now come to declare open war on humanity, attacking not only our possibilities for living, but our chances of survival" (Debord, 1998: 39); and "accumulation now constitutes the pre-eminent danger to the continuation of all forms of human life" (Harvey 2020: 116). Capitalism has exploited the human and natural resources that sustain it to their limit. It is a threat to their reproduction and, therefore, a threat to its own reproduction. The continuation of capital accumulation poses a direct threat to "species life" *and capitalists know this*; what they are not sure about is whether capitalism can survive the catastrophe it has unleashed.

Threat governmentality is the continuation of biopolitics by means of its collapse. It is the power modality of a capitalism that represents nothing but a threat to life, is conscious of this, and therefore fears life.

16 From "*there is no alternative*" to "*whatever it takes*"

The response to the twin crises involved mass mobilisation of state resources, both in the economic and the public health front. The magnitude of this mobilisation, we are continuously told, was unprecedented — implying that it was an anomaly, a one-off occurrence. Dictated by necessity, it was unparalleled, but also meant to be unrepeatable. Be that as it may, the more important feature of the state mobilisation was not its magnitude but its quality. It is not the tremendous volume of resources, but the character of the measures that bears political significance. In combating the twin crises, the state completely jettisoned the neoliberal rulebook, the set of established rules and protocols that determined state activity for four decades, together with their underpinning logic and ideology. From paying workers to remain idle; to suddenly spending billions in a public health system it had systematically starved for decades, the state had within weeks overwhelmed its deeply set parameters of action: it went off the rails. Instantaneously and without hesitation the state discarded the *there is no alternative* (TINA) doctrine, the neoliberal dogma that governed government. In its place emerged a state that does *whatever it takes* (WIT) — a state that combats crisis decisively without hesitating to overshoot.

Once again, the origins of the WIT state can be found in counterterrorism and the Bush administration's declaration that the US would combat the enemy by all means available (Bush 2008; also: Boukalas 2014: 95). It later became the rallying cry of the fight against the financial crisis in Europe, when then Director of the European Central Bank Mario Draghi declared that the bank would do "whatever it takes" to save the euro (Tooze 2021: 130). In the context of the twin crises, it is roared by heads of state, public health ministers, central bankers and finance ministers across Europe, North America and beyond (Blakeley 2020: 21; Boyer 2021: 31, 100, 149; Brenner 2020: 14–15; Hancock 2020; IMF 2020c; Tooze 2021: 161).

Whatever it takes denotes strong and decisive state action in response to a major emergency: a potent state rising to meet a devastating crisis. Demanded by necessity, the state's response is truly forceful: it is robust, and relies on force rather than law. *Whatever it takes* denotes a state that breaks the rules: laws, the rule of law, established protocols, traditions and

DOI: 10.4324/9781003302988-19

dogmas — everything the state had set in place to guide, and limit, the exercise of its power. While *there is no alternative* is dogmatic, a stringent set of restrictions to state power and strategy applied regardless of circumstance; WIT is anti-dogmatic. It denotes radical departure from dogma, even the smashing of dogma. In counterterrorism, the dogma departed from was that of civil liberties, human rights and the rule of law (Boukalas 2017a; Gearty 2010; Miller 2009). Now, biosecurity makes this departure ecumenical, applicable to all rather than a fringe category of suspects. The counterterrorist departure from the rule of law is permanent. The biosecurity departure is, officially, temporary. Still, it has conditioned society to the deprivation of its rights in exchange for protection.

Crucially, in the economic crisis ensuing from biosecurity, the jettisoned dogma is TINA itself — and the departure from TINA is (meant to be) strictly temporary. This departure is not only forceful, but also forced. The state jettisons TINA *because there is no alternative* but to do so if TINA — the neoliberal economy — is to be saved. The WIT state acts beyond and against the dogma in order to save the dogma: WIT is akin to commissarial dictatorship in the realm of economic policy (Chapter 14). The WIT state is the TINA state in crisis-combating mode.

Nonetheless, the stubborn fact remains that, even for the purpose of being saved, TINA has been wrecked. Incredibly, its smashing satisfied the market and earned its applause. Thus, TINA has been de-naturalised. It can be re-imposed, but it has lost the aura of inevitability and is no longer unquestionable. It is no longer a natural fact — like "autumn following summer" (Blair 2005 in Tooze 2021: 3). It is revealed to be a political choice.

As political regimes go, TINA and WIT share a fundamental trait. They both denote decisive government without decision. Political action can be radical and devastating, but it is moved only by necessity and premised on inevitability; this is a government of "forced decisions" (Gentili 2021: 95). In TINA, the non-existence of alternatives means that government is reduced to following a strict, pre-determined course from which it has neither the will or the ability to diverge. In WIT, government ceases to merely observe (its) movement on a preset trail. It intervenes forcefully on the course of things and alters it. Yet, the intervention is not its choice. It is dictated by an irresistible reality: a crisis, a threat. Thus, in both TINA and WIT government is a-political; it is determined by nature (TINA) or necessity (WIT). The true political choice the state makes is to choose TINA or WIT — to pick the path from which it cannot diverge. Once this fundamental choice is made, its political character is denied and concealed through the invocation of nature and necessity.

In sum, the state response to the twin crises has destroyed TINA. But it has only done so *because* "there is no alternative", because of necessity. We are still in the realm of government though inevitability, without genuine choice or decision. Nonetheless, the neoliberal TINA as an ontological, undeniable and inescapable condition, is shuttered. The only undeniable thing about it now is that it has been de-naturalised, re-politicised, contested. Moreover, the economic crisis showed—again—that the neoliberal order needs its own suspension in order to be saved. It cannot maintain and reproduce itself by itself. Far from alternative-less, it is contingent: constituted by, and relying on, political determination and intervention.

Thus, the WIT state represents a paradox. Its power is decisionist, unleashed from rules, institutional limitations and conventions; it manoeuvres on a blank canvas, is massive and massively productive: it reshapes the institutionality of the state and, through a vast array of programmes, regulations, policies and measures, it operates in novel ways on parts of social life it did not address before. Yet, it does all this not out of will but out of necessity: because it must. The forceful state acts forcefully because it is forced to do so. The omnipotent state is compelled to be so. Just like TINA, it acts only as, and when, it must. And it only acts in order to secure TINA from challenge or collapse: it only acts as needed to secure the social order over which it presides. This, in turn, reveals the true nature of security as a relation.

Security always appears as a relation between society and the state, where society is the object to be secured and the state the subject that provides this security. In reality, the object of protection is not society "as such", but a specific ordering of society, an established social order. The state is not just a part of the established social order. It is a social meta-relation, the relation of relations, into which the social order crystallises (Poulantzas 1978). The state pertains to the established social order: its institutionality and the modalities of its power are determined by the dynamics that mark the social order; and intervene in the field of social dynamics to promote and maintain that order. In short, the state is defined by a given social order *and* helps to create and reproduce it—its overall purpose is the establishment and reproduction of the social order that creates it. Every social order and its state are mutually constituted. Thus, if we understand the state as the encapsulation of a given social order—as "the official résumé of society" (Marx 1936: 156)—security becomes a relation between the state and the state, a relation where the state *as social order* is the object that must be secured and the state *as institutional depository of effective social power* is the subject that provides security. Crucially, what the state-as-social-order needs securing *from* is precisely society "as such": the innate, multifarious and opaque faculties of society and the possibility that they may come to challenge the established social order. This potentiality is what the state will do *whatever it takes* to avert. When state-society relations are framed as relations of security, this can only mean that society is perceived by the state as a threat—as a threat to its present ordering.

Seen as a security-relation, we can appreciate the WIT state from a new angle: its only purpose is to fight fires. It is not meant to do anything else, but only ensure that things stay as they are. If it takes the WIT state an extraordinary effort—a tremendous excess of power—to achieve this, it means that the existing social order takes a lot of securing, that it has become very unstable. This points to a second paradox in the constitution of the WIT state: it does all it must, but it must not and cannot do anything. The overwhelmingly forceful WIT state is, at the same time, a state unable to articulate strategy and envision a future. While WIT implies the full mobilisation of state power, including in authoritarian ways and beyond the confines of rules, law and rights, this power has no purpose, no goal — and, consequently, no plan of how to achieve it and no coordination in attempting it. The WIT state is determined, omnipotent and barren. It cannot create.

As for the specific order that the WIT state aims to secure, its parameters are rather narrow. *Whatever it takes* applies exclusively to securing capital valorisation and accumulation. It does not encompass the condition and living standards of workers, nor any public service and necessity — not even public health — as such. These come into consideration only inasmuch their misadventures threaten to negatively impact accumulation. Indeed, workers are "encouraged" and compelled to go to work, as long as enough of them can return home in a state of health that enables them to go again next day; they have their sick leave earnings, their wages and their social wage repressed, while the state invites capital to a "Keynesian" banquet. Moreover, just like the pandemic fell from the sky, so does the inflation of basic goods and energy prices. The state declares inability to do anything about them. All these are peripheral concerns to the state, collateral to its focus on securing smooth accumulation. People's lives, living conditions, the natural environment they exist in, their political rights and freedoms — society as such — are conditional to the end of accumulation; often, their impairment is part of "whatever it takes" to achieve it.

Finally, what brings the WIT state to life is crisis — and crises are scheduled to occur abundantly and with absolute certainty: economic crises, security crises, war, public health crises caused by new epidemics that are now seen as inevitable, the environmental crisis with its unthinkable magnitude, universality and endless percolations. While the state assumes unimpeded authority to fight these crises when they erupt, it does not accept responsibility for them. First, it is not responsible for mitigating their causes. Indeed, in a political epistemology that holds causes of threats as unknowable and denies causality relations, such preoccupation would make no sense (Chapter 7). Crises are inevitable, but are generated mysteriously. And, second, the state does not accept responsibility for failings in crisis management — these are either due to the crisis being impossible to confront, or due to mistakes made by anyone but the state (Chapter 6). This state, then, claims jurisdiction over, and intervenes, in all aspects of social and personal life, but denies all responsibility for the phenomena that call forth its interventions, as well as the failure of the latter. As crisis, in some shape or other, is set to be a perennial fixture of social life, so does the supposedly temporary *whatever it takes* modality of state power.

The state then does not so much govern *in* (or during crisis); it governs *through* crisis. Indeed, a state set to preserve the social order, to avert change, is only activated when this order is challenged, when change is threatened; in crisis. Then it emerges in full *whatever it takes* armoury, it takes and implements forceful decisions that are preordained and forced. They are dictated by the need to combat the crisis, and the need to do so only to secure the existing order. They are doubly bound: determined by the exigencies of the crisis and overdetermined by the exigency for the social order to be maintained intact.

In sum, the WIT state is a security state. It is mobilised to defend the social order. The latter comprises capital accumulation in its integral sense: accumulation and anything it needs for its smooth continuation. This is under threat, actual or potential, from society and the dynamics that it may develop. The WIT state presents some peculiar, rather paradoxical, features. It claims jurisdiction over everything, but is responsible and accountable for nothing. It is perennially temporary. It moves heaven and earth only in order to stand still. Its hyperactivity is focused on achieving nothing; it is focused on averting change, on preventing and denying events, on imposing stasis. And, everything it does stems not from political deliberation or decision, but is imposed on it by necessity: it is highly decisionist, but decides nothing. The WIT state is an authoritarian *energoumeno* of necessity.

17 The rule of law and endless pseudo-necessity

The necessity that brings the *whatever it takes* state into being also determines the medium through which it acts. For liberal states, this medium is, typically, the rule of law. State actions are based on law and anticipated in it; state strategies are codified in law; and the institutional architecture of the state, its competencies, powers and their limits are also set out in law. In short, the state is constituted and acts through law — through law that itself produces (Boukalas 2014: 23–26). Crucially, not any state-issued rule qualifies as law. The hallmark of a liberal state is a separation of powers, which is essentially a division of labour concerning the production, implementation and distribution of law, between three distinct institutions — the Executive, the Legislature and the Judiciary. Accordingly, if law is to be valid it must emanate from the state institution dedicated to its production: the Legislature; and, it must be produced according to the rules and procedures specified for its production. There are also formal requirements that state-issued rules need fulfil to be acknowledged as law: they must be universally and equally applicable, clear and accessible to citizens and state personnel, and compatible with already existing laws, especially the fundamental ones provided by the constitution and the international human rights framework. Finally, all conflict in law — between state institutions and actors; between state and citizens; or between citizens — is adjudicated by another state institution dedicated to this work, the Judiciary. In specifying the competences and function of each institution, this liberal arrangement aims to impose some limit to state power over the individual and society; it especially aims to restrict the power of the Executive, the branch of the state that *acts* (and carries weapons). The terrain demarcated by limits to state power is the realm of freedoms and rights. In sum, the state exists and acts through, and in accordance with the law; and the law exists and operates in accordance to the framework of the rule of law.

To be sure, the state is not just law. It makes the law; therefore, as every producer, it always maintains a surplus of capacity relevant to its product. Thus, the state can create law to legalise its intended actions, and also circumvent, ignore or suspend the law it has made (Poulantzas 1978: 84–86). The overwhelming of the law by the state signals trouble for the existing social order. Either the state is embarking in a social project that necessitates its alteration

DOI: 10.4324/9781003302988-20

(e.g. the New Deal); or the social order is put under threat, and the state under pressure, by an external enemy or, more usually, from sections of society. Typically, the state's overwhelming of its legality combines empowerment of the Executive relative to the the other two branches; and a limitation, suspension or cancellation of rights, which allows state power to operate in realms and ways it normally would not. The biosecurity experience and the *whatever it takes* state bear clear marks of such an overwhelming of the law by the state under conditions of danger to the social order, under conditions of necessity.

A first remarkable feature is the eclipse of the Legislature and the courts during the pandemic. Regarding the Judiciary, in Britain Johnson's government is set to diminish the scope and potency of judicial review over the actions and decisions of executive agencies (Davis 2021); and Germany offers an example of the relation between the courts and the WIT state. Its Federal Constitutional Court ruled, in May 2020, that the European Central Bank's (ECB) Public Sector Purchase Programme did not abide with the proportionality principle — and was therefore unlawful (*Bvr 859/15*, 5 May 2020; Bundesverfassungsgericht 2020; also: Grimm 2020). This judgement was ignored by the executive branches of both the EU and Germany, and the ECB refused to address it and continued with its bond-buying scheme as if the court's decision did not exist (Tooze 2021: 182–183, 188).

Regarding the Legislature, it is notable that all policy, concerning either the biosecurity or the economic crisis, was introduced by Executive decree. The countless biosecurity regulations, the changes in public health infrastructure and practices, tax relief measures, grants and loans to enterprises, were all determined by Ministers and Secretaries of State. These actors did not break the law or act beyond their powers in issuing regulations and imposing measures. They draw from existing authorisations that empower them to do so, authorisations set in the constitution or, in the case of Britain, in legislation produced by Parliament. These authorisations invite the Executive to essentially do "whatever it takes" — whatever it decides — to combat the crisis (Chapter 4). They are, emergency authorisations, allowing the Executive to overwhelm the law. Much like the Executive's subsequent actions, these authorisations were also dictated by necessity: the combination of a perceived emergency necessitating a quick and robust action, combined with the perception that the Executive is the branch best suited to undertake such action (Scheuerman 2002). Notably, neither the failures of the Executive to control the pandemic, nor the chaotic nature of its measures or the persistence of the crisis for almost two years managed to shake these perceptions. Legislatures were occasionally called to rubber-stamp some of the Executive-issued regulations; and, theoretically, maintain their power to outlaw specific measures and to vitiate the authorisations that underpin them — something that, to my knowledge, has yet to happen anywhere. Still, even if the power of legislatures is inert, rather than compromised or neutralised, this does not deny that the twin crises have been managed through Executive decree (Cowan 2021: 17–20).

Crucially, the legislation and constitutions that underpin these decrees do not convey any obligations to the Executive. Characteristically, all that the UK Coronavirus Act 2020 does is to grant discretionary powers to the Executive. It does not impose any obligation or responsibility on it to, for example, provide health workers with PPE; prevent the discharge of untested patients into care homes; impose measures that prevent the spread of the disease in workplaces; test people so that the spread of disease can be estimated. The drastic empowerment of the Executive does not entail any strengthening of accountability. The Executive has powers but not duties. Thus, the state deregulates its power: it deposes of obligations and accountability, and restricts or augments its powers in an ad hoc way, mediated by law only in appearance.

Nonetheless, even if inert, the capacity of the Legislature to bloc, amend or cancel executive measures and powers remains intact. This is important: it shows that, while the Executive is drastically empowered in the context of necessity, it has not usurped power; the source of authority — the power to grant powers — remains in the hands of the Legislature. The management of the twin crises does not constitute a dictatorial derailment that smashes the rule of law framework. Rather, it denotes that state branches — the Executive *and* the Legislature — act in synergy to relax and even evade rule of law requirements in the context of necessity. This circumvention of the rule of law becomes more apparent when we consider the highest legal codification of power between the state and society: the framework of rights and liberties.

We have seen that state policy during the pandemic was determined through, often vague and intuitive, calculi between harm to public health and harm to the economy (Chapter 8). Rights and liberties *were never a factor in these calculi.* Indeed, biosecurity signals a sudden retreat of certain rights — to movement, association, assembly and privacy — before the right to health and, ultimately, life. The collapse of the former set of rights in the face of the latter is so complete that it raises the fundamental constitutional question of whether there are limits to the restriction of rights and, therefore, of whether rights have an untouchable core or are subordinate and conditional to the rights to life and health (Contiadis 2020: 81–82).

Importantly, the rights to health and life impose a duty on the state to safeguard them. The response of the state to this duty remains, however, ambiguous. We have seen that, in the UK, the prolonged failure to provide hospital and care home personnel with PPE, and the casualties resulting from it, made Parliament's Human Rights Committee question the government's compliance with its duty. A host of state practices raise the same question: the sacrificial treatment of workers; the chronic undermining of the NHS; triaging; the clear-out of hospitals; the reckless endangerment of care homes; the refusal to provide viable sick-pay; the tardiness of adopting restrictive measures; the lifting of measures when disease indices were rising; the lack of any obligations to protect health and life in biosecurity legislation; and the apparent pursuit of a policy aiming to herd immunity in all but name — they all point to a systematic neglect of the state's duty to safeguard health and life. The state disengages from its duty, and imposes it instead on the citizens. The protection of public health and life are now a duty each person owns to her fellows and to herself. Biosecurity evidences the withdrawal of the state from the duties stemming from rights, and the transfer of these duties on to the citizen (Contiadis 2020: 83). In short, all rights retreat before the necessity to safeguard the rights to health and life; but, as the state disengages from ensuing duties, these rights are transformed into a duty of the citizen, leaving the latter with no rights at all.

Thus, our contemporary state distinguishes itself from the judicial and political civilisation based on rights. It is determined to dispatch political rights — as witnessed in counterterrorism, biosecurity and beyond. While in counterterrorism political rights are compromised in order to safeguard the right to life; in biosecurity this right too, along with health, is undermined, as the state evades the obligations that ensue from it. Instead of rights, the citizen receives conditional, often reluctant, permissions. This points to the deep structure of rights: they are not *powers*. They are permissions handed by the state to the citizen; they are guaranteed on the condition that the citizen denounces political power and consents to be governed, i.e. acknowledges the power of the state to decide on all matters social. Accordingly, rights are always individual. By being so, they atomise society (Poulantzas 1978: 63–92) and render it judicially invisible. This individualisation of rights and its concomitant atomisation of society, leave the state with a juridical monopoly over the "public". Thus, the state can, almost automatically and almost fully, overrun individual rights whenever issues concerning the "public good", "general interest", "national security" or any combination of such terms arise — according to the state.

This is precisely the case with biosecurity. It leaves the citizen with compromised rights and a host of arbitrary duties, obligations and permissions. None of these are stable, coherent or clear. They are haphazard, temperamental and ever-shifting: now travel, now don't; wear a mask while standing up but not while sitting down, while outside but not inside; show proof of vaccination to bouncers but not to nurses; drink beer if you eat pizza...The law, if it can be called that, is spasmodic, a sheer reflex. It cannot cohere, not even as mere instrumentality. Among the hundred ad hoc regulations, it is unclear which, if any, have contributed (and how much) in achieving their purpose — not least because the purpose is not defined: to protect the NHS? to save lives? to tolerate the virus? to eliminate it? to preserve the economy? to restructure it?

The purposeless character of state actions belies the very notion of necessity on which the state purports to govern. In necessity, state force, unhindered by law, is focused on achieving a vital, specific and clear purpose. Instead, what we experience is a pandemonium of open-ended, ill-defined purposes and random "targets". They are often complementary to one another, often contradictory, and constantly shifting. What is perceived, or at least invoked, as a state of necessity is a state of a myriad urgencies, arising from a pandemonium of threats. Importantly, the state of necessity is mobilised to achieve a specific purpose; once this is done necessity is lifted. The innate purpose, and measure of success, of the state of necessity is to cancel itself, to become redundant, unnecessary. The state of necessity is inherently temporary. By contrast, the threats and urgencies that determine the current legal instrumentality spring eternal: they are ill-defined, open-ended and set to be replaced or complemented by new ones. Our state of jeopardy is therefore perpetual. Having no clear aim, its overarching purpose is to perpetuate itself.

Thus, the state that combats the twin crises is not a juridical state of necessity. Such thing would have involved a temporary instrumentalist alignment — or suspension — of the law to the achievement of a specific purpose. Instead, the twin crises signal the advent of a new juridico-political regime, one deeply hostile to the rule of law. The jettisoning of key rule of law requirements — for clarity, universality and stability; for comportment of state power according to rights and freedoms — is symptomatic of a more fundamental shift. The new order defines and treats society as a compound of right-less subjects to be governed through an endless barrage of arbitrary decrees. That these are typically authorised by parliament, occasionally rubber-stamped by it and can even be stroke down by it, does not alter the reality that executive decree is now the predominant legal format. The new juridical regime denotes a right-less society and a state whose arbitrary power is not limited by law, but authorised by it.

More profoundly: whereas the rule of law is a legal constellation emanating from the subjectivity of the "free man", a creative person who is primarily concerned with the maintenance and expansion of her freedom, which she cherishes because she intends to develop herself and her world through it; at the heart of the new constellation we find an individual that is indifferent to — and rather fearful and suspicious of — freedom. He eagerly surrenders it in order to be protected from a threat. For he lives in a threatening world and cannot do anything about it. In place of the autonomous, creative citizen, the new legal order is premised on the subjectivity of the fearful slave.

The rule of law, at its very core, expresses the determination of society *not to be treated as scum* (Bloch 1996: 220). By contrast, our society eagerly welcomes the new juridico-political regime that effectively renders it right-less. It consents to the cancellation of its rights and often demands it. It self-polices the observance of state-imposed duties. It desires to be secured and places no conditions to the protective state — not even that its measures are effective for its security. Taking account of the nature of the security relation, this means that — ultimately — people yearn for the maintenance of the existing social order and their place in it. To this end they exercise their right to counterfeit rights, their freedom not to have freedoms, their autonomous will to be treated like matter. The desire to be protected and the will to obey make the rupture with any form of democratic, or even liberal, juridico-political constellation irredeemable.

18 Personal responsibility and the irresponsible state

A constant feature of the *whatever it takes* state, is its irresponsibility. The WIT state claims jurisdiction on anything and responsibility for nothing, including its own acts and omissions; and its departure from the rule of law juridico-political constellation portrays its power as essentially arbitrary and unaccountable. In combating the twin crises, the state makes extraordinary interventions on society in order to avert the dangers to "life and livelihood", to public health and the economy. While it reaps the accolades for successful interventions, it *never commits itself to a duty towards society*. However salvaging its interventions, they do not stem from any particular role, function or duty the state is obliged to fulfil. They are essentially favours. By contrast, when state interventions prove inadequate or harmful, the responsibility for the failure is ours. All power to the state, all responsibility to society: this distribution of power/responsibility saturates the state response to the twin crises.

Throughout the pandemic, the response of the state was marked by contradictions. The first, between protecting the population from the pandemic and securing the smooth operation of the economy, defined the range of state operations and led to strategic confusion, resulting to contradictory and mutually sabotaging strands of policy. The second contradiction marks its biosecurity policy. On the one hand, the state exercised an unparalleled amount of force that penetrated the innermost interstices and folds of society, including the household and the body. It reshaped the social environment beyond recognition and even cancelled society as such. Yet, at the same time the state was insisting that the decisive factor in biosecurity was citizens' common sense and personal responsibility.

Notably, the invocation of common sense occurred precisely at the moment when biosecurity had upended the entire system of social relations and practices; and arbitrary, particularistic regulations had proliferated to such an extent that it became impossible for anyone — including those who issued them — to follow or even know them with certainty. In short, citizens' common sense became the vanguard of biosecurity precisely at the moment when common sense was upended by the state. While fronting the biosecurity effort, common sense would not be a defence to criminal liability for citizens' failure to observe the state's unfathomable regulations.

DOI: 10.4324/9781003302988-21

Common sense was a duty imposed on the citizen, in circumstances that made its fulfilment impossible. Personal responsibility was dictated to citizens when the state decided to lift all biosecurity restrictions whilst a new wave of the pandemic was unfolding. It was meant to fill the void resulting from the state's abandonment of biosecurity. Thus, common sense and personal responsibility are imposed upon society at the moment when the state failed its effort or decided to abort it. They are calls to society to fend for itself; and they transfer the burden of responsibility for failure from the state to society. Notably, responsibility is denied as a socio-political relation. It is seen strictly as an individual, personal attribute.

Interestingly, the British Prime Minister framed the decision to lift biosecurity restrictions as a "move from a universal government diktat to relying on people's personal responsibility" (Johnson cited in Williams 2021). It is, then either "personal responsibility" or "government diktat": dictatorship. Personal responsibility denotes a type of power and indicates a form of state. Both its opposition to dictatorship and its individualised character, place personal responsibility in a political constellation that is emphatically liberal.

The core of liberal political ideology is the individual. This individual is inherently creative. It creates wealth and, incidentally, its society and its history. Liberalism as a revolutionary ideology replaces "god" with "man" as the creator of the social universe. This creative faculty makes the individual responsible for its actions. However, the individual's creative scope is limited. It is always already restricted by nature, its laws and its "natural rights", above all the right to property (Locke 2016). Thus restricted, creativity takes the form of choice. Individuals are free to choose and, consequently responsible for the choices they make. Further: since society is nothing but the sum of the individuals operating within the natural realm of property exchange (the market); and since agency is restricted to individual free choice; the common good is the aggregate of individual choices. It is the collateral outcome of individuals making self-interested choices (Smith 1982). Thus far, the Prime Minister's mantra is textbook classical liberalism: the collective good results from the personal choice-hence-responsibility of each individual. But that is not all.

Neoliberalism departs from classical liberalism in that it does not assume the market, and free choice therein, as undeniable natural conditions — it has experienced their partial or full suspension by democratic, socialist, corporatist, and fascist movements and regimes. For neoliberalism, free choice is not the point of departure, but that of arrival. It is a moral good, an imperative that needs to be pursued and achieved (Böhm 1937; Hayek 2013; Oksala 2017). The market, and the freedom of choice reigning therein, is a political regime and needs to be created. Thus, neoliberalism demands that society is shaped so that free choice is imposed as a universal relation and undeniable condition. This is a core responsibility of the neoliberal state — which duly reshapes social relations and their meaning, so that citizens, patients, students etc become clients: market participants exercising free choice (Mol 2008: 16–32).

For neoliberalism, the duty to shape society on the basis of free choice does not end with the state, but envelops every individual. Citizens must constantly exercise their freedom of choice, cherish it, demand and protect it. In a social environment awash with choice, they are responsible for making the proper ones, thus promoting the common good while pursuing their self-interest. But the core of their responsibility is to maintain the social order that attributes them choices and responsibilities. To uphold choice and responsibility is a responsibility for the citizens; it is a choice that they are not free to not make. Thus, the core of neoliberal responsibilisation is not so much the (liberal) responsibilisation for one's own choices, but the responsibility of each to promote a society based on free choice. The Prime Minister is fully attuned to political neoliberalism: abruptly, *by diktat*, he turns a society ruled by diktat into one (self-)governed by individual choice and personal responsibility.

The circumstances under which the sudden shift from "diktat" to "responsibility" occurred point to another important difference between liberalism and neoliberalism. Whereas liberalism understands freedom of choice as creative agency of the individual; for neoliberalism it is primarily the modality through which individuals are forced to cope with the adversities that society and, above all, the market throws at them. Free choice, in other words, operates within the confines of resilience (Chandler 2016: 27–48; Neocleous 2017a: 64–67, 71–72; Reid 2016: 53–55, 66–71). Individuals have to survive, endure and make the best of their fate, without seeking to influence the forces that govern it (Chapter 15). Finally, the state's abrupt abandonment of the biosecurity field reveals another feature of the neoliberal state. While it is responsible for imposing, promoting, expanding and securing market relations, including those of free choice and personal responsibility, this is the limit of its obligations. It has no (other) responsibility to society —and it must forcefully resist any attempt to be drawn into any. This void is filled by responsibilising the individual. "Blaming the victim here rules: whoever is sick has not adequately looked after his health" (Bröckling 2012: 261). The responsibilisation of the citizen is the absolution of the state from responsibility. Personal responsibility is the corollary of the irresponsible state.

This irresponsible state is *the strong state* envisioned and demanded by the frontrunners and highest to date theoretical exponents of neoliberalism: F.A. Hayek, the Ordoliberals as well as Carl Schmitt. In sharp contrast with the weak welfare state (pluralist, social-democratic or corporatist), which would succumb to pressures from different sections of society and endlessly attempt to arbitrate, reconcile, and synthesise their conflicting and proliferating demands, the neoliberal state is strong precisely because it is impervious to social and democratic pressures. Instead, the strong state concentrates all its power to a singular objective: to promote, secure and expand the conditions for the free market. The neoliberal state does "whatever it takes" to secure and expand capital accumulation, private property and profitability. This is its sole purpose and all its efforts are oriented to it. Anything that is not aligned, relevant or beneficial to capital accumulation in a free market is beyond the remit and the competence of the state (Biebricher and Vogelmann 2017; Bonefeld 2017a; Cristi 1998; Jessop 2019b). Rather, it falls within state competence and deserves intervention only in order to be eradicated; and the violence the state should exercise in order to protect the market is boundless (Bonefeld 2017b: 48; Hayek in Cristi 1998: 168; Kirkpatrick 1979; von Mises 1985: 51; Zevin 2019: 286–289). Secluded from democratic pressures and hostile to popular demands, the neoliberal state is, by constitution, authoritarian.

To come full circle, personal responsibility entails the de-responsibilisation of the state in relation to society. This is explicitly declared by the British Prime Minister; more importantly, it is practically expressed in the incapacity of the state to provide basic services and functions, from caring for the elderly to distributing PPE or collecting tax from the rich. This incapacity is the result of systematic sabotage of the state by the state: the most effective way to seclude the state from society is to render it genuinely incapable to respond to its needs. When this seclusion is threatened, the state resorts to force. Indeed, the long year of the pandemic was punctuated by a parade of force, as states — from Belgium to Chile, from Turkey to the US — engaged with citizens' protest through violence and *only* through violence. Far from being a form of society's self-government, the doctrine of personal responsibility is an invitation to state violence. It *a priori* legitimises the latter towards anyone doing things that the state deems irresponsible. Given that irresponsibility is quite distinct from illegality; and that the neoliberal state is prompt to deregulation, departure from the rule of law and arbitrariness, the only certain way to know what the state deems irresponsible is the police baton.

The state and society do not confront each other as two separate entities. They are mutually instituted in all their aspects, including their separation. The state is always the state of a particular society. The balance of power among different social forces and, especially, the interests and strategies of the dominant social force, determine the institutional shape and the powers of the state, as well as its relation to society. At the same time, and because it is a social creation, the state affects the social realm. Through its form and its policies it (re)shapes society (Jessop 2016; Poulantzas 1978). This shaping of society by the state is evident in the atomisation of society by the liberal state. To create the necessary conditions for generalised market exchange, the state dissolves collective communal bonds — hence both choice and responsibility can only be personal. Through law and disciplinarian regimentation, the liberal state forges society as a constellation of distinct, isolated individuals whose relations to each other are mediated by the state, and whose unity as a society is defined by it (Jessop 2008: 142–147; Poulantzas 1978: 63–120). Biosecurity brings atomisation to its apex. As disciplinarian regimentation takes the form of physical isolation, society is pulverised. Each isolated particle partakes in the social only through its surveillance and the mechanisms of coercion and propaganda. The only social synthesis the state can produce is series of statistics on infection and death.

The participation of the isolated individual in this horrific society is to shoulder the blame for it. It becomes the scapegoat for all wrongs, thus extricating the state from responsibility for its systemic, structural, strategic and operational shortcomings and failures. The contribution of capital accumulation in the generation of disease; the austerity measures that destroyed the capacity of the public health system to cope with disease; the strategic confusion of policy between health and accumulation; and even the failure to stockpile and distribute tests and PPE — are all overlooked as the blame is placed on individuals being candid with their mask wearing (Antithesis 2020: 27–28). Once the invention of vaccines established a plausible route out of the twin crises, the blame for the persistence of epidemic spread focused on those who refused to be vaccinated. They are bereft of the proscribed "common sense" — indeed they are derided for their ignorance and stupidity. Their refusal to subscribe to the solution sabotages the entire social effort: they defy "personal responsibility" — confirming that the summoning of personal responsibility is in fact a duty the state has imposed on society. Notwithstanding the monumental role of the state in raising vaccine scepticism (Davies 2022), the state conjures up a new social category: the "non-vaccinated" or, more polemically, the "anti-vaxxers" is a category construed to be the scapegoat for all the limitations and failings of the biosecurity effort. Notably, the "non-vaccinated" is not treated as someone who is most vulnerable to the virus; she is treated as the most dangerous subject. For, she refuses to mitigate the threat she embodies, she refuses to make herself less threatening. This reveals the character of biosecurity: while it is guided by care, it is at core a coercive relation. It also offers a crucial insight into security as a social relation. Security appears to be a universal good — all-inclusive and beneficial for everyone in society. It is in fact an intolerant relation that aims to the radical exclusion and neutralisation of threatening groups, persons, thoughts and behaviours (Neocleous 2017b:: 11–12).

Society keenly takes up its scapegoat role. Individuals blame each other for the spread of the disease (Golby 2020). In their isolation, they have no notion of the commons other than that emanating from the telescreen. Their restricted experience, poor in inter-personal communication, acquires meaning only by reference to state narratives. Under biosecurity, atomisation is perfected as society becomes a field of interaction between *mutually threatening privacies*. The only sense of commonality, of a higher unity of society, is that of mutual mistrust, fear, suspicion and intolerance — a sense of commonality that renders society impossible. "Eliminate trust and put every slave under the surveillance of the other slaves"; Aristotle (1994: V, 11) already knew that the dissolution of social bonds of trust was the necessary condition for tyranny and its crowning achievement (Sanguinetti 2018: 20–21).

19 Neoliberal despotism

The discussion of the state-form in the three previous chapters identifies two paradoxes. First, this is a state that intervenes in all aspects of social life, but accepts no responsibility towards society — it is therefore not responsible for its interventions and their effects. And, second, this is a state that employs its powers expansively, but does nothing. Unwrapping these paradoxes and the tensions they imply brings us to a fuller understanding of the emerging state-form.

Neoliberal despotism

Biosecurity connotes a state that, forced by necessity, exercises unlimited power over society. It intervenes in social relations and dictates social practices — to the point of suspension — *ex cathedra* and unconcerned by limitations posed by rights. This authoritarian power is motivated by care. Its purpose is not to injure or punish society, but to save it from the lethal threat of the virus. The state oppresses society in order to protect it. Biosecurity, then, appears to outline a relation between the state and society defined by pastoral power, the kind of power that relates the shepherd to the flock. It is a power of care and worry for the welfare of the flock and of each individual sheep. It is premised on thorough knowledge of each individual member and of the whole. Above all, it is benevolent and protective; but demands prompt, unconditional obedience. It is a power that aims to save society from itself (Foucault 2007: 126–128, 165, 182–185). Pastoral power is deeply paternalist — indeed, pre-modern. Its archetype is the parent-child relation. This makes it "natural": a power funded not on reason, consent or law, but on nature (Bobbio 1997: 72–73). Its ultimate aim is to reproduce itself as such: to maintain the relation between rulers and ruled as a natural relation between adult and child. To negate, in short, the ability of the governed to grow up into political equality with their rulers.

The pandemic experience confirms these tropes of pastoral power in its reach, modality (obedience in exchange for protection), and in its anti-democratic paternalist character. In biosecurity, the state's security drive, its determination to know society in order to secure the social order, dovetails with the commodification of personal and relational data, the extraction

DOI: 10.4324/9781003302988-22

of which has become a driving force of capital accumulation. The merging of state and capital's capacity to extract and analyse information in the context of biosecurity (Oswald et al 2021: 16–17) is an obvious sign of this trend; the storing of classified intelligence in Amazon's databases (Syal 2021) completes the move. The emerging state-form will therefore involve an intelligence-industrial complex; it will be a regime of omni-surveillance (Boyer 2021: 264–265, 278, 281). This is not all. Throughout the pandemic the state was not concerned only with biosecurity but also with the economy. Because it was not a "pure" biosecurity state, key features of pastoral power are missing: namely, those associated with care. Thus, the protection of public health has been conditional on the operation of the market. Moreover, the protection of individual health varied according to the market value of each person. Throughout the pandemic, the ultimate object of the state's care was the market. Finally, while demanding obedience, the state released itself from any responsibility, any care, towards society. With this, the idyllic of the pastorale is shuttered.

The state strives to disengage "itself" from society: it seeks to affect society, while at the same time cut itself free from social influence. It seeks to intervene in society while making it impossible for society to interfere with the state. The state conceives social interference as a threat. It engages with it accordingly.

The move appears innocuous: during the pandemic, the UK Parliament kept on renewing schedules 21 and 22 of the Coronavirus Act, the clauses that allow the police to arrest anyone they deem to be potentially infected with the virus; and to ban or disperse gatherings in private and public space. To arrest and disperse: these powers effectively allow the police to remove people from public space at will, granting the police absolute authority to decide if, when and who can be where. Crucially, these powers where not justified by the need for epidemic control: scientific evidence suggests that the contribution of open air gatherings to the spread of the epidemic is minimal; while, of course, everyone is likely to be or become affected, so unless everyone is arrested this power resolves nothing. And, while the government has officially declared the pandemic to be over, these emergency powers are still in force[1]. It seems then that their purpose is not to contain the pandemic, but to control society. They denote a state fearful of society's post-pandemic return. The anti-racist riots in Bristol in March 2021 occurred at the moment parliament was renewing these powers. They indicated *what* the state is anticipating and fearing. Soon after, the police outlawed, under CVA powers, gatherings in commemoration of Sarah Everard, a woman raped and killed by a police officer; and then proceeded to thrash the vigil in her memory — signalling what society can expect from the state when it emerges from lockdown.

Indeed, the power to disperse gatherings is so coveted by the state that it is set to become permanent. The *Police, Crime, Sentencing and Courts* Bill currently under consideration by Parliament, will authorise a State Secretary to outlaw a public demonstration, even an ongoing one. She will be able do so if she finds that the demonstration produces noise or is likely to cause distress to some members of the public. In other words, the Secretary will be able outlaw a protest whenever she wants. Protest then becomes an activity allowed exceptionally on the condition that the government tolerates its form and content. From being the culmination of civil liberties, protest becomes a mere permission the state grants or withholds at will. In a dress rehearsal of what the law will signify, the Home Secretary ordered the police to thrash the vigil for Sarah Everard; and she invariably refers to protesting people as *criminals* (Dodd 2020; Dodd and Grierson 2021; Messmer 2021). This attitude to protest is not a British peculiarity. In France which, like Greece, legislated during lockdown Executive powers to outlaw protest, police violence has intensified to such a degree that protesters often suffer serious injury and even risk death (Chrisafis 2019; Kivotidis 2021: 149–150); and in the Netherlands the police confronted anti-lockdown protesters with live ammunition. Meanwhile, in confronting the mass anti-racist movement in summer 2020, the US showed that it conceptualises, and engages with, protesters as insurgents in an occupied country (Marie 2020). Moreover, operating at arm's length from the official state, but with strong ties to centres therein, a fascist movement is being nurtured. It made spectacular demonstrations of force in the US (Becker 2020; Seymour 2021) and has also been mobilised in the UK (Sabbagh 2020; Steinberg 2021). We realise that, while the raison d'être of the protector-state is to exclude and neutralise the violence of others — including its citizens — against its "population", it does not exclude its own violence. Indeed, violence is inherent in its logic: the protector is, necessarily, a punisher.

Not limited to outlawing protest, the UK seeks to make it impossible at the first place, by sabotaging the ability of society to associate and organise in political terms. Legislated during lockdown, the *Covert Human Intelligence Sources (Criminal Conduct) Act 2021* grants intelligence agents that infiltrate a criminal organisation or a political group impunity for any crimes they commit in the course of their infiltration or for purposes related to it. All a covert agent needs in order to rape, murder or torture with impunity is his line manager's permission. We note here that two key elements of the state-form — omni-surveillance and the state's disregard to the rule of law — are tightly related to the intelligence apparatus. Further: intelligence, by its constitution, intervenes in society in any way it determines necessary; and it is unaccountable for its interventions and can deny responsibility for them. Its interventions are politically motivated, in defence of the social order. Thus, in the emerging state-form, intelligence is the *dominant state apparatus* (Boukalas 2020: 11–13). It is the mechanism whose logic is the predominant state logic, whose interests are supported by the state as a whole (Jessop 2008: 127–128; Jessop 2016: 67–69; Poulantzas 1978: 136–139) and, in our case, the mechanism whose operational principles define those of the entire state.

Finally, more than unlawful and impossible, protest — social interference with the state — should be unthinkable. The UK nurtures plans to create a *sui generis* crime of "extremism" (Commission for Countering Extremism 2021). Defined as any act or word that diverges from the values of political liberalism, extremism is already heavily policed across social settings: schools, hospitals, nurseries, prisons, mosques, universities, the internet (Boukalas 2019; Heath-Kelly 2013; 2017). Moreover, the Department for Education instructs teachers to not use in class anything produced by a person or organisation that has been critical of capitalism (Busby 2020). The government's plans for a *sui generis* offence will complete, and make official, what is already imposed in practice: the criminalisation of critique.

The state aims to seclude itself from society. We now see how it plans to achieve this: through force. A defining feature of the emergent state is that it is "deaf to words and reason"; it acts through force and responds only to force — with force (Frade 2020: 18–19). In disposing of the right to protest, the state denies society the only way it has left to influence it (Boukalas 2014: 100). The state is determined to achieve this seclusion by all means: it institutes it in law; practices it through police violence; and establishes it semiotically: there are no protesters or radicals, only criminals and enemies. At the same time, the state institutes its right to intervene in society — to rape, murder and torture it; and declares that its agents are not legally accountable. The state secures its seclusion from society through violence; it does so with relish. It openly parades its excess of violence declaring that it can treat society as it likes, thrashing the slightest hint of resistance. This is a provocative, unapologetic state, proud in its brutality. If society is the enemy, the mode of engagement is overkill.

It is this exclusion of society from influencing the state that marks the emerging state-form as authoritarian. The term *authoritarianism* denotes precisely this: the expansion of state power's reach into society *combined with* the forceful exclusion of society from influencing the state (Poulantzas 1978: 203–209, 238). The state determines social affairs, while society is banned from interfering with the state — from interfering, i.e. with its government, life and destiny.

Yet, the state can never be separated from society. For, the state is not a subject with its own will, interests or power. The state is a social relation. Its institutionality is a crystallisation of the dynamics between different social forces; and its power — remit, limits and modality — is determined by the interests of social forces in their dynamic interplay (Boukalas 2014: 13–19; Jessop 2016: 53–90; Poulantzas 1978: 125–129). Thus, rather than a — practically impossible and conceptually absurd — autonomy of the state from society, the state's authoritarian hardening prevents from influencing state power the social forces that have no institutional means to do so: the subaltern classes. Thus, the state is not cut off from society; there is one social force that can, and is invited to, influence the state: capital.

Capital's capture of the state — and the state's eagerness to surrender — is evident in state policy throughout the pandemic period: the suppression of wages; the intensification of workfare; the undermining of small businesses; the "countercyclical" unconditional transfer of public funds to capitalist enterprises; the "pro-cyclical" encouragement of wealth concentration; the sacrifice of "low-value" people; the idle contemplation of energy and food price rises and the ensuing devastation of living standards; the cheerleading for "green" capitalism; the expansion of the working day; the prioritisation of "livelihoods" over "lives", of the "life of the factory" over the life in the factory, of the economy over health...Throughout the pandemic, the state has been unequivocally declaring that it is "simply, and only, a service provider to capital" (dell'Umbria 2020: 63). If this is what the state has in store for the material interests of the vast majority of people, then its authoritarian hardening is a sensible move.

In sum, the state becomes an attachment to capital, serving its needs. At the same time, the state fully secludes itself from popular pressures, social needs and demands. This is, then, an authoritarian neoliberal state — rather: this authoritarian state is *neoliberal.* Its heavy, "countercyclical" intervention in the economy is irrelevant to this classification. The central texts of neoliberal ideology (Friedman 2002; Hayek 1993; 2013), let alone the practice of neoliberal politicians and economists, make obvious that for neoliberalism *the question has never been whether the state can intervene in the economy. The question has always been whether society can intervene in the state.*

The fortification of the state against society and its capturing by a single social force has a far-reaching consequence: it renders the state incapable of strategy, of coherent long-term planning and action. The strategic capacity of the state has been the result of its relative, and always selective, openness to society, of its attempt to synthesise the conflicting demands and interests of different social forces (Boukalas 2021). As capital becomes the only force that determines policy, the strategic capacity of the state evaporates — the state indeed becomes a mere service provider for capital. The loss of strategic ability affects, in turn, the way in which the state relates to capital. It is no longer able to express the interests of the capitalist class as a whole, but rather engages with it in a piecemeal (sector-by-sector, case-by-case and just-in-time) basis, responding to the requests of specific capitals and sectors as they arise, without cohesion or coordination (Sayer 2016: 122). The close proximity between state actors and specific capitals, combined with the lack of a cohesive plan that would guide state-capital relations, makes corruption a structural feature of the state-form (Chapter 13). By becoming structural, the term "corruption" loses its meaning, for it is premised on the distinction between a public political power and a private economic one, a distinction that in the emerging state-form is lifted (Tsoukalas 2021: 90–93). *Once there were scandals, but not anymore* (Debord 1998: 22).

The loss of strategy is concomitant to an erasure of the temporal perspective, of the future. Strategy entails the vision of a future: it is coordinated action and planning that occurs now, but will be fulfilled in the future. Without strategy the state has no future tense. Its only cognitive and operational horizon is the present. Thus, the monumental mobilisation of state power aims only to preserve things as they are. *The strategy of a state incapable of strategy is to impose stasis* — and, the more unstable the social arrangements it needs to preserve are, the greater the mobilisation of powers must be. Imposing stasis is the only thing this state is able to do. This informs my labelling of the state-form as *despotic* rather as, more generically, *authoritarian*. Despotism is a subset of authoritarianism: every despotic state is authoritarian — it combines extensive reach of state power in society with the expulsion of the latter from state affairs. But, not every authoritarian state is despotic. There are two key distinctions. First, in despotic regimes, the extreme concentration of power at the hands of the state, especially the Executive, is matched by an extreme concentration of wealth — and its proud display. Indeed, for neoliberalism, concentration of wealth is the ultimate, existential, goal; and the open, even provocative, display of opulence is a cultural imperative and ethos. Second, and more importantly, authoritarianism can connote the mobilisation of power towards a goal. Typically, authoritarian state power seeks to smash social resistance and thus reshape society to the detriment of the majority of people. It seeks to achieve something; its purpose is outside itself. Despotic power, by contrast, has no goal, does not aim to alter or to reshape society. Its purpose is perpetuation of the social order, including "itself". It seeks to maintain society as it is, securing the concentration of wealth. It is a power that imposes stasis. In short, despotism is an authoritarianism set to prevent social change and thus perpetuate the concentration of wealth.

Finally, this despotic neoliberal state governs through fear (Chapters 8, 15). Being despotic, its overall purpose is to condemn society to an eternal present. Being neoliberal, the present that the state aims to perpetuate is marked by inequality, exploitation and destitution. The combination of the state's aversion to the future and society's aversion to the present gives rise to a dialectics of government through fear. At a first remote, the state that cannot offer society a vision of a better future is reduced to justifying its authority through fear: it requires society to accept its authority and comply to its power, or face untold catastrophe. In essence the state blackmails society — it threatens it. Thus, at a second remote, government through fear refers to a fearsome state: the state is prone to terrify society, as evidenced in its overkill against social resistance, actual and potential. This decisive, and very open, parade of force against society means that the state fears society. At a third remote, government through fear is determined by the state's fear of society. It conceptualises society as a threat, forcefully and meticulously prevents it from influencing the state and, at the limit case of biosecurity, suspends it altogether — all in order to secure the present social order from the threat society poses to it. Finally, at a fourth remote, the state fears society because it knows that the neoliberal order it seeks to secure is a threat to society: it cannot offer it anything but degradation, agony and death (Chapter 15).

In sum, the emerging state is preoccupied, exclusively, with securing the social order and averting the possibility of its change. The social order in question is a neoliberal one. It comprises an accumulation regime based on extraction, rather than production, of wealth; and distribution policies aimed at the concentration of wealth. It is, in short, a social order detrimental to the vast majority of society. It entails material deprivation, misery and existential agony for the poor, and the making of the majority of people poor. Securing this order means that the state has forfeited its function to synthesise conflicting social interests; it exclusively promotes the interests of capital. By losing its socially synthetic function, it also loses its strategic ability. Without it, the state, first, cannot promote the interests of the capitalist class over a long term horizon — it merely responds to demands of specific capitals in an ad hoc, spasmodic, manner. And, second, the state is not only averse to change, towards a future, but genuinely incapable for it. The eternal present of the existing social order is not just the only thing it wants; it is the only thing it can. It achieves it by becoming a private club for select capitals, excluding society from politics. It denies any responsibility, obligation or duty to society, and engages with it through flattery, deception and violence. Its violence is not only excessive, but also pronounced and unapologetic. Through a parade of force, disregard to law, and self-issued impunity, the state seeks to make social resistance impossible, even unthinkable. It treats society as an enemy for it fears society's potentiality to alter its existing order, to produce a future for itself. It fears this potential because it knows that the existing social order is a threat to society.

Friedmanian, workfare, national apparatus

The above discussion outlines the mode in which the state relates to society. To complete the outline of the emerging state-form I now address its structure and institutionality. The account that follows is loosely modelled on Jessop's (2002) seminal outline of the shift in the state-form during the last decades of the 20th century: from a *Keynesian, welfare, national state* (KWNS) to a *Schumpeterian, workfare, post-national regime* (SWPR). My assessment uses SWPR as the point of departure from which the distance with the emerging state-form can be perceived. It also replicates the outlining of the state-form in terms of: (a) the key approach to political economy that determines state policy (Keynes, Schumpeter, and now Friedman); (b) the key approach towards labour and society (workfare); the key cultural and spatial reference of the state (from post-national back to national); and the decisive feature of the state's institutional assemblage (from a (meta-) governance regime, to a (security) apparatus). While modelled on Jessop's account, my outline does not claim to replicate its rigour. Jessop's account encompasses the length of an entire monograph; and — more importantly — it outlines an established state-form, while I am grappling with a form still in emergence which moreover, as I will argue, is an unstable one. While Jessop's account was definite, mine is tentative. Finally, it is important to note that, in hindsight, SWPR, which crystallised during the 1990s, marked the peak of neoliberalism and provided the ideal form for the neoliberal state. The departure from SWPR is commensurate with a modulation and partial reversal of neoliberalism, and possibly with its crisis and demise.

The seclusion of the capitalist state from society appears to bring to fruition the ordoliberal vision of a "strong state and a free economy". This vision calls for the state to establish, maintain and safeguard the cultural and institutional conditions for a fully competitive market. These conditions comprise a constitutional framework and a configuration of the rule of law forged on the basis of, and aiming to protect and promote, private property, free markets, and a competitive price mechanism (Jessop 2019b:: 3–4). Establishing and perpetually policing this "economic constitution" is the sole role of the state. The state should be constitutionally restricted from responding to social pressures and demands and institutionally unable to do so. Thus, ordoliberalism demands a limited state: its power is limited by the rule of law framework; and its function is limited to securing the social conditions for the competitive market. This limitation is precisely what makes it a "strong" state: its actions are focused and it is impervious to popular-democratic pressures (Bonefeld 2017b; Cristi 1998; Hayek 1993; Hayek 2013; Rüstow 1932). The state bares no responsibility to society other than maintaining the smooth function of the market.

The state emerging from the twin crises displays marked ordoliberal features: it is pre-occupied with securing the smooth operation of the market, is aloof to social demands and hostile to democratic pressures. Yet, the "constitutional" elements of an ordoliberal state are missing. Our state shows disregard to the rule of law and resists legal regulation of its actions: it is a "whatever it takes" state. There is no sign of a constitutional order for the operation of the market either: this state promotes capitalist interests not by establishing a favourable legal and institutional framework, but by arbitrarily selecting specific sectors and capitals as privileged interlocutors and satisfying their demands. The emerging state is therefore closer to the Chicago variant of neoliberalism, which demands the full deregulation of economic activity, reduces social order to the free-play of force among market actors, and demands of the state to neutralise social resistance to market forces — by means of dictatorship if necessary (Jessop 2019b:: 6). Whereas ordoliberalism is avert to disorder, American neoliberalism seeks it out, for it enhances the opportunities, expands the terrain and innovates the methods for profitability and accumulation. This makes the neoliberal economy unstable and prone to crisis — but crisis is not an unwanted occurrence. It relieves the market from underperforming players and re-orients investment to new fields. Thus, the environmental crisis becomes an opportunity for accumulation, by means of the "green" economy. Similarly, bio-technology, the production of life-forms with a view to their exploitation, was greatly enhanced thanks to the pandemic. The omni-surveillance of society and the commodification of ensuing data took off thanks to the support of the state in the context of security crises: terrorism and, later, the pandemic. In other words, the three sectors that will drive accumulation in the immediate future owe their prominence to state support offered in the context of crisis. They are, in turn, inserted in an accumulation mode that relies on profit deriving from rent, especially in financial assets (Lapavitsas 2013; Piketty 2014). The complexity that unregulated financial circuits develop make this mode of accumulation prone to financial crisis; its extractive nature puts a drag on the broader economy and make it likely to cause economic crisis. Finally, the overall regime of accumulation is one based on the perception of scarcity, instability and conflict (Chapter 14). More than a structural tendency, crisis is also a strategic choice for sectors of capital. The capacity of the neoliberal state-form to increase capital profitability is reaching its asymptote and, often, is an impediment to enhanced profitability. Accordingly, sectors of capital, led by high finance, are seeking to further enhance their extractive accumulation by sabotaging the structures and institutions of the neoliberal state: by causing and exploiting institutional crises (Bourgeron 2021).

On every count, this is an economy that thrives on disorder, one where the main driver of accumulation is crisis. If political economy is the set of knowledges that informs the capitalist state and guides its actions; then the emerging state is informed and guided by the political economy of the Chicago School. I therefore call it after that School's emblematic figure: *Friedmanian*.

The spatial horizon of this Friedmanian state is significantly reduced. Geopolitical and geo-economic arrangements are shifting at a pace comparable to that in the early 1990s, but to the opposite direction. The space for capital accumulation is no longer a smooth terrain enveloping virtually the entire planet; it is syncopated and restricted by intra-state antagonisms. International institutions are severely weakened without new ones taking their place (Boyer 2021: 184); transnational supply chains are crumbling; and war becomes more that merely possible. In short: the envelope for accumulation has shrank. Rather than being global, the new envelope will comprise regional blocs of economic integration — south-east Asia, continental Europe and the "Anglo" world seem to emerge as early forerunners. While the process of regionalisation remains molten, the determination of economic policy increasingly refers to the national scale. It seeks its legitimacy and justification within the national framework, does not hesitate to adopt protectionist measures, and is marked by a nationalist ideology that comes to inform economic policy. In one word, rather than trans-national, the emerging state appears to be a *national* one.

This national state-form is more state-like — or statist — than its previous iteration. The sub-national scales, local and regional, are politically neutralised and power emanates from the national centre, from the political capital of a country. While this centralisation of power is unequivocal in the management of the economic crisis and the drawing of economic policy; the picture is more complicated in the management of the biosecurity crisis. On the one hand, there is a centripetal tendency — notable in the German *Länder* succumbing to policy determined in Berlin. But there are also centrifugal tendencies: in the US several states defied President Trump's *laissez faire* approach to the pandemic; and in the UK the devolved governments in Scotland and Wales occasionally departed from London's policy. In extreme instances, they even took the unthinkable step of closing their borders with England. These frictions, however, do not necessarily negate the tendency towards centralisation; they may rather signify a tendency towards the break-up of the UK, or to denote a centralisation in *three* centres — Cardiff, Edinburgh and London — each "sovereign" over its own jurisdiction and nation. Centralisation of power is also evident in the EU, but here it occurs at supranational level. The management of the Eurozone crisis (2010–2015) entailed a transfer of power from member states to the central, unelected, governance institutions of the EU: the Commission, the European Central Bank and the EU Court of Justice, who came to define and police the macroeconomic policy of member states. This formal shift of power from the members to the EU entailed another, informal one: from debtor states to creditor ones, especially Germany, who are able to determine the policy of central EU institutions (Menéndez 2017: 70-74). In the course of the twin crises, these shifts are entrenched and expanded. The conditionality of EU funds (loans and grants) brings economic policy *tout court*, its modalities and objectives, to be dictated by the EU's unelected institutions. Member states are limited to adjusting and implementing it at their national context. This, in turn, galvanises and extends the power of those member states who can influence central EU policy at the expense of that of those that cannot. Thus, in the EU concentration of power entails, for most member states, loss of a core state capacity: their competency to devise economic policy. Concentration of power in the EU signals a drastic disempowerment of the national state, combined with the transformation EU itself from a loose "quasi-federal polity into a centralised, hierarchical, and deeply asymmetrical *state* (Menéndez 2017: 73; original emphasis). In every case, what is absent during the twin crises is the "governance regime", i.e. the byzantine milieu of semi-formal, informal or shadowy public-private forums, which operated across scales of governance and was responsible for determining and implementing policy during the height of the neoliberal era. The absence of this governance regime, combined with the centralisation of "properly public" power denotes a return to statism. There are, however, two important caveats.

First, statism involves the gradual transmission of command from the summit of the state to society, through defined lines of hierarchy — which double up in the opposite direction as lines of accountability. In its previous iteration, the neoliberal state had largely replaced these hierarchical-bureaucratic lines of command with a public-private governance regime. Now, that regime seems to be replaced with nothing. Policy and command descends from the summits of the state upon society *directly*, without hierarchical mediation. And, of course, there are no lines of accountability connecting the state to society. Second, and more important, while the term "state" denotes a unifying entity that synthesises conflicting social interests into a national-general interest; the emerging state has neither appetite or ability to do anything like that. Indeed, it cannot even synthesise and promote the "general interest" of the capitalist class — but only responds to direct requests by selected capitals. It seems, therefore that, as the governance regime of public-private fora is eclipsed, the state itself has become one.

This lack of synthetic role inevitably results to the state's loss of strategic ability. This lack of strategy — of planning, mobilisation and coordination of state powers towards a purpose — reduces the state to mere machinery. Its agency is mechanical. The emerging state is just an *apparatus*. For the select capitals that are its privileged interlocutors, the apparatus-state resembles a vending machine: they put money at one end, and get policy at the other. For society, the state is a coercive apparatus; it imposes prohibition, surveillance and violence.

This coercive apparatus aims to impose workfare — its determination to do so is palpable, it has been noticed throughout the book, and Chapter 12 has focused on it. Workfare — the political, ideological and economic devaluation of labour — is not just a feature of the neoliberal state; it is the decisive element. All other structural elements are meant to align so that workfare is imposed, expanded and secured (Boukalas 2014: 135, 215–216). Here the emerging state-form is deeply problematic: its elements are not solid supports for workfare. The first problem is the centralisation of power and the eclipse of the governance regime. The latter comprised a nebula of ad hoc fora that, while decisive for policy planning, were unfathomable and even imperceptible to society. In the emerging state-form the centre — the source of unpopular policies — is too visible, indeed, highlighted: senior ministers and, above all the head of government. However secluded, the centre is a focal point for resistance. Hence, protest must be criminalised and critique prohibited. The second, perhaps more problematic, element is the de-globalisation of economic policy and its re-anchoring in the national framework. This produces two competing perspectives for labour. The first is that, as it becomes more secluded from the competition of lower labour costs in other regions of the planet, the price of labour in western countries will increase, and so will the workers' bargaining power. This threatens to upend workfare. It is paramount for capital to re-introduce labour cost discrepancies by zoning labour: spatially, so that ample pools of cheap labour are created within each regional bloc and nation state; and along the lines of business sector and workers' skillset. Capital needs to maintain the devaluation of labour in the face of structural trends that push to the opposite direction. The state is mobilised to this cause: it does whatever it takes to suppress wages, services and the social wage; and employs a panoply of violence to respond to awkward social demands.

Further, the "Friedmanian" crisis-seeking mode of accumulation this state is called to promote is, as such, absurd. Crisis can be a regular and even a perpetual occurrence — but it cannot be constant. Accumulation tends to settle in a concrete, predictable framework of regular rules and modalities, in a regime of normality — and it *must* do so soon if it is to continue. Without such a framework it will not be able to proceed beyond the immediate term. Moreover, without a framework of normality, the notion of crisis will lose all meaning and become conceptually impossible — for if there is no normality there is nothing that can fall into crisis, only emergency painting its red upon red (paraphrased: Hegel 2008: 16).

Finally, the broadest and most profound misalignment of the emerging state-form is that between a neoliberal state set to suspend time in an eternal present, and capitalism — which is by constitution a dynamic and future-oriented system. A despotic state fixated with preserving and perpetuating the present cannot serve capital for long. Indeed, the "bourgeois state" has always been a future-oriented state based on "leadership", one that envisioned, designed and effectuated projects (Kojève 2020: 61–66). Despotism and capitalism are incompatible. A deep structural fissure appears to open between capitalism and the capitalist state. This means either that the neoliberal-despotic state is a temporary abomination; or that capitalism has been transformed. Indeed, the rapid acceleration of turnover times towards zero indicate an orientation of capital towards the present. More importantly, the turn, during the neoliberal era, of capital investment away from wealth-creating production and towards wealth-extracting rent (especially finance and real estate), signal that the capitalist class is avert to change. It has lost its dynamism and now aims to protect its gains, to keep social wealth concentrated — and concentrating — in its hands. For *this* capitalism the despotic state appears to be a good fit. Even then, two key problems remain. First, the authority of the despotic state is weak. An authority fixed on the present, unable to draw support from either the past or the future (as, respectively, conservative and liberal states did) is a shallow authority, prompt to disintegrate into administration and force (Kojève 2020: 64–65, 75). And, second, as the concentration of social wealth at the hands of capital is approaching its asymptotes (Bichler and Nitzan 2012) its continuation becomes increasingly hard; it demands ever increasing force.

Thus, the emerging *Friedmanian, workfare, national apparatus* (FWNA) is a misaligned and unstable state-form: it subscribes to a strand of political economy and ideology that is chaotic and actively promotes instability; and some of its structural elements tend to undermine its core feature. This is a state-form that emerges from the dissolution of the neoliberal social order and it is charged to keep it together. This self-contradictory form is kept together only through coercion — hence its markedly authoritarian characteristics. For this form, state violence is a necessary structural element. *A regime that needs to be protected by so much violence cannot be good or secure* (Machiavelli 2021: III, 26).

Note

1. They are scheduled to expire with the rest of the Act in late March 2022.

20 Overcoming the order of fear

Implosion

There are two ways in which political orders die, i.e. expire through discontinuity. The first is explosion. It occurs when social dynamics can no longer be accommodated by the institutional shell that contains it. To fulfil its potential it smashes this shell. Explosion is expressed in, and as, a white-hot moment. Its development may be prolonged, and so can be its aftermath; but its manifestation is abrupt and marks an identifiable point in time. The second way is implosion. Implosion occurs when social dynamics has shrunk to such a point that it can no longer sustain the shell that contains it. Implosions, then, are cool, prolonged in their development and protracted in their manifestation.

The archetypal form of explosion is revolution. In revolutionary situations, social dynamics accelerates and intensifies to such a degree that it overwhelms the institutional order that contains it. It can no longer be accommodated in, and expressed through, existing institutional frameworks and channels (Poulantzas 1974: 313–329; Poulantzas 1976). Social antagonism outpaces the ability of the institutional framework to change and adjust to social dynamics so that it can continue to accommodate them. The institutional incapacity to change in accordance to social pressures reflects the unwillingness or inability of state actors — and, ultimately, the ruling class — to adapt to accelerated social dynamics that challenge some aspects of their rule, or their rule *tout court*. In such a juncture, the state and the ruling class will attempt to marginalise, corrupt, co-opt and oppress antagonistic forces. If successful, they can either proceed to reform the institutional order so that it can now accommodate the shift in social dynamics — albeit in ways that guarantee the long term reproduction of their rule. Or, they can seek to reinstall their upset institutional framework intact —an effort that typically involves a round of vengeful violence, a campaign of terror, aiming to exterminate antagonistic forces. If state attempts to corrupt, co-opt and repress social antagonism fail, the state is lost: social dynamics will smash it and the order it represents.

DOI: 10.4324/9781003302988-23

Implosion, by contrast, occurs when the degree of social antagonism necessary to sustain an institutional order is missing. Institutional orders are an outcome of social antagonism; they are partial (in both senses of the word) and shifting crystallisations of social antagonism. They are shaped by it and shape it (Boukalas 2014: 15–18; Jessop 2008: 37–45; Poulantzas 1978: 44–45, 147–152). Without it, they collapse. Without antagonism, institutional orders have no content or purpose; they become empty shells, they linger and collapse —they implode. Implosion, then, occurs when social dynamics is atrophic, when society has become too pacified. When there are no resistances, challenges, alternative modalities, priorities and purposes of practice, competing social projects and temporal perspectives. In short, when society becomes unilateral, operating under a singular uncontested logic, for a singular purpose, without tensions caused by alterity. This was the situation on the eve of the pandemic (Boukalas 2021). Here is a danger for the state: while it can easily identify explosive situations and grapple with them; it may mistake implosive ones, and the social peace and apathy they involve, as its triumph over social antagonism.

Biosecurity achieved a unique feat: palpable implosion. As biosecurity pulverised society into isolated, enclosed household units and removed it from public space, it effectuated a complete eclipse of social antagonism. Politics — especially popular, "unofficial" politics — necessitates assembly and culminates in its expression in public space; it was therefore erased. During more than a year of partial and full lockdowns, politics was reduced to an eternal televised litany of a singular official monologue. Biosecurity achieved perfect implosion. It did this abruptly, for a prolonged period, and it condensed the force of implosion to such a degree that it became visible, audible and tangible: in the silent streets and clean air of quarantined cities.

Faced with the absence of social dynamics, the institutional order shrunk so that it could be sustained by minimal antagonism. Thus, the televised official bulletins that stood in for politics were concerned with only one thing: biosecurity. They were addressing it within narrow technical parameters, dictated (supposedly) by science. Political "debate" was reduced to addressing the deployment and efficacy of techno-scientific measures. Even the weak, inconsequential criticism articulated within this framework and the allusions to state responsibilities, were castigated for "politicising" the issue. In short, the only political issue was the pandemic, a (supposedly) a-political, technical matter, which allowed only a restricted range of questions and actions and an even more restricted scope for critique.

The state did indeed mistake implosion for victory. Its police forces fully controlled the evacuated public space; and its ideologues fully occupied ether and airwaves with paternalist admonitions backed by threats. The arrogance and intolerance of state actors resulted from a combination of panic before a rapid implosion that they could not control; and the elation that their actions were motivated by the imperative moral duty to protect society. Biosecurity was the state's mission and its zeal. The acts of its ministers, however relevant, successful or sincere, were *a priory* legitimate and popular. Thus, the state engaged in a ventriloquist dialogue with society (Hall et al 1978): the latter craved for security; the state duly obliged by expanding its powers and placing them beyond questioning or accountability. Society demanded protection and in exchange was offering obedience. Biosecurity established the ideal, from the point of view of the state, relation between rulers and ruled.

This, however, is only the observable part of political reality. Biosecurity never suspended social antagonism. It was absorbed by it and laid a new terrain for it. Form the start, when the virus arrived in Italy, factory workers resisted the sacrificial role assigned to them and demanded safety measures in the workplace. Wildcat strikes erupted, and the very condition of biosecurity made them morally irresistible. The ill-concealed reluctance of capital and the state to satisfy workers' demands burst the idyllic of patriotic unity against the "invisible enemy". By contrast, the state was more perceptive to a second set of demands. These were demands against biosecurity, expressed mainly by small business owners who biosecurity measures threatened with extinction. Once sectors of big capital joined the opposition to prolonged closures, governments promptly lifted lockdowns as soon as public health appearances would permit — or sooner. In other words, the "life or livelihood", "health or economy" dilemma was an ideological expression of social conflict; the state's prioritisation of the economy stems from its class allegiance. Still, the petit bourgeois rebellion had further political ramifications. Expressed as a defence of freedom from the threat of an authoritarian state, it challenged biosecurity power. Its social resonance was limited, for its liberal demands were expressed and exploited by a nascent fascist movement currently going under the "alt-right" pseudonym. This milieu is part of a parallel network of power that has strong links, and can act in coordination, with actors within the official state. In the US —were it is more developed, has fraternal relations with the police, and its political allies reside as high up as the Senate and, occasionally, the White House — its hit-squads made spectacular shows of force.

Thus, rather than eradicating social antagonism, biosecurity became its object. A "civil war" broke out between those "for" and those "against" lockdown —the "socially responsible" and the "freedom lovers", known to each other as "covidiots" and "sheeple". The object, camps and terms of engagement in this "war" were determined and controlled by the state. It allowed the latter to evade implosion by staging and directing an anodyne antagonism that spitefully divides society without antagonising the social order. It allows the state to pick and change sides, without coming under social pressure. Characteristically, at the start of the pandemic, societies, especially in Europe, where articulating demands for the strengthening of the health system and the reversal of a decade of austerity; by the end of the pandemic, these demands are forgotten: instead everyone blames the "anti-vaxxers" for everything. Society has fallen in the "personal responsibility" trap letting the state continue with business as usual undisturbed (Wu Ming 2021).

In sum, biosecurity was a moment of political implosion, unique in magnitude. The state managed to overcome it by expanding its authoritarian powers with the eulogies of society; reducing the scope of politics; and staging anodyne and exploitable "civil wars" to compensate for the missing antagonism. The state has been very *effective* in grasping the opportunities biosecurity offered. But it has not been *successful* — for biosecurity was thrashed.

If they don't fear this, they won't fear anything

Biosecurity suspended society and turned public space into a vacuum. In doing so, it would erase social antagonism and reduce politics to the initiatives of the state — themselves also apolitical, for they were dictated by necessity. Biosecurity should have cancelled politics, but didn't.

To begin with, lockdowns were perforated by countless acts of individual deviance, including by politicians and their sage advisers who imposed the restrictions. While these acts lack any identifiable political motivation and do not constitute a political expression, the very condition of biosecurity vests them with political significance: they were, strictly speaking, acts of illegality.

While these were opportunistic, atomised, acts of deviance, the same cannot be said about another phenomenon that flourished under lockdown: street parties. These improvised events were a fixture of the lockdown experience across Europe. Again, they were expressions of illegality that lacked an identifiable political motivation — but their political character is unmistakable. They were genuine popular assemblies that reclaimed public space from its state-imposed vacuum. They did not oppose the lockdown, they openly defied it. And, at least in Belgium, France, Greece and the UK, they engaged in violent confrontations with the police; even when such clashes did not materialise, those attending knew they were a real possibility.

If street parties were de facto political events, another type was consciously and explicitly so. In the US, lockdown was smashed by the rise of an anti-racist movement, which was unparalleled in recent history in terms of mass, perseverance and ferocity; notably, its anti-racist agenda was interwoven with socialist demands (Robinson 2020; Shemon 2020). Mobilisations in solidarity to the US movement took place across Europe. In the UK, they challenged the sanctity of the country's colonial past, triggering the hysterical reaction of the government and the mobilisation of fascist groups to counter it. Elsewhere, the peace of quarantined cities was upset by the protest of workers (France, Greece), women (Turkey, UK) environmentalists (UK) and anti-fascists (Greece); and the banning of protest was met with mass protests (France, UK). All these movements and gestures of resistance were confronted by intense police violence. This highlights the state's conception of society as a threat and its inability to deal with it in ways other than force. All it achieved was to trigger mass protests against the police. Thus, the character of biosecurity as a counter-insurgency strategy, and its implication that the state views society as the enemy, is largely confirmed. It seems, however, that the strategy has failed: rather than pacifying the public realm by emptying it of people, it brought the latter to the fore in a multiplicity of unexpected expressions. Rather than paralysing social antagonism, it radicalised it.

The eruption of protest under lockdown defeated biosecurity, its operation and its logic. Protest overcame the biopolitical reduction of society into a "population", an object-matter of power, and affirmed its existence as a relation-in-action. In protest, society re-constituted itself by itself, overcoming its state-imposed reduction to isolated atoms. It reinstalled itself as a creative agent and author of its history. Moreover, protest had a reason. It rose against authoritarianism, police violence, racism, exploitation, misogyny, fascism. Against an exploitative, oppressive and murderous state. Protest's intensely political nature means that society reconstitutes itself for a reason. This shutters biosecurity's reduction of life to metabolism. For society, life is purpose, it is meaning. To pursue its purpose and gain its meaning, life can be risked. Everyone involved in protest believed that doing so is a risk to the life of herself and others. Her participation testifies that there are things worth risking life for; things that differentiate life from its metabolism, things that make life life.

Protest involved risk to life. To do it, it took courage. Society overcame the fear of a lethal virus, the fear of being outlawed, the fear of police violence and, above all, the state-induced universal fear and suspicion of everyone against everyone. In doing so, it not only destroyed the condition of biosecurity; it dealt a blow to threat governmentality. To rule society, the state offers it security. Society *returned the gift* (Neocleous 2008: 185–186). This is a worrying development, for the state. It suggests that government through fear has a saturation point beyond which it becomes self-negating. Society can develop immunity to fear. It can overthrow the fear emanating from a specific threat and become insubordinate to the authority stemming from it. Possibly, it can shift its attitude towards fear *tout court*. The problem for the state is this: if society ceases to fear a highly contagious, malleable, and lethal disease, what on earth *will* it fear? This is a problem because, if fear is overcome, state actions lose their legitimacy and their authority becomes flimsy: supported only by force. With fear gone, the state is left without a platform on which to govern; it can only dominate.

Thus, biosecurity's promise of complete implosion, of erasure of social antagonism, abruptly turned into a reality that is potentially explosive. Social uprising during lockdown washed away biosecurity and its conceptual and operational paraphernalia; and jeopardised the basis of state authority and legitimacy. The implosive moment of biosecurity is, in short, superseded by a situation of indeterminacy — a situation were established relations, meanings and practices are reassessed, challenged and undermined and their evolution remains an open question. This indeterminacy is the most obvious, and profound, legacy of the pandemic experience.

Retour à la normale...

The experience of the pandemic has eroded a lot of our unquestioned premises. The normality in which we used to live can no longer exist, or be returned to, as an *a priory* given order of things (Tsoukalas 2021: 30). The pandemic has been an "ideal suspension". It temporarily neutralised the sense of normality and naturalness of social life under capitalism. It showed it as an artificial condition, the aspects of which can be — and were — put on pause and even upended (Penzin 2020: 11–12). The sense of bewilderment has been universal, encompassing all aspects of social life: from tourism to budgetary limits; form pollution to drinks with friends; from sport spectating to office work and commute. Even the practices that were not suspended acquired new meanings and significance. Walking, working, shopping — they all continued but were not the same. As a crisis, the pandemic had a revelatory effect. It laid bare what was previously swept under the blanket of naturalness: loneliness; race, class and gender injustice; homelessness; exploitation; job insecurity (Stimilli 2020: 392). Finally, few have failed to notice that, in order to sustain capitalist relations — first and foremost the wage relation and the dependency and division it encapsulates — neoliberal governments, in unison, resorted to measures of "socialist" providence: they nationalised railways, suspended rent and mortgage payments, banned evictions, provided something that resembles universal basic income, halted consumption and directed production towards the satisfaction of "basic needs" (Penzin 2020: 12). In short, the entire network of capitalist relations and practices, their settings and their meanings, have been upended, making it impossible to recover as a natural or inevitable order.

As if that was not enough, attitudes towards the constitutive elements of the social order — work, politics, the law — have also been upset. For instance, whatever its contribution to saving lives, the NHS or the economy has been, the only certain achievement of biosecurity omni-regulation was to make the social majority experience *illegality*. People's relation to the law changed. It can no longer be taken as gospel; its exigencies are evaluated, rationally or emotionally, and compliance depends not on the legal command as such, but on the result of this evaluation.

Further, the prolonged display of state irresponsibility during the pandemic is pregnant with a mortal danger for the state: If the state does not acknowledge its failures, is not accountable for its actions, declares impotence to influence "inevitable" developments and abruptly abandons society to face the moment of danger by itself; then society can reasonably wonder *what the use of the state is* — and if there is any.

Finally, nested as it was in the clashing fears for "life" and "livelihood", the pandemic experience can raise another radical question: "what good is biological life if…it simply exists for the benefit of economic activity and what good is dedicating so much of our lives to economic activity if it simply exists to maintain biological life?" (Situations Collective 2020: 13). It can make, in other words, both "live to work" and "work to live" become unbearable *simultaneously*.

Still, the deepest legacy of the pandemic is the realisation that change is possible. For almost half a century we have been instilled with the consciousness that there is no alternative, that society cannot change — certainly not by us — that history has ended, that the future can only be a repetition of the present, at best. Politicians, the media, "radical" philosophers and "melancholic" revolutionaries, catechise that change is impossible. That our social order, even if it is not natural or perfect, it is the best we can hope for and, in any case, it is unshakable. Then, within a week, all our social relations — with each other, with ourselves, with space, time, property, work, law, the state, the wage and death — they all changed completely, at once. This was revolutionary change: it forced a radical re-evaluation of social practices, relations, purposes and meanings. Yet, unlike revolutionary risings, this was not driven by society, but imposed — reluctantly and incoherently — by the state. It had no programme or purpose except to preserve the social order intact. Still, it exposed the artificiality, brittleness and neediness of the social order, and thus made the notion of its impregnability sound absurd. Against the dogma that change is impossible, it forced the notion than no-change might be impossible too. Ironically, in its urgency to save the capitalist order, the state undermined its conceptual foundations.

Its comportment during the pandemic is therefore deeply embarrassing for the state. If possible, it would make everyone forget it, avert people from talking, writing or pondering about the collective experience we had in isolation, blindside it like an ignominious episode in the family history. Failing that, it would raise maximum noise about the event — for instance through "forensic" examinations of incidents and apportioning of praise and blame to specific ministers — until the pandemic experience is reduced to petty insignificance. *Nothing has happened*. The state is instructing everyone to push ahead with the return to normality — a return it has been idiotically promising ever since it took the first biosecurity measures. Indeed, a speedy, full recovery of the status quo ante is the only purpose of the state and the height of its ambition and ability.

Such a return to normality is far from certain. The cognitive, conceptual and affective battering normality took during the pandemic will make its restoration precarious. Worse, there are some signs that, despite the state's cheerleading, a return to normality is not what society desires. Early in the pandemic, opinion polls suggested that only a small fraction (between 6 and 12 percent) of UK citizens were keen to return to (their) economic normality (Proctor 2020). At the other end of the pandemic, a majority of UK youth incredibly declared its conversion to socialism (Niemietz 2021). Their continental counterparts think that an authoritarian state is better suited to combat the environmental crisis than a democratic one (Abramska-Wyss and Honsel 2021: 39–40)[1]. In short, society seems keen on anything other than the normality the state offers it. Under this light, the self-satisfaction with which the state makes this offer suggests a discrepancy. Society and the state seem to be at cross-purposes — and this is a dangerous position for the state to be in.

Back to neoliberal despotism — and beyond

As western societies "return to normality", they are at once hit by another crisis: one of energy and food shortage that, as it pushes prices upwards, has ignited inflation. The prospect of economic turmoil becomes a distinct possibility, involving the architecture of supply chains, the labour conditions therein, interest rate policy, living standards, weakening demand and syncopated supply. The state, in other words, cannot deliver the only thing it promises: normality. It seems to stumble from one crisis to the next. Every occurrence seems to trigger a crisis. The state cannot cope even with predictable and avoidable developments, developments that largely stem from its own initiatives. It cannot anticipate the effects of its interventions. It policies are devised on the hoof. They lack coordination and cohesion because they do not pertain to a strategy.

Indeed, rather than a cohesive social agent, the despotic state is a jumble of paradoxes and contradictions, of unresolved tensions. The first among them is that this state is both hyperactive and impotent. It constantly mobilises powers and intervenes in all aspects of social life; but has no idea what it tries to achieve with this, for it lacks strategic perspective and ability. Manoeuvring through this paradox, the state directs its efforts to securing that things remain as they are; it embarks on the strategy of a state incapable of strategy.

Instead of lifting the paradox, this manoeuvring gives rise to a second one: the state dedicates all its efforts to impose social stasis, at the moment when change is inevitable. The social order it seeks to preserve is not preservable: its sliding into crisis with every opportunity is symptomatic of its instability. Its instability results, in turn, from popular resentment towards it. For an ever-increasing social majority the present order entails ever-increasing hardship, degradation and agony. Matched as this is with provocative displays of opulence and contempt by an ever-decreasing minority, it is marked by injustice. As neither the state nor society can envision a path out of it, the existing order becomes unbearable.

The expansion and intensification of state powers results precisely from the state's aim to evade the inevitable: change. This is its sole preoccupation, and it constantly brings it face to face with myriad inevitabilities —"inevitable" crises, of all shapes and sizes, stemming from the state's determination to suppress the real inevitability. The state's attitude to change is not a Lampedusian one, where *everything must change for everything to remain the same* — i.e. an organised, methodic retreat that acknowledges the inevitability of change, identifies its direction, and seeks to secure a privileged place in the new arrangement (Di Lampedusa 2007). It neither is a Gramscian hegemonic manoeuvre that would alter the terrain of social dynamics and tactically concede ground to the opposition in order to preserve the core of power relations (Gramsci 1998). Either of these tactics would involve strategic planning and cohesion. Instead, the state is simply kicking against the pricks. Its attitude to change is reactionary and, moreover, it is ad hoc and haphazard, dictated only by the exigencies of the moment. Ironically, instead of preventing change, this effort changes the state. It triggers the expansion of its powers and the shift in its form. The tension between state-imposed stasis and socially induced change, becomes inscribed in the form of the state. Hence, the emerging state-form is maladjusted and comprises misaligned and contradictory structural elements. The FWNA is a transitional and moribund state-form.

The tension between the inevitability of social change and the state's determination to repress it shapes the state's overall logic. Here, it morphs into a curious dialectic of fear. For a state determined to preserve an anti-popular and un-popular social order and unable to promise society a better future, fear is the only platform on which it can govern. State authority and legitimacy are premised, exclusively, on the invocation of catastrophe. This invocation is, somehow, supposed to make the deterioration of life over which the state presides palatable. The spectre of exotic threats, spectacular and external to the social order, also serves to conceal the reality that the main threat to society is endogenous, it stems from the social order itself. The latter can now produce nothing but hardship, agony and death. The state knows that the social order it strives to secure has nothing good in store for society and is abhorred by the latter. Hence, the state fears society. It conceptualises it as a threat, and seeks to neutralise its inherent potential for change.

In short, the state is in fear of society, a fear that ensues from the threat that the social order poses to society. This threat is projected, by the state, as a phantasmagoria of threats, which beg for the state's protective intervention and legitimise the state's securing of the social order that threatens society. This dialectic of fear informs threat governmentality, the logic that informs and traverses state activity.

In sum, this state fears society and tries to scare it in order to govern it; it strives to secure a social order that is both anti-social and unsustainable; so is the state itself, for the structural elements of its emerging form are mutually contradictory and hard to align; and, while it is determined to do whatever it takes to secure the social order, the state lacks — or should lack — confidence in its ability to do so; to come full circle, this is a state in fear. Its structure, its relation to society, its logic and purpose are crammed with contradictions, unresolvable tensions and unreconcilable dialectics. The only means to hold these elements together is force.

In overcoming the paralysing fear of the pandemic, society's reconstitution in protest destroyed any state plans to turn it into a biosecurity colony. To do so it neutralised the spectacular fear that is the only remaining platform for state authority and legitimacy. Overcoming fear injures the authority of the protector — the state's only remaining source of authority. From now on, state power is grounded only on force. And this means the loss of authority — for authority is the ability to direct the conduct of others without opposition from their part, even though they are able to offer such opposition. Authority, then, is incompatible with the exercise of force (Kojève 2020: 7–14). The parade of violence of the neoliberal state is, precisely, the proclamation of its loss of authority. Worse still, the realisation that the real threat to society is its established social order is already fermenting. If society manages to express this realisation politically, threat governmentality will collapse and the political dialectic of fear will reach a (final?) resolution. For, the despotic state will respond with a paroxysm of violence. From fearful fear-monger it will transform into fear's author. Any pretence that its government aims to secure society from a threat will evaporate as the state assumes this role itself. This will constitute a genuine, universal crisis, which will end with society's subjugation to brute force, or initiate its renaissance.

Note

1. This trend is instructive. First, like all reductions of politics to a singular moral imperative, environmentalism has inherent authoritarian tendencies (Riesel and Semprum 2014). Second, an authoritarian state is better suited to combat any existential crisis — this is what the democratic state itself has been declaring since 9/11 including, and with renewed urgency, during the pandemic. The authoritarian hardening of the crisis-combating state is the only political model the youth have known. By contrast, third, it is not clear what benefits the youth have reaped from living under a democratic regime, or if they have experienced such a thing in their lifetime.

21 Postscript: Pericles and the plague

In 430 BC, Athens was struck by a plague. It was the only Greek city to be visited by the disease. However, the disease was not autochthonous to Athens; it found its way there, probably, from Ethiopia via Egypt. The disease was wildly contagious. The first, and hardest, hit were those caring for the ill: relatives, friends and doctors. The ministrations of the latter were largely irrelevant, for there was no treatment for the illness and each person would fare according to their physical constitution and luck. The disease came in recurrent waves: it would ebb and flow seasonally over the next few years (Thucydides 2009: II, §47–48, 51; III, §87). It is estimated to have caused the death of a quarter of the city's population (Littman 2009).

This is where the similarities with our predicament end. And thankfully so, for the hallmark of the Athenian plague was the savage pain, blindness and amnesia it caused[1] and its very high mortality rate. Its spread, violence and deadliness resulted to a collapse of the moral order. With families decimated, people would ditch dead friends and relatives into other people's graves or pyres. With this ultimate taboo broken, the entire moral system of the city was breeched. The arbitrary and indiscriminating nature of a plague that would not differentiate between the rich and the poor, the fair and the vile, the lawful and the criminal, the honest and the fraudulent; combined with the consciousness of death's imminence, resulted to complete disregard for legal and moral constraints, and the citizenry proceeded to a generalised orgy of pleasure and cruelty (Thucydides 2009: II, §49–50).

Crucially, Athens suffered the plague at the moment that it was fighting a war against Sparta, a war between the two "superpowers" of the age that enveloped every Greek city from the middle east to Italy and also involved the Persian empire. The war destroyed civilian populations and, given its political undercurrent as a fight between democracy and oligarchy, also ignited internal wars within each city. In short, Athens had to fend off the plague and at the same time fight what, by analogy, was a world war. Worse, the plague broke out at the very moment the enemy was at the gates: the Spartan army was ravaging the planes of Attica, Athens's food basket. Thus, the plague was coupled with famine. The two crises dovetailed: the sick population could not work on the land, perpetuating the famine; while the famine further worsened

DOI: 10.4324/9781003302988-24

the ability of citizens' bodies to resist the illness. Further, the extra-mural farmer citizens who entered the city to escape the Spartan army, are said to be mainly responsible for reigniting the plague within the city. Finally, under the circumstances, Athens lost its grip over its allied cities. Unable to continue exploiting them, Athens suffered a collapse of its public finances (Thucydides 2009: II, §52–53, 55–57).

In sum: Athens was facing a deadly, incurable disease, war, famine, economic collapse and acute anomy — at once. What is worth marvelling at is that, amidst all that, its political institutions remained standing — and, through them, the city recovered at all fronts[2].

As the leader of Athenian democracy in that period, Pericles became the lightning rod for citizens' desperate fury at their dire circumstances. They blamed him for persuading them to go to war and for the ensuing misfortunes of the plague and the famine (Thucydides 2009: II, §59). Indeed, he was temporarily suspended from public office, but was reinstalled a year later and remained a general until he died — of the plague. Pericles countered these accusations before the assembly of citizens. As was his habit, he intertwined his own, individual defence with that of the city and its institutions. His argument is founded on the axiomatic premise that the strength of the city is collective, and so is its fate: prosperous individuals will be ruined in a ruined city, while personal misfortunes will be overcome in a city that prospers. The horror of the plague, added on the travails of the war, has caused Athenians' judgment to shrink to mere contemplation of their immediate individual misfortune, losing sight of the their collective prospects. This stunned reasoning, resulting from fear and shock, is feeble and wrong-headed. It fails to contemplate the enduring strength of the city, a strength residing in their undisputed naval dominance, but also in their "conviction of superiority", the informed and prudent knowledge that they are better, braver and stronger than the other Greeks — a pride that is distinct from arrogance, for every moron can be arrogant if he gets lucky a few times. Pericles then duly reminds his fellow citizens that the decision to go to war was one between the city's freedom and its subjugation to Spartan rule; and explains that surrendering to Sparta would mean the loss of Athens's empire over other cities. Weaving past present and future together, he admonishes the citizens that forfeiting the empire their progenitors created would unleash the hatred of their subjects against them, and deprive them of their exalted place in the world and the pride they take in it. Instead, if they summon the determination and courage to continue fighting and keep their empire in the face of extreme adversity, future generations will revere them as much as the earlier generation of empire-builders (Thucydides 2009: II, § 60–65).

Our broad familiarity with the epidemiological situation and the political-institutional framework in which Pericles's discourse was uttered invite reflection on our contemporary state[3]. A lot in Pericles's exposition resonate with the modern reader: the weaving of the prospects of the individual with those of the collective is an established trope of republican political theory; the establishment of an inter-generational community of fate is replicated by republicans and nationalists alike. Other elements in Pericles's discourse are more bewildering, like the peculiar combination of freedom *and* empire as sources of pride; the explicit declaration by a democratic leader that the empire is tyranny to those under it — a declaration the frankness of which is banished from modern political discourse.

Crucially, Pericles could point out to the Athenians that going to war with Sparta was *their own* decision. This demonstrates the democratic understanding of the political subjectivity as a creative one: its society and its history are its own, exclusive, work (Castoriadis 1983). Society and history are determined by the citizens' decisions and hence the citizens bear the responsibility for these decisions and their consequences. This trope has reverberated down the centuries to reach us as "personal responsibility" (Chapter 18). Our political leaders stress the latter at every opportunity; but, in contrast to Pericles, they cannot point to a decision we took. The capacity of citizens to take political decisions, to govern themselves, has evaporated; but its correlative responsibility remains acute. It acquires, moreover, a strictly individualist character and thus the political decision-making organ, the state, is exempt from it. In Athens, in other words, the decision and the responsibility are attributes of one and the same political subject, the *demos*; while in contemporary democracies, decision and responsibility are mutually exclusive attributes, attached to two separate subjects. The one that decides, the state, is exempt from responsibility; and the individual, the bearer of responsibility, does not decide anything. In short, the state bears no responsibility for the decisions it makes; and individuals are burdened with a duty to execute and cope with decisions they never took — to be resilient — and to shoulder the cost and the blame for the consequences. Thus, while both notions — collective decision-making and personal responsibility — are premised on a conceptualisation of the individual and society as historically-creative; personal responsibility without collective decision-making capacity pertains to a polity that is not democratic but, at best, merely liberal.

At the heart of Pericles's argument is the value that the Athenians attribute to themselves and their polity — rather: to themselves *as* their polity. This value is communicated by the statesman and acknowledged by the citizens not as an anxious exhortation but simply as a fact. It is the "conviction of superiority", the pride Athenians took in their collective achievements and their political constitution however paradoxical it was: pride in both the freedom of their democratic constitution *and* the tyranny they exercised on others. Pericles emphasises the perils and sacrifices of the endeavour, and the determination, prudence and civil-mindedness necessary to carry it through. The result would be expanded freedom; enhanced collective prosperity, through the extension of the Athenian empire ensuing from Sparta's defeat; and an augmentation of citizens' pride in themselves and their inclusion in the pantheon of exalted generations. In short, Pericles could invoke collective resources of value, offer prospects of a better collective future, and name the core mental requirements to get there. The contrast with our current democratic leaders is devastating. Our leaders are unable to articulate a reason that makes our socio-political life, our social order, worth cherishing. This, in turn, makes their nationalist trumpeting sound hollow. They do not appeal to a common, fortifying, conviction because there is — or they have — none. Instead, they establish their claim to authority on fear: if we do not obey their decrees we shall perish, cause our fellows to perish, and sabotage the economy (and, hence, perish). Their role is to issue orders for our protection; our responsibility is to obey.

Finally, the Athenians' decision was correct. Pericles outlines the ills that the wrong decision — the decision to appease rather than confront Sparta — would have entailed. More importantly, he outlines a brave future that is within the Athenians' grasp if they stick to the course they have decided. Notably, he does not promise or guarantee the desired outcome of a pan-Grecian Athenian empire and its associated glory and wealth. For this to come, Athenians should not only stick to their original decision, but also continue to act in a certain manner: with courage, perseverance and prudence (and the fleet!). Even then, the outcome is not certain: they will also need luck. The wise decision is, in other words, a necessary condition for a desired outcome; it makes it possible, but does not, by itself, bring it to fruition. Success is not certain unless it is achieved. This contrasts sharply with our present situation. Political leaders constantly offer (constantly falsified) promises and guarantees for an imminent, definite victory in the "war" against the virus — and place the blame for its repeated failure to materialise on us. Yet, they fail to disclose what realities or possibilities this victory will bring. In a complete reversal of the Periclean schema, while success is certain, there is no future after it, only a return to the past.

In contrast to democratic Athens, the state's predominant relation with society is not based on conviction and commitment to a social order recognised as good and desirable, but on fear that biological survival will be disrupted. Unable to discover value in the present of our social order, our political leaders are, naturally, unable to offer a perspective for its future. If, thanks to their best ministrations, we come out of this alive, all we can look forward to is a return to the *status quo ante*. The best and only vision our leaders can offer is the return of a fabled "normality", of the capitalist pre-pandemic arcadia, which for society entailed a generalised condition of precarious, prospect-less, and meaningless existence (Boukalas 2021). As they have no vision for the future to offer, their desired and only conceivable, outcome is the erasure of the event and its time. In short, the future will be the past; for this, the present must be erased.

Without anything valuable to identify in the present, or desirable to offer in the future, political authority will again be based on fear: fear that without our leaders' leadership, the perpetuation of an unpleasant, deteriorating and prospect-less reality will be violently disrupted by yet another catastrophe. Here is precisely lies the danger of the pandemic's legacy. Biosecurity has been government-by-fear in overdrive. By being so, it has debased the currency of fear as a platform for political authority and legitimacy. Indeed, people — even during the most frightening stages of the pandemic — have sought meaning in relations and activities that are not defined by fear, and have overcome fear in order to engage in them (Chapter 20). In short, security underpinned by fear is the only thing that the state can offer; and people are starting to "return the gift" (Neocleous 2008: 185–186). This means that the state's loss of its last remaining platform of legitimacy becomes a real possibility. Equally possible becomes the prospect that, deprived of legitimacy, the state will seek to rule on the basis of sheer force. Government will continue to be premised on fear — the fear of the government.

Notes

1. The established position was that the disease was a bubonic plague variant; recent research has shaken this certainty, but has not conclusively identified the disease, which is variously thought to have been a version of typhus, smallpox, salmonella or Ebola. See: Olson et al 1996; Shapiro et al. 2006.
2. The war was eventually lost, but much later and for reasons unrelated to the plague, namely the strategic "overreach" of the expedition to Sicily and the tactical mistakes that pestered it, as well as the strategic blunter of neglecting the navy.
3. Notably, the advent of the pandemic caused several scholars to retrieve Thucydides' account, to draw parallels and lessons for our predicament (e.g. Bass 2020; Kelaidis 2020; Malbeuf et al 2021; The Economist 2020a). They invariably fail to read Thucydides a bit further — they do not register the crucial, in political terms, Periclean response to the collapse of communal life and the citizens' protest. It is therefore unclear what the point of revisiting the ancient text was — their accounts merely inform us that there was once a plague in Athens.

Bibliography

2&3Dorm (2020) "Ημερολόγια Καραντίνας" ["Quarantine diaries"]. *Το Διαλυτικό* 4: 85–96, Athens, December

Abramska-Wyss, Reja and Victoria Honsel (2021) "Climate change". In T. Garton Ash (ed.) *Young Europeans speak to EU*. Oxford: Oxford University European Studies Centre (https://europeanmoments.com/sites/default/files/2021-08/young-europeans-speak-to-eu-rev20210808.pdf)

Adorno, Francesco Paulo (2014) "Power over life, politics of death: Forms of resistance to biopower in Foucault". In V. Lemm and M. Vatter (eds) *The government of life: Foucault, biopolitics and neoliberalism*. New York: Fordham University Press, pp. 98–111

Agnoli, Johannes (2020) "Το κρατος του κεφαλαίου" ["Der Staat des Kapitals"]. In *Κειμενα για το κράτος και την πολιτικη*. Athens: ΚΨΜ, pp. 103–176

Agustin, Bianca, Chuck Collins, Jonathan Heller, Sara Mykleburst and Omar Ocampo (2020) "Billionaire wealth vs community health". *Institute for Policy Studies* (https://ips-dc.org/billionaire-wealth-vs-community-health/)

Allegretti, Aubrey and Rajeev Syal (2021) "Creating a charity to pay for PM's flat refurb would be 'an outrage'". *The Guardian*, 2 March (https://www.theguardian.com/politics/2021/mar/02/creating-a-charity-to-pay-for-pms-flat-refurb-would-be-an-outrage)

Allsop, Rachel, Claire Bessant and Sneha Dawda et al (2021) "Snapshot report 1: Data-driven public policy". *MDDAC Research Compendium*, 18 May

Amnesty International (2020) *As if expendable*. London: Amnesty International

Antithesis (2020) "Σημειώσεις για τη διαχείρηση της πανδημικής κρίσης από το καπιταλιστικό κράτος και τους αγώνες εναντίον της" ["Notes on the management of the pandemic crisis by the capitalist state and the struggles against it"]. *Το Διαλυτικό* 4: 25–32

Aradau, Claudia and Rens van Munster (2011) *Politics of catastrophe*. Abington: Routledge

Aratani, Lauren (2022) "US inflation reached 7% in December as prices rise at rates unseen in decades". *The Guardian*, 12 January (https://www.theguardian.com/business/2022/jan/12/us-inflation-rate-december-2021)

Arendt, Hannah (1970) *On violence*. New York: Harcourt

Aristotle (1992) *Politics*. London: Penguin

Armstrong, David (1995) "The rise of surveillance medicine". *Sociology of Health and Illness* 17: 393–404

Asquith, Shelly (2021) "Workplace covid outbreaks are at an all-time high. Where is the action?". Trade Union Council, 21 January (https://www.tuc.org.uk/blogs/workplace-covid-outbreaks-are-all-time-high-where-action)

Austermühl, Frank (2014) *The great American scaffold*. Amsterdam: John Benjamins

Bank of England (2020) "The impact of Covid-19 on businesses' expectations: Evidence from the decision making panel". London: Bank of England, 25 September

Barbaria (2020) "Οι μαριονέτες το κεφαλαίου" ["The puppets of capital"]. *To Διαλυτικό* 4: 79–84

Barr, Caelainn and Robert Booth (2021) "Covid deaths higher among low-paid workers in England and Wales, analysis shows". *The Guardian*, 25 January (https://www.theguardian.com/world/2021/jan/25/covid-deaths-higher-among-low-paid-workers-in-england-and-wales-analysis-shows)

Barr, Caelainn, Pamela Duncan and Niamh McIntyre (2020) "Coronavirus UK death toll: why what we think we know is wrong". *The Guardian*, 4 April (https://www.theguardian.com/world/2020/apr/04/why-what-we-think-we-know-about-the-uks-coronavirus-death-toll-is-wrong)

Bass, Gary (2020) "The Athenian plague, a cautionary tale of democracy's fragility". *The New Yorker*, 10 June (https://www.newyorker.com/culture/culture-desk/the-athenian-plague-a-cautionary-tale-of-democracys-fragility)

BBC (2019) "Nato alliance experiencing brain death, says Macron". 7 November. https://www.bbc.co.uk/news/world-europe-50335257

BBC (2020) "Coronavirus: UK failed to stockpile crucial PPE". *BBC*, 28 April (https://www.bbc.co.uk/news/newsbeat-52440641)

BBC (2021) "Covid: Boris Johnson's 'bodies pile high' comments prompt criticism". *BBC News*, 27 April (https://www.bbc.com/news/uk-politics-56890714)

Berry, Christine (2021) "Nursery staff are being treated like cannon fodder so 'higher value' work can go on". *The Guardian*, 28 January (https://www.theguardian.com/commentisfree/2021/jan/28/nursery-staff-work-covid-crisis-early-years-support)

Bichler, Shimshon and Jonthan Nitzan (2012) "The asymptotes of power". *Real World Economics Review* 60: 18–53

Biebricher, Thomas and Frieder Vogelmann (eds) (2017) *The birth of austerity: German Ordoliberalism and contemporary neoliberalism*. London: Rowman and Littlefield

Big Brother Watch (2021) "Access denied: the case against a two-tier Britain under covid certification". (https://bigbrotherwatch.org.uk/wp-content/uploads/2021/04/Access-Denied-Big-Brother-Watch.pdf)

Blakeley, Grace (2020) *The corona crash*. London: Verso

Bloch, Ernst (1996) *Natural law and human dignity*. Cambridge: MIT Press

Bloom, Dan (2020) "Panorama PPE scandal: UK Government admits overcounting gloves during coronavirus pandemic". *Edinburgh News*, 28 April (https://www.edinburghlive.co.uk/news/edinburgh-news/panorama-ppe-scandal-uk-government-18165038)

Bobbio, Noberto (1997) *Democracy and dictatorship*. Cambridge: Polity

Böhm, Franz (1937) "Economic ordering as a problem of economic policy and a problem of the economic constitution". In T. Biebricher and F. Vogelmann (eds) *The birth of austerity: German Ordoliberalism and contemporary neoliberalism*. London: Rowman and Littlefield, pp. 115–120

Bonefeld, Werner (2017a) "Authoritarian liberalism: From Schmitt via ordoliberalism to the Euro". *Critical Sociology* 43(4–5): 747–761

Bonefeld, Werner (2017b) *The strong state and the free economy*. London: Rowman and Littlefield

Bordiga, Amadeo (1949) "Class struggle and 'bosses' offensives'". *Battaglia Comunista* 39. (https://www.marxists.org/archive/bordiga/works/1949/class-struggle.htm)

Boukalas, Christos (2012) "Government by experts: Counterterrorism intelligence and democratic retreat". *Critical Studies on Terrorism* 5(2): 277–296

Boukalas, Christos (2014) *Homeland security, its law and its state.* Abington: Routledge

Boukalas, Christos (2017a) "UK counterterrorism law, pre-emption and politics. Towards authoritarian legality?" *New Criminal Law Review* 20(3): 355–390

Boukalas, Christos (2017b) "L'anti-terrorisme, entre Étatisme Autoritaire et Captation de l'Avenir". In S. de Simoni, P. Guillibert and M. Krickerberg (eds) *Critique de la Sécurité.* Paris: Eterotopia

Boukalas, Christos (2019) "The Prevent paradox: destroying liberalism in order to protect it". *Crime, Law and Social Change* (https://doi.org/10.1007/s10611-019-09827-8)

Boukalas, Christos (2020) "Overcoming liberal democracy: 'threat governmentality' and the empowerment of intelligence in the UK Investigatory Powers Act". Studies in Law, *Politics and Society* 82: 1–25

Boukalas, Christos (2021) "No future: pre-emption, temporal sovereignty and hegemonic implosion —a study on the end of neoliberal time". *Constellations* 28: 252–268

Bourdelais, Patrice (1998) "La construction de la notion de contagion: entre médecine et société". *Communications* 66: 21–39

Bourgeron, Théo (2021) "'Let the virus spread'. A doctrine of pandemic management for the libertarian-authoritarian capital accumulation regime". *Organizations* 29(3): 401–413

Boyer, Robert (2021) *Οι καπιταλισμοί στη δίνη της πανδημίας [Les capitalismes à l'épreuve de la pandémie].* Athens: Πόλις

Bratsis, Peter (2007) *Everyday life and the state.* London: Paradigm

Brenner, Robert (2020) "Escalating plunder". *New Left Review* 123: 5–22

Breu, Christopher (2012) "Time, biopolitics and the capitalist world-system". In Institute on Globalisation and the Human Condition (Working Papers 12/3) *An interdisciplinary forum on time and globalization.* Hamilton, Canada:, McMaster University

Brewer, Mike, Adam Corlett, Karl Handscomb and Daniel Tomlinson (2021) "The living standards outlook 2021". London: Resolution Foundation, January

Bröckling, Urlich (2012) "Human economy, human capital: A critique of biopolitical economy". In U. Bröckling, S. Krasmann and T. Lemke (eds.) *Governmentality: Current issues and future challenges.* Abington: Routledge, pp. 247–268

Brown, Lauren (2021) "One in 10 workers told to reapply for their jobs on worse terms, TUC reveals". *People Management*, 25 January (https://www.peoplemanagement.co.uk/news/articles/one-in-10-workers-told-to-reapply-for-their-jobs-on-worse-terms#gref)

Brown, Olen (2020) "Asymptomatic covid-19; we don't know what we don't know". *Preprints* (https://doi.org/10.20944/preprints202007.0681.vl)

Brown, Wendy (2015) *Undoing the demos.* New York: Zone

Bundesverfassungsgericht (2020) "ECB decisions on the Public Sector Purchase Programme exceed EU competences". *Press Release No. 32/2020*, 5 May 2020 (https://www.bundesverfassungsgericht.de/SharedDocs/Pressemitteilungen/EN/2020/bvg20-032.html)

Bush, George W. (2008) *Highlights of accomplishments and results 2001-2009: The administration of George W. Bush.* Washington, DC: White House Archives

Buther, Patrick (2020) "Growing numbers of 'newly hungry' forced to use UK food banks". *The Guardian*, 1 November (https://www.theguardian.com/society/2020/nov/01/growing-numbers-newly-hungry-forced-use-uk-food-banks-covid)

Butler, Patrick (2022a) "Universal credit claimants face tough sanctions in UK job crackdown". *The Guardian*, 27 January (https://www.theguardian.com/society/2022/jan/27/universal-credit-claimants-face-tough-sanctions-in-uk-job-crackdown)

Butler, Patrick (2022b) "Report on effectiveness of benefit sanctions blocked by DWP". *The Guardian*, 27 January (https://www.theguardian.com/society/2022/jan/27/report-on-effectiveness-of-benefit-sanctions-blocked-by-dwp)

Caduff, Carlo (2020) "What went wrong: corona and the world after the full stop". *Medical Anthropology Quarterly* 34(4): 467–487

Calvert Jonathan and George Arbuthnott (2021) *Failures of state*. London: Mudlark

Campbell, Denis (2021a) "Non-NHS healthcare providers were given £96bn in a decade, says Labour". *The Guardian* 3 May (https://www.theguardian.com/society/2021/may/03/non-nhs-healthcare-providers-given-96bn-in-a-decade-says-labour)

Campbell, Denis (2021b) "Number of doctors retiring early trebles in England and Wales". *The Guardian*, 23 June (https://www.theguardian.com/society/2021/jun/23/number-of-doctors-retiring-early-trebles-in-england-and-wales)

Castoriadis, Cornelius (1983) "The Greek polis and the creation of democracy". In D.A. Curtis (ed) *The Castoriadis Reader*. Oxford: Blackwell

Castoriadis, Cornelius (2002) *On Plato's statesman*. Stanford: Stanford University Press

Castrillón, Fernando and Thomas Marchevsky (eds) (2021) *Coronavirus, psychoanalysis and philosophy*. Abington: Routledge

Chan, Szu Ping (2022) "Don't ask for a big pay rise, warns Bank of England boss". *BBC*, 4 February (https://www.bbc.co.uk/news/business-60206564)

Chancellor of the Exchequer (2020) "Spending Review 2020". CP 330. November. London: Her Majesty's Stationary Office

Chandler, David (2016) "Resilience: The societalisation of security". In D. Chandler and J. Reid (eds) *The neoliberal subject*. London: Rowman and Littlefield, pp. 27–49

Chapoutot, Johann (2021) *Ελεύθερος να υπακούς [Libres d'obéir]*. Athens: Αγρα

Chrisafis, Angelique (2019) "French police weapons under scrutiny after gilets jaunes injuries". *The Guardian*, 30 January (https://www.theguardian.com/world/2019/jan/30/french-police-tactics-scrutiny-gilets-jaunes-injuries-paris)

Commission for Countering Extremism (2021) "Operating with impunity — Hateful extremism: the need for a legal framework". *Commission for Countering Extremism*, February.

Connolly, Rachel (2020) "The pandemic has taken surveillance of workers to the next level". *The Guardian*, 14 December (https://www.theguardian.com/commentisfree/2020/dec/14/pandemic-workers-surveillance-monitor-jobs)

Contiadis, Xenophon (2020) *Πανδημία, βιοπολιτική και δικαιώματα [Pandemic, biopolitics and rights]*. Athens: Καστανιώτης

Corporate Europe Observatory (2020) "Power and profit during the pandemic". *Brussels*, 21 September (https://corporateeurope.org/en/2020/09/power-and-profit-during-pandemic)

Corporate Watch (2021) "Vaccine capitalism: a rundown of the huge profits being made from covid-19 vaccines". London, 18 March (https://corporatewatch.org/vaccine-capitalism-a-run-down-of-the-huge-profits-being-made-from-covid-19-vaccines/)

Cortés, Juan Donoso (2000) "Speech on dictatorship". In Jeffrey P. Johnson (ed) *Selected works of Juan Donoso Cortés*. Westport: Greenwood Press, pp. 45–59

Costello, Anthony (2020) "The government's secret science group has a shocking lack of expertise". *The Guardian*, 27 April (https://www.theguardian.com/commentisfree/2020/apr/27/gaps-sage-scientific-body-scientists-medical)

Cowan, Dave (2021) "Ruling the pandemic". In D. Cowan and A. Mumford (eds) *Pandemic legalities*. Bristol: Bristol University Press

Crispin, Jessa (2021) "Welcome to dystopia: getting fired from your job as an Amazon worker by an app". *The Guardian*, 5 July (https://www.theguardian.com/commentisfree/2021/jul/05/amazon-worker-fired-app-dystopia)

Cristi, Renato (1998) *Carl Schmitt and authoritarian liberalism*. Cardiff: University of Wales Press

Cutler, A. Claire (2003) *Private power and global authority*. Cambridge: Cambridge University Press

Davies, Caroline (2022) "Harm to AstraZeneca jab's reputation 'probably killed thousands'". *The Guardian*, 7 February (https://www.theguardian.com/society/2022/feb/07/doubts-cast-over-astrazeneca-jab-probably-killed-thousands-covid-vaccine)

Davies, William (2017) *The limits of neoliberalism*. London: SAGE

Davis, David (2021) "Be warned: this government is robbing you of your right to challenge the state". *The Guardian*, 25 October (https://www.theguardian.com/commentisfree/2021/oct/25/judicial-review-peoples-right-fight-government-destroy-courts-undemocratic)

Davis, Nicola, Peter Walker and Denis Campbell (2021) "Boris Johnson urges Covid caution amid warnings of 200 deaths a day". *The Guardian*, 12 July (https://www.theguardian.com/politics/2021/jul/12/boris-johnson-urges-covid-caution-amid-warnings-of-1000-hospitalisations-a-day)

Debord, Guy (1994) *The society of the spectacle*. New York: Zone Books

Debord, Guy (1998) *Comments on the society of the spectacle*. London: Verso

dell'Umbria, Alessi (2020) "Full metal yellow jacket". *Το Διαλυτικό* 3: 55–70

Demirović, Alex (2012) "Υπερεθνικοποίηση του κράτους και κρίση του καπιταλισμου της χρηματοπιστωτικής αγοράς" ["State supra-nationalisation and the crisis of financial capitalism"]. In C. Golems and I. Oikonomou (eds) *Ο Πουλαντζάς σήμερα [Poulantzas today]*. Athens: Νήσος, pp. 235–252

Department for Education (2021) "What to do if a child or adult is displaying symptoms, or is a confirmed case of coronavirus (covid-19) in an early years setting". (https://assets.publishing.service.gov.uk/government/uploads/system/uploads/attachment_data/file/958657/What_to_do_if_a_child_or_adult_is_displaying_symptoms_or_is_a_confirmed_case_of_coronavirus_COVI.pdf)

Department for Work and Pensions (2022) "New jobs mission to get 500,000 into work". Press Release, 27 January (https://www.gov.uk/government/news/new-jobs-mission-to-get-500-000-into-work)

D'Eramo, Marco (2020) "The philosopher's epidemic". *New Left Review* 122: 23–28

Di Lampedusa, Tomasi (2007) *The leopard*. London: Vintage

Dodd, Vikram (2020) "Extinction Rebellion 'criminals' threaten UK way of life, says Priti Patel". *The Guardian*, 8 September (https://www.theguardian.com/environment/2020/sep/08/extinction-rebellion-criminals-threaten-uks-way-of-life-says-priti-patel)

Dodd, Vikram and Jamie Grierson (2021) "Priti Patel wanted police to stop people gathering at Sarah Everard vigil". *The Guardian*, 19 March (https://www.theguardian.com/uk-news/2021/mar/19/priti-patel-wanted-police-stop-people-gathering-sarah-everard-vigil)

Elgot, Jessica (2022) "Boris Johnson: nobody warned me No 10 party was against the rules". *The Guardian*, 18 January (https://www.theguardian.com/politics/2022/jan/18/boris-johnson-nobody-warned-me-no-10-party-was-against-the-rules)

Elliott, Larry (2020) "UK jobs support should end only when Covid crisis is over". *The Guardian*, 22 December (https://www.theguardian.com/business/2020/dec/22/uk-jobs-support-covid-haldane-employment)

Elliott, Larry (2021) "What we can learn from British history about unemployment". *The Guardian*, 3 February (https://www.theguardian.com/society/2021/feb/03/what-we-can-learn-from-british-history-about-unemployment)

Emerson, Carl, Isabel Stockton and Ben Zaranko (2021) "What does the changing economic outlook mean for the Spending Review?". *Institute for Fiscal Studies*, 21 July (https://ifs.org.uk/publications/15542)

Esposito, Roberto (2008) *Bios: Biopolitics and philosophy*. Minneapolis: University of Minnesota Press

Esposito, Roberto (2021) "Cured to the bitter end". *Autonomie and European Journal of Psychoanalysis* (https://www.journal-psychoanalysis.eu/coronavirus-and-philosophers/)

Euken, Walter (1942) "Competition as the basic principle of the economic constitution". In T. Biebricher and F. Vogelmann (eds) *The birth of austerity: German Ordoliberalism and contemporary neoliberalism*. London: Rowman and Littlefield

European Commission (2021) *SURE: Taking stock after six months*. Brussels: European Commission, 22 March

Farrar, Jeremy (2021) *Spike: The virus vs the people* (with Anjana Ahuja). London: Profile

Ferguson, Daniel and Brigid Francis-Devine (2021) "Briefing Paper: Public Sector Pay". House of Commons Library, 10 March. CPB 8037

Ferguson, Neil, Daniel Laydon, Gemma Nedjati-Gilani et al (2020) "Report 9: Impact of non-pharmaceutical interventions (NPIs) to reduce COVID-19 mortality and healthcare demand". Imperial College Covid-19 Response Team, 16 March (https://www.imperial.ac.uk/media/imperial-college/medicine/sph/ide/gida-fellowships/Imperial-College-COVID19-NPI-modelling-16-03-2020.pdf)

Foucault, Michel (1995) *Discipline and punish*. London: Vintage

Foucault, Michel (1996) *The birth of the clinic*. London: Vintage

Foucault, Michel (2007) *Security, territory, population*. Basingstoke: Palgrave-Macmillan

Foucault, Michel (2008) *The birth of biopolitics*. Basingstoke: Palgrave-Macmillan

Frade, Carlos (2020) "Pandemic politics, oligarchic times and the idiotic subject of 'freedom'". *Open Democracy*, 21 May

Friedman, Milton (2002) *Capitalism and freedom*. Chicago: University of Chicago Press

Gallas, Alexander (2017) *The Thatcherite offensive*. Chicago: Haymarket Books

Garrison, Joey and Ledyard King (2021) "'We have a deal': Biden reaches $1.2 trillion infrastructure compromise with bipartisan group of senators". *USA Today*, 24 June (https://eu.usatoday.com/story/news/politics/2021/06/24/biden-senators-agree-1-2-trillion-infrastructure-deal/5333841001/)

Garside, Juliette and Rupert Neate (2020) "UK government 'using pandemic to transfer NHS duties to private sector'". *The Guardian*, 4 May (https://www.theguardian.com/business/2020/may/04/uk-government-using-crisis-to-transfer-nhs-duties-to-private-sector)

Gearty, Conor (2010) *Can human rights survive?* Cambridge: Cambridge University Press

Gentili, Dario (2021) *The age of precarity*. London: Verso

Global Labour Journal Editorial Board (2020) "Global labour studies in the pandemic: Notes for an emerging agenda". *Global Labour Journal* 11(2): 74–87

Golby, Joel (2020) "Don't blame the government for its handling of Covid. It's our fault, apparently". *The Guardian*, 14 October (https://www.theguardian.com/commentisfree/2020/oct/14/covid-blame-government-public-fault)

Good Law Project (2021a) "The judgement is in". 19 February (https://goodlawproject.org/update/the-judgment-is-in/)

Good Law Project (2021b) "Failure to publish". 16 March (https://goodlawproject.org/update/failure-to-publish/)

Good Law Project (2021c) "Permission granted on our cronyism challenge – we're going to Court". 28 March (https://goodlawproject.org/update/permission-granted-cronyism/)

Good Law Project (2022) "Breaking: High Court finds government PPE 'VIP' lane for politically connected suppliers 'unlawful'". 12 January (https://goodlawproject.org/update/high-court-vip-lane-ppe-unlawful/)

Gramsci, Antonio (1995) *Further selections from the prison notebooks*. London: Lawrence and Wishart

Gramsci, Antonio (1998) *Selections from the prison notebooks*. London: Lawrence and Wishart

Green, Penny and Tony Ward (2004) *State crimes*. London: Pluto

Gregory, Andrew (2021) "England's Covid test and trace spending over £1m a day on consultants". *The Observer*, 21 November (https://www.theguardian.com/world/2021/nov/21/england-covid-test-and-trace-spending-over-1m-a-day-on-consultants)

Grimm, Dieter (2020) "A long time coming". *German Law Journal* 21: 944–949

Gros, Frédéric (2019) *The security principle*. London: Verso

Guittet, Emmanuel-Pierre and Fabienne Brion (2017) "The new age of suspicion". In E. Eklundh, A. Zenvik and E-P Guittet (eds) *Politics of anxiety*. London: Rowman and Littlefield, pp. 79–99

Hall, Stuart, Chas Critcher and Tony Jefferson et al (1978) *Policing the crisis*. London: Cobden Trust

Halliday, Josh (2020) "Lockdown tightened in parts of northern England with ban on indoor meetings". *The Guardian*, 30 July (https://www.theguardian.com/uk-news/2020/jul/30/lockdown-tightened-in-parts-of-northern-england-with-ban-on-indoor-meetings)

Halliday, Josh and Simon Murphy (2020) "Cabinet minister Robert Jenrick visited his parents during Covid-19 lockdown". *The Guardian*, 9 April (https://www.theguardian.com/world/2020/apr/09/cabinet-minister-robert-jenrick-visited-his-parents-during-covid-19-lockdown)

Handler, Joel (2004) *Social citizenship and workfare in the United States and Western Europe*. Cambridge: Cambridge University Press

Hansard (2020a) "Covid-19: test, track and trace". Commons Chamber debate. *Hansard*, vol. 675, 5 May

Hansard (2020b) "Covid-19 strategy". Commons Chamber Debate, vol. 676, 11 May

Hansard (2020c) "Prime Minister". Commons Chamber Debate. *Hansard*, vol. 676, 20 May

Hansard (2020d) "Public health: Coronavirus regulations". Commons Chamber Debate. *Hansard*, vol. 682, 13 October

Hansard (2021a) "Covid-19 update". Commons Chamber Debate. *Hansard*, vol. 689, 9 February

Hansard (2021b) "Coronavirus". Commons Chamber Debate. *Hansard*, vol. 691, 25 March

Harding, Rosie (2021) "Covid-19 in adult social care: futures, funding and fairness". In D. Cowan and A. Mumford (eds) *Pandemic legalities*. Bristol: Bristol University Press

Harvey, David (2003) *The new imperialism*. Oxford: Oxford University Press

Harvey, David (2005) *Neoliberalism*. Oxford: Oxford University Press

Harvey, David (2020) "Value in motion". *New Left Review* 126: 99–116

Harvey, Fiona (2021) "Treasury blocking green policies key to UK net zero target". *The Guardian*, 13 August (https://www.theguardian.com/environment/2021/aug/13/treasury-blocking-green-policies-key-to-uk-net-zero-target)

Hayek, F.A (1988) *The fatal conceit: The errors of socialism*. Chicago: University of Chicago Press

Hayek, F.A (1993) *The road to serfdom*. Abington: Routledge

Hayek, F.A (2013) *Law, legislation and liberty*. Abington: Routledge

Hayes, Lydia J.B. (2017) *Stories of care: A labour of law*. Basingstoke: Palgrave McMillan

Health and Safety Executive (2020–2021) "Management information: Coronavirus (covid-19) disease report" (https://www.hse.gov.uk/statistics/coronavirus/index.htm)

Heath-Kelly, Charlotte (2013) "Counter-terrorism and the counterfactual: Producing the 'radicalisation' discourse and the UK Prevent strategy". *The British Journal of Politics and International Relation* 15: 394–415

Heath-Kelly, Charlotte (2017) "The geography of pre-criminal space: Epidemiological imaginations of radicalisation risk in the UK Prevent strategy, 2007-2017". *Critical Studies on Terrorism* 10 (2): 297–319

Hegel, G.W.F. (2008) *Outlines of the philosophy of right*. Oxford: Oxford University Press

Heine, Heinrich (1847) "The stability of the Guizot ministry". In *The Works of Heinrich Heine vol. VIII (Lutetia)*. London: William Heinemann

Helm, Toby, Robin McKie and Lin Jenkins (2020) "Fearful Britons remain strongly opposed to lifting coronavirus lockdown". *The Guardian*, 3 May (https://www.theguardian.com/world/2020/may/02/fearful-britons-oppose-lifting-lockdown-schools-pubs-restaurants-opinium-poll)

High Court (2021a) The Queen vs Secretary of State for Health and Social Care. Case Number: CO/3610/2020. [2021] EWHC 346 (Admin). 18 February 2021

High Court (2021b) The Queen vs Minister for the Cabinet Office. Case Number: CO/2437/2020 [2021] EWHC 1569 (TCC). 9 June 2021

High Court (2022) The Queen vs The Secretary of State for Health and Social Care. Case Numbers: HT-2020-000226; HT-2020-000291; HT-2020-000292; HT-2020-000419 [2022] EWHC 46 (TCC). 12 January 2022

Hinsliff, Gaby (2020a) "Boris Johnson's Covid-19 dice are loaded against our struggling towns". *The Guardian*, 2 July. (https://www.theguardian.com/commentisfree/2020/jul/02/boris-johnsons-covid-19-dice-loaded-towns-pandemic)

Hinsliff, Gaby (2020b) "Why is the government so pig-headed about free school meals?". *The Guardian*, 26 October (https://www.theguardian.com/commentisfree/2020/oct/26/government-pig-headed-free-school-meals)

HM Government (2020a) *Our plan to rebuild: The UK Government's Covid-19 recovery strategy*. CP 239. London: Her Majesty's Stationary Office

HM Government (2020b) "National restrictions: support for jobs and businesses". *Economic Support Factsheet 5*. 5 November.

HM Government (2020c) "Covid-19 winter plan". CP 324. November. London: Her Majesty's Stationary Office

HM Government (2020d) "Analysis of the health, economic and social effects of covid-19 and the approach to tiering". 30 November. London: Her Majesty's Stationary Office

HM Treasury (2020a) "Forecasts for the economy: a comparison of independent forecasts". November 2020.

HM Treasury (2020b) "Spending Review 2020". CP 330, 25 November. London: Her Majesty's Stationary Office

HM Treasury (2020c) "HM Treasury coronavirus business loan statistics". Published: 27 May; Updated: 17 December (https://www.gov.uk/government/collections/hm-treasury-coronavirus-covid-19-business-loan-scheme-statistics)

HM Treasury (2021a) "Budget 2021". HC1226. Published: 3 March 2021

HM Treasury (2021b) "Autumn budget and spending review 2021". HC822. 27 October

Hobbes, Thomas (2008) *Leviathan*. Oxford: Oxford University Press

House of Commons Liaison Committee (2020) "Oral evidence from the Prime Minister". HC322, 27 May. HC322

House of Commons Public Accounts Committee (2021) "Covid 19: Test, track and trace (part 1)". *House of Commons*, 10 March. HC932

House of Commons Science and Technology Committee (2021) Oral evidence: Coronavirus: Lessons learnt, 26 May. HC95

House of Commons Treasury Committee (2020) "Economic impact of coronavirus: the challenges of recovery". *House of Commons*, 8 September. HC 271

House of Commons Work and Pensions Committee (2021a) "The temporary increase in Universal Credit and Working Tax Credit". *House of Commons*, 9 February. HC 1193

House of Commons Work and Pensions Committee (2021b) "Universal Credit and 'survival sex'". *House of Commons*, 2 March. HC 1225

House of Lords (2020) "Coronavirus bill: explanatory notes". *The House of Lords*, 24 March. HL Bill 110-EN 58/1

Hunt, Adrian (2013) "From control orders to TPIMs". *Crime, Law and Social Change* 62(3): 289–321

Hyde, Marina (2020a) "The truth about why Cummings hasn't gone: Johnson is too terrified to sack him". *The Guardian*, 26 May (https://www.theguardian.com/commentisfree/2020/may/26/dominic-cummings-boris-johnson-terrified-sack-him)

Hyde, Marina (2020b) ""Over by Christmas": now, where have we heard Johnson's new slogan before?" *The Guardian*, 17 July (https://www.theguardian.com/commentisfree/2020/jul/17/christmas-johnson-slogan-prime-minister-pmqs)

Hyde, Marina (2021) "The Tories have worked out how to pull off an NHS data grab: do it during a pandemic". *The Guardian*, 4 June (https://www.theguardian.com/commentisfree/2021/jun/04/tories-nhs-data-grab-pandemic)

IFS (2021) "The IFS Deaton Review of Inequalities: a New Year's message". *Institute for Fiscal Studies Briefing Note*, 5 January (https://www.ifs.org.uk/publications/15241)

Illitch, Ivan (1982) *Medical nemesis*. New York: Random House

IMF (2020a) "World economic outlook: The Great Lockdown". *International Monetary Fund.* April, Washington DC

IMF (2020b) "Fiscal Monitor: Policies for the recovery". *International Monetary Fund.* October, Washington DC

IMF (2020c) "Regional economic outlook. Europe. Whatever it takes: Europe's response to Covid-19". *International Monetary Fund.* October, Washington DC

IMF (2020d) "United Kingdom: staff concluding statement of the 2020 Article IV mission". *International Monetary Fund.* 29 October, Washington DC

IMF (2021a) "World economic outlook. Managing divergent recoveries". *International Monetary Fund,* April, Washington DC

IMF (2021b) "Fiscal monitor: A fair shot". *International Monetary Fund.* April, Washington DC

Inman, Phillip (2022a) "UK inflation rises to highest level in almost 30 years at 5.4%". *The Guardian,* 19 January (https://www.theguardian.com/business/2022/jan/19/uk-inflation-hits-near-three-decade-high-rising-to-54)

Inman, Phillip (2022b) "£40bn profits for BP and Shell fuel calls for windfall tax on energy firms". *The Guardian,* 5 February (https://www.theguardian.com/business/2022/feb/05/40bn-profits-for-bp-and-shell-fuel-calls-for-windfall-tax-on-energy-firms)

Isidore, Chris (2021) "Here is what Covid vaccines are worth to big pharma". *CNN Business,* 15 March (https://edition.cnn.com/2021/03/13/business/business-of-covid-vaccine/index.html)

Jayanetti, Chaminda (2021) "Benefits freeze will leave tenants across Britain facing rent arrears of £1,000". *The Observer,* 13 March (https://www.theguardian.com/money/2021/mar/13/benefits-freeze-will-leave-tenants-across-britain-facing-rent-arrears-of-1000#:~:text=From%20April%2C%20the%20government%20is,including%20those%20on%20universal%20credit)

Jessop, Bob (1990) *State theory.* Cambridge: Polity

Jessop, Bob (2002) *The future of the capitalist state.* Cambridge: Polity

Jessop, Bob (2008) *State power: A strategic-relational approach.* Cambridge: Polity

Jessop, Bob (2015) "The symptomatology of crises, reading crises and learning from them: Some critical realist reflections". *Journal of Critical Realism* 14(3): 238–271

Jessop, Bob (2016) *The state — Past, present, future.* Cambridge: Polity

Jessop, Bob (2018) "Elective affinity or comprehensive contradiction? Reflections on capitalism and democracy in the time of finance-dominated accumulation and austerity states". *Berlin Journal of Sociology* 28: 9–37

Jessop, Bob (2019a) "Valid construals and/or correct readings? On the symptomatology of crises". In B. Jessop and K. Knio (eds) *The pedagogy of economic, political and social crises.* Abington: Routledge

Jessop, Bob (2019b) "Ordoliberalism and neoliberalisation: governing through order or disorder". *Critical Sociology* 45 (7–8): 967–981

Johnson, Boris (2020a) "Prime Minister's statement on coronavirus: 10 May 2020". *Prime Minister's Office,* 10 May

Johnson, Boris (2020b) "PM economy speech: 30 June 2020". *Prime Minister's Office,* 30 June

Johnson, Boris (2020c) "Prime Minister's statement on coronavirus (COVID-19): 22 September 2020". *Prime Minister's Office,* 22 September

Johnson, Boris (2021) "PM statement at coronavirus press conference: 5 July 2021". *Prime Minister's Office,* 5 July

Joint Committee on Human Rights (2020) "The government's response to covid-19: human rights implications". *House of Commons and House of Lords*, 14 September. HC 265/HL Paper 125

Jones, Jonathan (2021) "The government's hasty Covid law-making cannot become a template for the future". *The Guardian*, 18 February (https://www.theguardian.com/commentisfree/2021/feb/18/governments-hasty-covid-law-making-template-future)

Justice Alliance (2020) *Justice matters – Essays from the pandemic*. London: Legal Action Group

Klein, Naomi (2007) *The shock doctrine*. London: Allen Lane

Kant, Immanuel (2017) *The metaphysics of morals*. Cambridge: Cambridge University Press

Knio, Karim and Jessop Bob (2019) "Introduction: Organisational perspectives on crisiology and learning". In B. Jessop and K. Knio (eds) *The pedagogy of economic, political and social crises*. Abington: Routledge

Kassovitz, Mathieu (director) (1995) *La haine*. Paris: Productions Lazennec and Le Studio Canal

Kelaidis, Katherine (2020) "What the great Plague of Athens can teach us now". *The Atlantic*, 23 March (https://www.theatlantic.com/ideas/archive/2020/03/great-plague-athens-has-eerie-parallels-today/608545/)

Kirkpatrick, Jean (1979) "Dictatorships and public standards". *Commentary Magazine* 1, November (https://www.commentary.org/articles/jeane-kirkpatrick/dictatorships-double-standards/)

Kivotidis, Dimitris (2021) "Ο 'εχθρός-λαός' και η συνταγματική αντμιμετώπισή του" ["The 'people-enemy' and its constitutional treatment". In *Ιδεολογική Επιτροπή και Τμημα Δικαιοσύνης της ΚΕ του ΚΚΕ (ed) Η συνταγματική έκφραση της δικτατοριας του καφαλαίου*. Athens: Συγχρονη Εποχή, pp. 105–166

Kojève, Alexandre (2020) *The notion of authority*. London: Verso

Kollewe, Julia (2021a) "From Pfizer to Moderna: who's making billions from Covid-19 vaccines?" *The Guardian*, 6 March (https://www.theguardian.com/business/2021/mar/06/from-pfizer-to-moderna-whos-making-billions-from-covid-vaccines)

Kollewe, Julia (2021b) "UK business activity at four-month low due to staff shortages amid 'pingdemic'". *The Guardian*, 23 July (https://www.theguardian.com/business/live/2021/jul/23/uk-retail-sales-rise-in-july-helped-by-euro-2020-food-and-drink-spending-business-live)

Kollewe, Julia (2021c) "Pfizer raises Covid-19 vaccine sales forecast to $36bn for 2021". *The Guardian*, 2 November (https://www.theguardian.com/business/2021/nov/02/pfizer-covid-19-vaccine-sales-2021-biontech)

Kropotkin, Peter (1902) *Mutual aid: A factor in evolution*. (https://theanarchistlibrary.org/library/petr-kropotkin-mutual-aid-a-factor-of-evolution)

Labour Behind the Label (2020) *Boohoo and covid-19*. Bristol: Labour Behind the Label

Lapavitsas, Costas (2013) *Profiting without producing*. London: Verso

LBC (2020) "What are the Government's five tests for lifting coronavirus lockdown?" *LBC*, 27 April (https://www.lbc.co.uk/hot-topics/coronavirus/government-five-tests-to-end-lockdown/)

Lemke, Thomas (2012) "Beyond Foucault: From biopolitics to the government of life". In U. Bröckling, S. Krasmann and T. Lemke (eds.) *Governmentality: Current issues and future challenges*. Abington: Routledge, pp. 165–184

Leoni, Tristan and Celine Alkamar (2020) "Θα κάνουμε ο,τι είναι απαραίτητο. Ο ιός, το κράτος και εμείς" ["We shall do whatever it takes. The virus, the state and us"]. *Το Διαλυτικό* 4: 39–63

Lerner, Sharon (2020) "Big pharma prepares to profit from the coronavirus". *The Intercept*, 13 March (https://theintercept.com/2020/03/13/big-pharma-drug-pricing-coronavirus-profits/)

Linebaugh, Peter (2011) "The Tyburn riot against the surgeons". In D. Hay, P. Linebaugh, J.G. Rule, E.P. Thompson and C. Winslow (eds) *Albion's fatal tree*. London: Verso

Littman, Robert J. (2009) "The plague of Athens: Epidemiology and paleopathology". *The Mount Sinai Journal of Medicine* 76 (5): 456–467

Locke, John (2016) *Second treatise on government*. Oxford: Oxford University Press

Losurdo, Domenico (2014) *Liberalism*. London: Verso

Losurdo, Domenico (2015) *War and revolution*. London: Verso

Lydall, Ross and Sophia Sleigh (2021) "City Hall probe will examine Jennifer Arcuri's fresh claims over her relationship with Boris Johnson". *Evening Standard*, 29 March (https://www.standard.co.uk/news/politics/city-hall-probe-jennifer-arcuri-relationship-boris-johnson-b926813.html)

Lyon, David (2003) *Surveillance after September 11*. Cambridge: Polity

Machiavelli, Niccolò (2021) *Φιωρεντινές ιστορίες [Istorie Fiorentine]*. Athens: Αλεξάνδρεια

Macleavy, Julie (2010) "Remaking the welfare state: From safety net to trampoline". In K. Birch and V. Mykhnenko (eds) *The rise and fall of neoliberalism*. London: Zed

Macron, Emmanuel (2020) "We are at war with covid-19 says President of France". Speech by M. Emmanuel Macron, President of the Republic, on the COVID-19 coronavirus. Paris, 16 March (https://uk.ambafrance.org/We-are-at-war-with-COVID-19-says-President-in-national-broadcast)

Makortoff, Kalyeena (2021) "HSBC boosts bonus pool and dividend as profits more than quadruple". *The Guardian*, 2 August (https://www.theguardian.com/business/2021/aug/02/hsbc-bonus-pool-profits-covid-19)

Malbeuf, Jilene, Peter Johnson, John Johnson and Austin Mardon (2021) "The plague of Athens shedding light on modern struggles with covid-19". *The Journal of Classics Teaching* 22: 47–49

Mallet, Victor (2019) "Macron says G7 will not issue joint communiqué to avoid row among leaders". *Financial Times*, 21 August (https://www.ft.com/content/3ad32bd4-c447-11e9-a8e9-296ca66511c9)

Malnick, Edward (2020) "Boris Johnson exclusive interview: We will not need another national lockdown". *The Telegraph*, 19 July (https://www.telegraph.co.uk/politics/2020/07/18/boris-johnson-exclusive-interview-will-not-need-another-national/)

Marie, Aurielle (2020) "I was kidnapped by police for nine hours for being a Black Lives Matter protester". *The Guardian*, 28 August (https://www.theguardian.com/world/2020/aug/27/i-was-kidnapped-by-police-for-nine-hours-for-being-a-black-lives-matter-protester)

Marmot, Michael, Jessica Allen, Peter Goldblatt, Eleanor Herd and Joana Morrison (2020) "Build back fairer: The COVID-19 Marmot Review". *The Pandemic, Socioeconomic and Health Inequalities in England*. London: Institute of Health Equity, December

Marsh, Sarah (2021) "'Follow the rules': What Matt Hancock told us – And What he did". *The Guardian*, 25 June (https://www.theguardian.com/politics/2021/jun/25/follow-the-rules-what-matt-hancock-told-us-and-what-he-did)

Martin, Alice (2021) "Why are cases of Covid in the workplace not being reported in the UK?" *The Guardian*, 20 February. (https://www.theguardian.com/commentisfree/2021/feb/20/why-cases-covid-workplace-not-being-reported-uk)

Marx, Karl (1848) "On the question of free trade". *Marxists Archive* (https://www.marxists.org/archive/marx/works/1848/free-trade/index.htm)

Marx, Karl (1936) *The poverty of philosophy*. London: M. Lawrence

Marx, Karl (1977) *A contribution to the critique of political economy* (Preface). Progress: Moscow

Marx, Karl (1990) *Capital*, volume 1. London: Penguin

Marx, Karl (1992) *Capital*, volume.2. London: Penguin

Marx, Karl (1993) *Grundrisse*. London: Penguin

Marx, Karl and Friedrich Englels (2015) *The Communist manifesto*. London: Penguin

Massumi, Brian (2015) *Ontopower*. Durham: Duke University Press

Mazzucato, Mariana (2021) "Capitalism won't save us from Covid, no matter what Boris Johnson might think". *The Guardian*, 27 March (https://www.theguardian.com/commentisfree/2021/mar/27/capitalism-covid-boris-johnson-uk-vaccine-state-funding)

Mbebe, Achille (2003) "Necropolitics". *Public Culture* 15(1): 11–40

McQuade, Brendan and Mark Neocleous (2020) "Beware: Medical police". *Radical Philosophy* 2(08): 3–9

Menéndez Agustín (2017) "The crisis of the law and the European crises: From the social and democratic *Rechtsstaat* to the consolidating state of (pseudo-)technocratic governance". *Journal of Law and Society* 44(1): 56–78

Messmer, Alyse (2021) "Official calls protesters 'criminals,' will toughen laws against disruptions they create". *Newsweek*, 10 May (https://www.msn.com/en-us/news/world/official-calls-protesters-criminals-will-toughen-laws-against-disruptions-they-create/ar-AAPaj40)

Microsoft (undated) "The next great disruption is hybrid work—Are we ready?". Microsoft Work Trend Index (https://www.microsoft.com/en-us/worklab/work-trend-index/hybrid-work)

Miller, Chris (ed) (2009) *War on terror —the Oxford Amnesty lectures*. Manchester: Manchester University Press

Minakakis, Vassilis (2020) *Μετά την πανδημία Covid-19 [After the covid-19 pandemic]*. Athens: ΚΨΜ

Ming, Wu (2021) "Conspiracy and social struggle". *Ill Will*, 18 November (https://illwill.com/conspiracy-and-social-struggle)

Mirowski, Philip (2009) "Postface". In P. Mirowski and Dieter Plehwe (eds.) *The road from Mont Pelerin*. Cambridge, MA.:Harvard University Press, pp. 417–455

Mises, von Ludwig (1985) *Liberalism in the classical tradition*. San Francisco: Cobden Press

Mol, Annemarie (2008) *The logic of care*. Abington: Routledge

Monroe, Jack (2022) "We're pricing the poor out of food in the UK – that's why I'm launching my own price index". *The Observer*, 22 January (https://www.theguardian.com/society/2022/jan/22/were-pricing-the-poor-out-of-food-in-the-uk-thats-why-im-launching-my-own-price-index)

Morozov, Evgeny (2020) "The tech 'solutions' for coronavirus take the surveillance state to the next level'. *The Guardian*, 15 April (https://www.theguardian.com/commentisfree/2020/apr/15/tech-coronavirus-surveilance-state-digital-disrupt)

Muhle, Maria (2014) "A genealogy of biopolitics: The notion of life in Canguilhem and Foucault". In Vanessa Lemm and Miguel Vatter (eds.) *The government of life: Foucault, biopolitics and neoliberalism*. New York: Fordham University Press, pp. 77–97

Murphy, Simon and Archie Bland (2020) "Ministers add to confusion over England covid lockdown rules". *The Guardian*, 3 November. (https://www.theguardian.com/world/2020/nov/03/ministers-prompt-confusion-over-england-covid-coronavirus-lockdown-rules)

National Audit Office (2016) "Benefit sanctions". HC 628. 30 November

National Audit Office (2020) "Investigation into government procurement during the covid-19 pandemic". HC 959. 26 November

Neatte, Rupert (2020) "Ten billionaires reap $400bn boost to wealth during pandemic". *The Guardian*, 19 December (https://www.theguardian.com/technology/2020/dec/19/ten-billionaires-reap-400bn-boost-to-wealth-during-pandemic)

Neatte, Rupert and Jasper Jolly (2020) "Hedge funds 'raking in billions' during coronavirus crisis". *The Guardian*, 9 April (https://www.theguardian.com/business/2020/apr/09/hedge-funds-raking-in-billions-during-coronavirus-crisis)

Neocleous, Mark (2000) *The fabrication of social order*. London: Pluto

Neocleous, Mark (2008) *A critique of security*. Edinburgh: Edinburgh University Press

Neocleous, M. (2015) "The universal adversary will attack: Pigs, pirates, zombies, and the class war". *Critical Studies on Terrorism* 8(1): 15–32

Neocleous, Mark (2016) *The universal adversary*. Abington: Routledge

Neocleous, Mark (2017a) "Anxiety: Trauma: Resilience". In E. Eklundh, A. Zenvik and E.-P. Guittet (eds) *Politics of anxiety*. London: Rowman and Littlefield, pp. 61–77

Neocleous, M. (2017b) "Qu'est-ce qui git dans la Boue?" In S. De Simoni, P. Guillibert and M. Krickeberg (eds) *Critique de la Sécurité: Pacification et Accumulation*. Paris: Eterotopia

Neumann, Franz (1995) "The change in the function of law in modern society". In W.E Scheuerman (ed) *The rule of law under siege*. Berkeley: University of California Press

Newsham, Janet (2020) "The working dead! Hazards campaign demands the government take tougher action on preventing transmission of the virus". *Hazards Campaign*, 16 December (http://www.hazardscampaign.org.uk/blog/the-working-dead-hazards-campaign-demands-the-government-take-tougher-action-on-preventing-transmission-of-the-virus)

Ni, Vincent (2021) "China denounces US Senate's $250bn move to boost tech and manufacturing". *The Guardian*, 9 June (https://www.theguardian.com/us-news/2021/jun/09/us-senate-approves-50bn-boost-for-computer-chip-and-ai-technology-to-counter-china)

Niemietz, Kristian (2021) "Left turn ahead? Surveying attitudes of young people towards capitalism and socialism". *Institute of Economic Affairs*, July

NIESR (2021) "Destitution levels are rising across the country – and terribly worrying in certain regions, NIESR research shows". *National Institute of Economic and Social Research*. Press Release, 22 February (https://www.niesr.ac.uk/media/niesr-press-release-destitution-levels-are-rising-across-country-%E2%80%93-and-terribly-worrying)

Nigro, Roberto (2014) "From reason of state to liberalism: The coup coup d'état as a form of government". In V. Lemm and M. Vatter (eds.) *The government of life: Foucault, biopolitics and neoliberalism*. New York: Fordham University Press, pp. 117–140

Nitzan, Jonathan and Shimson Bichler (2009) *Capital as power*. Abington: Routledge

Office for Budget Responsibility (2022) "Economic and fiscal outlook". March. CP 648

Office for National Statistics (2022) "Labour market overview". 17 May (https://www.ons.gov.uk/employmentandlabourmarket/peopleinwork/employmentandemployeetypes/bulletins/uklabourmarket/may2022)

Olson, PE, CS Hames, AS Benenson and EN Genovese (1996) "The Thucydides syndrome: Ebola deja vu? (or Ebola reemergent?)". *Emerging Infectious Diseases* 2: 155–156

Oltermann, Philip (2021) "Austria plans compulsory Covid vaccination for all". *The Guardian*, 19 November (https://www.theguardian.com/world/2021/nov/19/austria-plans-compulsory-covid-vaccination-for-all)

Oksala, Johanna (2017) "Ordoliberalism as governmentality". In T. Biebricher and F. Vogelmann (eds) *The birth of austerity: German Ordoliberalism and contemporary neoliberalism*. London: Rowman and Littlefield, pp. 181–196

Opitz, Sven (2012) "Government unlimited: The security dispositif of illiberal governmentality". In Ulrich Bröckling, Susanne Krasmann and Thomas Lemke (eds.) *Governmentality: Current issues and future challenges*. Abington: Routledge, pp. 93–114

Orwell, George (2021) *Nineteen eighty-four*. London: Collins

Oswald, Marion, Rachel Allsopp, Claire Bessant et al (2021) "Data-driven responses to covid-19 —Lessons learned". *OMDDAC Research Compendium*, October

Papanikolopoulos, Dimitris and Dimitris Katsoridas (2021) "Από τη λιτότητα στην πανδημία" ["From austerity to the pandemic"]. In A. Kapsalis, V. Koumarianow and N. Kourahanis (eds) *Κοινωνική πολιτική, αυταρχικός νεοφιλελευθερισμός και πανδημία [Social policy, authoritarian neoliberalism and the pandemic]*. Athens: Topos

Partington, Richard and Alexandra Topping (2021) "Boris Johnson accused of backtracking on workers' rights pledge". *The Guardian*, 11 May (https://www.theguardian.com/law/2021/may/11/boris-johnson-accused-of-backtracking-on-workers-rights-pledge)

Partington, Richard and Ashley Kirk (2022) "In numbers: what is fuelling Britain's cost of living crisis?". *The Guardian*, 3 February (https://www.theguardian.com/business/2022/feb/03/in-numbers-britains-cost-of-living-crisis)

Parveen, Nazia, Heather Stewart and Josh Halliday (2020) "Boris Johnson apologises for getting north-east England lockdown rules wrong". *The Guardian*, 29 September (https://www.theguardian.com/world/2020/sep/29/tories-competence-questioned-as-minister-fails-to-clarify-lockdown-rules)

Pegg, David and David Conn (2020) "'No documentation, no justification': NAO criticism of Covid contracts". *The Guardian*, 18 November (https://www.theguardian.com/politics/2020/nov/18/no-documentation-no-justification-nao-criticism-of-covid-contracts)

Penzin, Alexei (2020) "Pandemic suspension". *Radical Philosophy* 2(08): 10–17

Philippides, Christos (2020) *"Είμαστε σε πόλεμο με έναν αόρατο εχθρό: πανδημία, βιοπολιτική και αντιεξέγερση"* ["We are at war with an invisible enemy: Pandemic, biopolitics and counterinsurgency"]. Athens: Futura

Piketty, Thomas (2014) *Capital in the 21st century*. Cambridge: Harvard University Press

Pilikington, Ed (2020) "Six months of Trump's Covid denials: 'It'll go away … It's fading'". The Guardian, 29 July (https://www.theguardian.com/world/2020/jul/29/trump-coronavirus-science-denial-timeline-what-has-he-saidPilkington)

Pollock, Allyson and Peter Roderick (2021) "If you believe in a public NHS, the new health and care bill should set off alarm bells". *The Guardian*, 7 December (https://www.theguardian.com/commentisfree/2021/dec/07/public-nhs-the-new-health-and-care-bill-alarm-bells-privatisation)

Poulantzas, Nicos (1973) *State power and social classes*. London: New Left Books

Poulantzas, Nicos (1974) *Fascism and dictatorship*. London: New Left Books

Poulantzas, Nicos (1976) *The crisis of dictatorships*. London: New Left Books

Poulantzas, Nicos (1978) *State, power, socialism*. London: Verso

Primrose, David, Robin Chang and Rodney Loeppky (2020) "Pandemic unplugged: Public health and the persistence of neoliberalism". *Journal of Australian Political Economy* 85: 17–28

Proctor, Kate (2020) "Just 6% of UK public 'want a return to pre-pandemic economy'". *The Guardian*, 28 June (https://www.theguardian.com/world/2020/jun/28/just-6-of-uk-public-want-a-return-to-pre-pandemic-economy)

Prozorov, Sergei (2016) *The biopolitics of Stalinism*. Edinburgh: Edinburgh University Press

Public Eye (2021) "Big pharma takes all". Lausanne and Zurich, March (https://www.publiceye.ch/fileadmin/doc/Medikamente/2021_PublicEye_BigPharmaTakesItAll_Report.pdf)

Quiggin, John (2020) "Crises and recession as the norm". *Journal of Australian Political Economy* 85: 39–43

Quinn, Ben, Tobi Thomas and Niamh McIntyre (2021) "Record 5.8m people in England waiting for hospital treatment". *The Guardian*, 11 November (https://www.theguardian.com/society/2021/nov/11/record-58m-people-in-england-waiting-for-hospital-treatment)

Rawlinson, Kevin (2021) "Matt Hancock: links to firm used by NHS fuels Tory cronyism row". *The Guardian*, 16 April (https://www.theguardian.com/politics/2021/apr/16/tory-government-infected-with-widespread-cronyism-labour)

Rawnsley, Andrew (2021a) "The record-beating cost to the taxpayer of Boris Johnson's wasteful government". *The Observer*, 14 March (https://www.theguardian.com/commentisfree/2021/mar/14/the-record-beating-cost-to-the-taxpayer-of-boris-johnson-wasteful-government)

Rawnsley, Andrew (2021b) "David Cameron and the Greensill scandal is just the tip of the fatberg". *The Observer*, 18 April (https://www.theguardian.com/commentisfree/2021/apr/18/david-cameron-greensill-scandal-tip-of-fatberg)

Rayner, Gordon (2020) "'Go back to work or risk losing your job': Major drive launched to get people returning to their office". *The Daily Telegraph*, 2 September

Reid, Julian (2016) "Resilience: The biopolitics of security". In D. Chandler and J. Reid (eds) *The neoliberal subject*. London: Rowman and Littlefield, pp. 51–71

Resolution Foundation (2020) "Time out". *Resolution Foundation*, December

Resolution Foundation (2021a) "Spending fast, taxing slow". *Resolution Foundation*, March

Resolution Foundation (2021b) "The Boris budget". *Resolution Foundation*. London, October

Roubini, Nouriel (2021) "Conditions are ripe for repeat of 1970s stagflation and 2008 debt crisis". *Project Syndicate/The Guardian*, 2 July (https://www.theguardian.com/business/2021/jul/02/1970s-stagflation-2008-debt-crisis-global-economy)

Riesel, Rene and Jaime Semprum (2014) *Catastrophism, disaster management and sustainable submission*. Amsterdam: Roofdruk Edities

Robinson, Idris (2020) "How it might should be done". *Red May TV*, 4 August (https://www.youtube.com/watch?v=cQeW7RPkCZQ)

Ross, Tim (2021) "U.K. Reopening in Chaos as Ministers Undermine Isolation Orders". *Bloomberg*, 20 July (https://www.bloomberg.com/news/articles/2021-07-20/isolation-optional-if-pinged-by-covid-app-u-k-minister-says)

Rousseau, Jean-Jacques (1992) "Letter from J.J. Rousseau to Mr de Voltaire". In: Roger D Masters and Christopher Kelly (eds) *Collected writings of Rousseau, vol.3*. Hanover: University Press of New England, pp. 108–121

Rumsfeld, Donald (2002) "US Department of Defence news briefing", 12 February

Rüstow, Alexander (1932) "State policy and the necessary conditions for economic liberalism". In T. Biebricher and F. Vogelmann (eds) *The birth of austerity: German Ordoliberalism and contemporary neoliberalism*. London: Rowman and Littlefield

Ryan-Collins, Josh (2021) "Is the UK housing bubble about to burst? These are the best and worst scenarios". *The Guardian*, 2 July (https://www.theguardian.com/commentisfree/2021/jul/02/housing-bubble-birst-uk-gdp-house-prices-interest-rates-economy)

Sabbagh, Dan (2020) "Campaigners fear far-right 'defence' of statues such as Churchill's". *The Guardian*, 10 June (https://www.theguardian.com/world/2020/jun/10/far-right-protesters-plan-defence-of-statues-such-as-churchills)

Sainato, Michael (2021) "Billionaires add $1tn to net worth during pandemic as their workers struggle". *The Guardian*, 15 January (https://www.theguardian.com/world/2021/jan/15/billionaires-net-worth-coronavirus-pandemic-jeff-bezos-elon-musk)

Samerski, Silja (2018) "Individuals on alert: Digital epidemiology and the individualisation of surveillance". *Life Sciences, Society and Policy* 14(13): 1–11

Sample, Ian and Natalie Grover (2021) "Chris Whitty: keeping Covid restrictions will only delay wave". *The Guardian*, 5 July (https://www.theguardian.com/world/2021/jul/05/chris-whitty-keeping-covid-restrictions-will-only-delay-wave)

Sanguinetti, Gianfranco (2018) *Το Μουνάκι, χθές και σήμερα*. Athens: Bibliothèque du Temps Perdu

Sanguinetti, Gianfranco (2020) *Ο δυτικός δεσποτισμός [Occidental despotism]*. Athens: Εκδόσεις των Συναδέλφων

Sayer, Andrew (2016) *Why we can't afford the rich*. Bristol: Policy

Savage, Michael, Tom Wall and James Trapper (2021) "Staff 'pressured to go back to work' in breach of UK Covid rules". *The Guardian*, 16 January (https://www.theguardian.com/world/2021/jan/16/staff-pressured-back-to-work-breach-of-uk-covid-rules)

Scheuerman, William E. (1994) *Between the norm and the exception*. Cambridge: MIT Press

Scheuerman, William E. (2002) "Rethinking crisis government". *Constellations* 9(4): 492–505

Scheuerman, William E. (2004) *Liberal democracy and the social acceleration of time*. Baltimore: John Hopkins University Press

Schmitt, Carl (1996) *The concept of the political*. Chicago: University of Chicago Press

Schmitt, Carl (2014) *Dictatorship*. Cambridge: Polity

Schwab, Klaus and Thierry Malleret (2020) *The great reset*. Geneva: Forum Publishing

Seymour, Richard (2021) "A return to civility will not begin to quell the threat of fascism in the US". *The Guardian*, 8 January (https://www.theguardian.com/commentisfree/2021/jan/08/threat-fascism-us-storming-capitol-far-right-trump)

Shapiro, Beth, Andrew Rambaut and M. Thomas P. Gilbert (2006) "No proof that typhoid caused the Plague of Athens (a reply to Papagrigorakis et al.)". *International Journal of Infectious Diseases* 10 (4): 334–335

Shemon (2020) "The rise of black counter-insurgency". *Ill Will*, 30 July (https://illwill.com/the-rise-of-black-counter-insurgency)

Sgaravatti, Giovanni, Simone Tagliapietra and Georg Zachmann (2022) "National policies to shield consumers from rising energy prices". *Bruegel*, 8 February (https://www.bruegel.org/publications/datasets/national-policies-to-shield-consumers-from-rising-energy-prices/)

Situations Collective (2020) "Revolution in the virocene—Near (or nearing) the end of time". *Institute for the Radical Imagination*, Pandemic Paper No. 1

Smith, Adam (1982) *The wealth of nations*. London: Penguin

Social Metrics Commission (2020) *Poverty and covid-19*. SMC: London, August

Sontag, Susan (1978) *Illness as metaphor*. New York: Farrar, Straus and Giroux

Stampnitzky, Lisa (2013) *Disciplining terror*. Cambridge: Cambridge University Press

Steel, Daniel (2015) *Philosophy and the precautionary principle*. Cambridge: Cambridge University Press

Steinberg, Jacob (2021) "Respect players taking the knee and do not boo, FA urges". *The Guardian*, 12 June (https://www.theguardian.com/football/2021/jun/12/respect-players-taking-the-knee-and-do-not-boo-fa-urges)

Stewart, Heather (2020a) "Neil Ferguson: UK coronavirus adviser resigns after breaking lockdown rules". *The Guardian*, 5 May (https://www.theguardian.com/uk-news/2020/may/05/uk-coronavirus-adviser-prof-neil-ferguson-resigns-after-breaking-lockdown-rules)

Stewart, Heather (2020b) "Covid: how chilling projection prompted Johnson to lockdown". *The Guardian*, 1 November (https://www.theguardian.com/world/2020/nov/01/chilling-prognosis-offered-cold-comfort-for-johnsons-top-quad)

Stewart, Heather and Denis Campbell (2020) "NHS workers angered at Hancock's warning not to overuse PPE". *The Guardian*, 10 April (https://www.theguardian.com/society/2020/apr/10/matt-hancock-urges-public-not-to-overuse-ppe)

Stimilli, Elettra (2020) "Apocalyptic time". *Political Theology* 21(5): 391–392

Storeng, Katerini and Antoine de Bengy Puyvallée (2021) "The smartphone pandemic: How big tech and public health authorities partner in the digital response to covid-19". *Global Public Health* 16 (8–9): 1482–1498

Streeck, Wolfgang (2014) *Buying time*. London: Verso

Sturgeon, Nicola (2020) "Coronavirus (Covid-19) update: First Minister's Speech". *Scottish Government, Edinburgh*, 27 April (https://www.gov.scot/publications/coronavirus-covid-19-update-first-ministers-speech-27-april-2020/)

Sunak, Rishi (2020) "Spending review 2020 and OBR forecast". *House of Commons*. Hansard, Volume 684, 25 November

Syal, Rajeev (2021) "Priti Patel pressed to explain award of spy agencies cloud contract to Amazon". *The Guardian*, 27 October (https://www.theguardian.com/uk-news/2021/oct/26/amazon-web-services-aws-contract-data-mi5-mi6-gchq)

Syal, Rajeev and Heather Stewart (2020) "Robert Jenrick under pressure to resign after donor-row documents released". *The Guardian*, 25 June (https://www.theguardian.com/politics/2020/jun/24/robert-jenrick-to-release-all-relevant-information-in-planning-row)

Tapper, James (2021) "Fury at "do not resuscitate" notices given to Covid patients with learning disabilities". *The Observer*, 13 February (https://www.theguardian.com/world/2021/feb/13/new-do-not-resuscitate-orders-imposed-on-covid-19-patients-with-learning-difficulties)

Tarrant, Alison and Lydia Hayes (2021) "Exposure to coronavirus in adult social care settings: A matter of safety or safeguarding?". *Public Law* 2: 223–232

The Economist (2020a) "When Athenians feared a disease would wreck their democracy". *The Economist*, 28 March

The Economist (2020b) "Everything's under control". *The Economist* 28 March–3 April

The Economist (2020c) "Building up the pillars of the state". *The Economist*, 28 March–3 April

The Economist (2020d) "Strategic pile-up". *The Economist*, 11–17 April

The Economist (2020e) "Absence of evidence is no evidence of absence". *The Economist*, 11–17 April

The Economist (2020f) "Undercut". *The Economist*, 25 April–1 May

The Economist (2020g) "Not quite all there". *The Economist*, 2–8 May

The Economist (2020h) "Goodbye globalisation". *The Economist* 16–22 May

The Economist (2020i) "Britain has the wrong government for the covid crisis". *The Economist*, 18 June

The Economist (2020j) "The next catastrophe". *The Economist* 27 June–3 July

The Economist (2020k) "What's the worst that could happen?" *The Economist* 27 June–3 July

The Economist (2020l) "Starting over again". *The Economist*, 25–31 July.

The Economist (2020m) "Putting the capital into capitalism". *The Economist*, 25–31 July

The Economist (2020n) "What a way to make a living". *The Economist*, 12–18 September

The Economist (2021a) "From whatever source derived". *The Economist*, 2–8 October

The Economist (2021b) "Flattened". *The Economist*, 9–15 October

The Economist (2021c) "Democratic discipline". *The Economist*, 9–15 October

The Economist (2021d) "The new order of trade". *The Economist*, 9–15 October

The Economist (2021e) "Stagflation sensation". *The Economist*, 9–15 October

The Economist (2021f) "Can't live without them. Yet". *The Economist*, 9–15 October

The Lancet Commissions (2021) "LSE–Lancet Commission on the future of the NHS: Re-laying the foundations for an equitable and efficient health and care service after COVID-19". *Lancet* 397: 1915–1978

The Guardian (2022) "The Guardian view on Boris Johnson and 'partygate': all played out". *The Guardian*, 19 January (https://www.theguardian.com/commentisfree/2022/jan/19/the-guardian-view-on-boris-johnson-and-partygate-all-played-out)

The Observer (2021) "Soaring house prices and cheap credit are creating the wrong sort of growth". Business Leader, *The Observer*, 2 May (https://www.theguardian.com/business/2021/may/02/soaring-house-prices-and-cheap-credit-are-creating-the-wrong-sort-of-growth)

The Observer (2022) "The Observer view on the use of dirty tactics to bolster Boris Johnson". *The Observer*, 23 January (https://www.theguardian.com/commentisfree/2022/jan/23/observer-view-on-dirty-tactics-to-bolster-boris-johnson)

Therborn, Göran (2021) "Inequality and world-political landscapes". *New Left Review* 129: 5–26

Thucydides (2009) *The Peloponnesian war*. Oxford: Oxford University Press

Tiltrecordings (2020) "I'll be damned". *Diaries of Infection*, 25 September (https://diariesofinfection.wordpress.com/2020/09/25/ill-be-damned/)

Tooze, Adam (2021) *Shutdown*. London: Allen Lane

Tooze, Adam (2022) "Why inflation and the cost-of-living crisis won't take us back to the 1970s". *The New Statesman*, 4 February (https://www.newstatesman.com/ideas/2022/02/why-inflation-and-the-cost-of-living-crisis-wont-take-us-back-to-the-1970s)

Townsend, Mark (2022) "Will Met inquiry into Downing Street lockdown parties 'neuter' Gray report?". *The Guardian*, 29 January (https://www.theguardian.com/politics/2022/jan/29/police-inquiry-into-downing-st-lockdown-parties-neuters-gray-report-say-critics)

Transparency International (UK) (2021) "Track and Trace". *Transparency International*, April https://www.transparency.org.uk/sites/default/files/pdf/publications/Track%20and%20Trace%20-%20Transparency%20International%20UK.pdf

Tsoukalas, Constantine (2021) *Το πολιτικό στη σκιά της πανδημίας [The political in the shadow of the pandemic]*. Athens: Καστανιώτης

Vaneigem, Raoul (2020) "Coronavirus". *Not Bored!* (http://www.notbored.org/coronavirus.pdf)

Virno, Paulo (2015) *Déjà vu and the end of history*. London: Verso

Waitzkin, Howard (2016) *Medicine and public health at the end of empire*. New York: Routledge

Waitzkin, Howard (2021) "Confronting the upstream causes of COVID-19 and other epidemics to follow". *International Journal of Health Services* 51(1): 55–58

Walker, Peter (2021a) "What is the Greensill lobbying scandal and who is involved?". *The Guardian*, 14 April (https://www.theguardian.com/business/2021/apr/14/what-is-greensill-lobbying-scandal-who-involved)

Walker, Peter (2021b) "Anger as ministers block 'fire and rehire' bill in Commons". *The Guardian*, 22 October. (https://www.theguardian.com/law/2021/oct/22/anger-as-ministers-block-fire-and-rehire-bill-in-commons)

Walker, Peter, Josh Halliday and Nicola Davis (2021) "England test-and-trace glitch blamed for spread of India Covid variant". *The Guardian*, 20 May (https://www.theguardian.com/world/2021/may/20/england-test-and-trace-delays-blamed-for-spread-of-indian-variant-of-covid)

Wall, Tom (2021a) "Firms accused of putting workers' lives at risk by bending lockdown trading rules". *The Observer*, 16 January (https://www.theguardian.com/politics/2021/jan/16/bosses-accused-putting-workers-lives-risk-bending-lockdown-trading-rules)

Wall, Tom (2021b) "Grant Shapps faces fury over mass Covid outbreak at DVLA". *The Observer*, 23 January (https://www.theguardian.com/world/2021/jan/23/minister-faces-fury-over-mass-covid-outbreak-at-top-government-agency)

Weale, Sally and Pamela Duncan (2021) "Teaching unions warn against 'big bang' return to school in England". *The Guardian*, 22 February. (https://www.theguardian.com/education/2021/feb/22/teaching-unions-warn-against-big-bang-return-to-school)

Westwater, Hannah (2021) "Universal Credit: What is it, and why does the £20 increase matter?". *The Big Issue*, 3 March (https://www.bigissue.com/latest/universal-credit-what-is-it-and-why-does-the-20-increase-matter/)

White House (2021a) "Fact sheet: The American Jobs plan". *The White House*, 31 March (https://www.whitehouse.gov/briefing-room/statements-releases/2021/03/31/fact-sheet-the-american-jobs-plan/)

White House (2021b) *Executive order on requiring coronavirus disease 2019 vaccination for federal employees*. Washington, DC: The White House Briefing Room, 9 September

White House (2021c) *Executive order on ensuring adequate COVID safety protocols for federal contractors*. Washington, DC: The White House Briefing Room, 9 September

White House (2021d) "Path out of the pandemic". Washington, DC: The White (https://www.whitehouse.gov/covidplan/)

Williams, Zoe (2021) "Boris Johnson ends Covid as a 'me problem' and makes it a 'you problem'". *The Guardian*, 5 July https://www.theguardian.com/politics/2021/jul/05/boris-johnson-ends-covid-as-a-me-problem-and-makes-it-a-you-problem)

Wood, Zoe (2021) "Higher taxes could leave low-paid frontline workers £1,000 worse off". *The Guardian*, 13 September (https://www.theguardian.com/politics/2021/sep/13/higher-taxes-low-paid-frontline-workers-worse-off)

Woodcock, Andrew (2020) "Coronavirus: Boris Johnson claims 'massive success' despite England having highest excess death rate in Europe". *Independent*, 20 July (https://www.independent.co.uk/news/uk/politics/coronavirus-boris-johnson-death-rate-england-covid-19-pandemic-a9645846.html)

Wright, Oliver, Chris Smyth and Philip Aldrick (2021) "Britain's tax burden will rise to highest in 70 years". *The Times*, 8 September (https://www.thetimes.co.uk/article/britains-tax-burden-will-rise-to-highest-in-70-years-qsrx0wxxw)

Zedner, Lucia (2007) "Preventive justice or pre-punishment? The case of control orders". *Current Legal Problems* 60(1): 174–203

Zevin, Alexander (2019) *Liberalism at large*. London: Verso

Zuboff, Shoshana (2019) *The age of surveillance capitalism*. London: Profile

Index